T0336814

VOLUME NINETY SEVEN

Advances in
COMPUTERS

VOLUME NINETY SEVEN

Advances in
COMPUTERS

Edited by

ATIF M. MEMON, Ph.D.
College Park, MD, USA

AMSTERDAM • BOSTON • HEIDELBERG • LONDON
NEW YORK • OXFORD • PARIS • SAN DIEGO
SAN FRANCISCO • SINGAPORE • SYDNEY • TOKYO
Academic Press is an imprint of Elsevier

Academic Press is an imprint of Elsevier
225 Wyman Street, Waltham, MA 02451, USA
525 B Street, Suite 1800, San Diego, CA 92101-4495, USA
125 London Wall, London, EC2Y 5AS, UK
The Boulevard, Langford Lane, Kidlington, Oxford OX5 1GB, UK

First edition 2015

Notices
Knowledge and best practice in this field are constantly changing. As new research and experience broaden our understanding, changes in research methods, professional practices, or medical treatment may become necessary.

Practitioners and researchers must always rely on their own experience and knowledge in evaluating and using any information, methods, compounds, or experiments described herein. In using such information or methods they should be mindful of their own safety and the safety of others, including parties for whom they have a professional responsibility.

To the fullest extent of the law, neither the Publisher nor the authors, contributors, or editors, assume any liability for any injury and/or damage to persons or property as a matter of products liability, negligence or otherwise, or from any use or operation of any methods, products, instructions, or ideas contained in the material herein.

ISBN: 978-0-12-802133-0
ISSN: 0065-2458

For information on all Academic Press publications
visit our web site at store.elsevier.com

Working together
to grow libraries in
developing countries

www.elsevier.com • www.bookaid.org

CONTENTS

PREFACE

This volume of *Advances in Computers* is the 97th in this series. This series, which has been continuously published since 1960, presents in each volume four to seven chapters describing new developments in software, hardware, or uses of computers.

This 97th volume is eclectic in nature. In the chapter on "Comparing Reuse Strategies in Different Development Environments," Dr. Varnell-Sarjeant and Prof. Andrews analyze and compare reuse success and failures in embedded versus nonembedded systems. Such a comparison is useful and timely because of the ongoing debate in the industry regarding whether lessons from reuse successes and failures in nonembedded software can be applied to embedded software. A survey of the literature identifies empirical studies of reuse that can be used to compare reuse outcomes in embedded versus nonembedded systems. Reuse outcomes include amount of reuse, effort, quality, performance, and overall success. The authors also differentiate between types of development approaches to determine whether and how they influence reuse success or failure. In particular, for some development approaches, quality improvements and effort reduction are low for embedded systems. This is particularly relevant to the Aerospace industry as it has been subject to reuse mandates for its many embedded systems.

In the chapter on "Advances in Behavior Modeling," Prof. Roubtsova provides a survey of existing approaches to discrete events behavior modeling. The survey is based on a series of successful international workshops on behavior modeling run by the author and is enriched by the results of her research experience. The survey is conducted on a selected set of semantic elements useful for major system life cycle activities, such as requirements engineering, analysis, system understanding, system design, and evolution. The semantic elements are identified in the observed approaches and illustrated with examples of models. The advantages of the semantic elements for the major system life cycle activities can be taken into account for the choice and for the design of behavior modeling approaches.

In the chapter on "Overview of Computational Approaches for Inference of MicroRNA-Mediated and Gene Regulatory Networks," Prof. Ristevski describes biological backgrounds of regulatory relationships in living cells, high-throughput experimental technologies and application of computational approaches in reverse engineering of microRNA-mediated and gene regulatory networks. The most commonly used models for gene regulatory networks inference based on Boolean networks, Bayesian networks, dynamic Bayesian networks, association networks, novel two-stage model using integration of *a priori* biological knowledge, and differential and difference equations models are detailed and their inference capabilities are compared. The regulatory role of microRNAs and transcription factors in microRNAs-mediated regulatory networks is described as well. Additionally, commonly used methods for target prediction of microRNAs and transcription factors are described as well as most commonly used biological regulatory relationships databases and tools are listed. The mainly validation criteria used for assessment of inferred regulatory networks are explained.

In the chapter on, "Proving Programs Terminate Using Well-Founded Orderings, Ramsey's Theorem, and Matrices," Prof. Gasarch discusses various ways to prove that a given program terminates. Many programs allow the user to input data several times during its execution. If the program runs forever the user may input data infinitely often. A program terminates if it terminates no matter what the user does. The proofs use well-founded orders, Ramsey Theorem, and matrices. These techniques are used by real program checkers.

In the chapter on "Advances in Testing JavaScript-Based Web Applications," Prof. Mesbah discusses recent advances in testing JavaScript, which is a flexible and expressive prototype-based scripting language used by developers to create interactive web applications. The language is interpreted, dynamic, and weakly typed and has first-class functions. It also interacts extensively with other web languages such as CSS and HTML at runtime. All these characteristics make JavaScript code particularly error-prone and challenging to analyze and test. This chapter explores recent advances made in analysis and testing techniques geared toward JavaScript-based web applications. In particular, the chapter presents recent empirical studies, testing techniques, test oracle automation approaches, test adequacy assessment methods, fault localization, and repair, and IDE support to help programmers write better JavaScript code.

I hope that you find these chapters of interest. If you have any suggestions of topics for future chapters, or if you wish to be considered as an author for a chapter, I can be reached at atif@cs.umd.edu.

Prof. ATIF M. MEMON, Ph.D.
College Park, MD, USA

CHAPTER ONE

Comparing Reuse Strategies in Different Development Environments

Julia Varnell-Sarjeant, Anneliese Amschler Andrews
Department of Computer Science, University of Denver, Denver, Colorado, USA

Contents

Abstract

There is a debate in the aerospace industry whether lessons from reuse successes and failures in nonembedded software can be applied to embedded software. This chapter analyzes and compares reuse success and failures in embedded versus nonembedded systems. A survey of the literature identifies empirical studies of reuse that can be used to compare reuse outcomes in embedded versus nonembedded systems. Reuse outcomes include amount of reuse, effort, quality, performance, and overall success. We also differentiate between types of development approaches to determine whether

Advances in Computers, Volume 97
ISSN 0065-2458
http://dx.doi.org/10.1016/bs.adcom.2014.10.002

and how they influence reuse success or failure. In particular, for some development approaches, quality improvements and effort reduction are low for embedded systems. This is particularly relevant to the aerospace industry as it has been subject to reuse mandates for its many embedded systems.

1. INTRODUCTION

Reuse supposedly reduces development time and errors. "If a software package has been executing error-free in the field for an extended period, under widely varying, perhaps stressful, operating conditions, and it is then applied to a new situation, one strongly expects that it should work error-free in this new situation [1]" and "In theory, reuse can lower development cost, increase productivity, improve maintainability, boost quality, reduce risk, shorten life cycle time, lower training costs, and achieve better software interoperability [2]." The aerospace industry was an early advocate of reuse. Chapter 8 of Ref. [1] discusses reuse in aerospace, including potential savings in quality, cost, and productivity. In July of 1992, the DoD released the DoD reuse: vision and strategy [3]. The government invested heavily in reuse, e.g., the Control Channel Toolkit (CCT) in 1997 and Global Broadcasting Service (GBS) beginning in 1998. Hence, one would expect large-scale planned reuse. Many government requests for proposals contain a requirement for quantifying expected savings from reuse.

However, from the beginning, there has been a debate on reuse success. In aerospace, not all reuse experiences have been as successful as expected. Some major projects experienced large overruns in time, budget, as well as inferior performance, at least in part, due to the wide gap between reuse expectations and reuse outcomes [4, 5]. This seemed to be especially the case for embedded systems. In many US government customer shops, reuse became a red flag when awarding contracts.

Many engineers believed that one of the root causes of the disconnect between reuse expectations and reuse realization was that too often estimated savings from reuse came from projects that differed from the target project. In particular, the reuse estimates for nonembedded systems were applied to embedded systems. There was an ongoing debate as to whether embedded systems and nonembedded systems were similar as far as reuse was concerned. Many systems and software engineers, especially those who worked on embedded systems, claimed that reuse could not be successfully used in their systems because the code was optimized to particular processors which may not be used in the new project. Many of the embedded systems software engineers claimed that reusing software was more costly than building the system from scratch. Further, many claimed that, in particular, trying to use model-based (MB) development (derived from the Initiative) was more costly than using other development approaches. Our major motivation was to investigate whether empirical studies exist that either support or contradict these opinions. Our research questions are:

- Are embedded systems different with respect to reuse?
- Do embedded systems employ different development approaches?
- Does the development approach have an impact on reuse outcomes?
- What types of empirical studies exist that analyze and/or compare reuse in embedded and nonembedded systems? Given that empirical studies can vary greatly in their rigor, this should give an indication how "hard" the evidence is.
- To what extent is there solid quantitative data paired with appropriate analysis?
- Are there studies that either deal with aerospace projects or can reasonably be generalized for this domain?
- What are the limitations of the current empirical evidence related to reuse?

In 2007, Mohagheghi and Conradi [6] conducted a survey assessing reuse in industrial settings. They studied the effects of software reuse in industrial contexts by analyzing peer-reviewed journals and major conferences between 1994 and 2005. Their paper's guiding question was "To what extent do we have evidence that software reuse leads to significant quality, productivity, or economic benefits in industry?" Reference [6] is a major step forward in identifying and measuring reuse effectiveness. Unfortunately, their work does not distinguish embedded versus nonembedded systems. By contrast, this chapter

- Compares reuse effectiveness in embedded versus nonembedded systems
- Compares reuse effectiveness for different development strategies

Section 2 describes these development strategies and defines embedded systems and types of empirical studies. Section 3 explains the review process used and the criteria for including or excluding papers. 4 analyzes reuse experiences for embedded versus nonembedded systems, the development approaches used, and the type of evidence available. Section 5 summarizes measures of reuse outcomes reported in these studies and compares differences between the types of metrics collected for embedded versus nonembedded systems. Section 6 analyzes the metrics in an attempt to answer the research questions above, by comparing size, development approach, and reuse success for embedded versus nonembedded systems. Section 7 discusses threats to validity. Section 8 summarizes results, limitations, and makes suggestions for improvements.

2. DEVELOPMENT APPROACHES FOR EMBEDDED AND NONEMBEDDED SYSTEMS WITH REUSE

2.1. Development Approaches

Reference [6] defines software reuse as "the systematic use of existing software assets to construct new or modified assets. Software assets in this view may be source code or executables, design templates, freestanding Commercial-Off-The-Shelf (COTS) or Open Source Software (OSS) components, or entire software architectures and their components forming a product line (PL) or product family. Knowledge is also reused, reflected in the reuse of architectures, templates, or processes." To simplify comparison, we use the [6]'s definition. If a study fails to report the development approach, we classify it as "unspecified." Table 1 summarizes the approaches.

Component-Based Software Engineering (CBSE). CBSE aims to design and construct software systems with reusable software components [7]. CBSE recognizes that the same capabilities are required in many different situations. There is no value in developing these same capabilities from scratch multiple times. In fact, nearly every developer has, in the process of developing software, remembered doing the same routines before and incorporated his or her own or a colleague's previous work rather than going through the full development process again. CBSE formalizes this approach by defining a method to create off-the-shelf components and an accompanying, well-defined architecture. This allows software engineers to develop large systems by incorporating previously developed or existing components. It supposedly leads to a significant reduction in development and testing time and cost [14] and reduces risk, in that, once validated, the components should behave the same in subsequent products as in the original. Further, there is an expectation of reduced maintenance costs associated with the upgrading of large systems.

Model-Based Software Engineering (MBSE). In aerospace, reuse is characterized as "the collection of related processes, methods, and tools used to support the discipline of systems engineering in a 'model-based' or 'model-driven' context...Model-Based Engineering (MBE) is about elevating models in the engineering process to a central and governing

Table 1 Development Approach-Specific Systematic Reuse Strategies

Development Approach	Definition	Reusable Assets
Component based (ex: Control Channel Toolkit)	Involves the use of existing components either developed for the purpose of reuse or already in use as components or both. "Component-Based Software Engineering (CBSE) is a process that emphasizes the design and construction of computer-based systems using reusable software 'components' [7]." CBSE is a process that aims to design and construct software systems with reusable software components. CBSE recognizes that the same capabilities are required in many different situations.	Code routines, functions, or methods contained in libraries or existing projects, COTS.
Model based (ex: DoDAF)	Reuse of preexisting models or prototypes. An MBSE methodology can be characterized as "the collection of related processes, methods, and tools used to support the discipline of systems engineering in a 'model-based' or 'model-driven' context...Model-Based Engineering (MBE) is about elevating models in the engineering process to a central and governing role in the specification, design, integration, validation, and operation of a system [8].	Architectures or design models, use cases, performance models, and simulations.
Product line (ex: Satellites)	Basic capabilities were determined in advance and the architecture, design, and code were generated to map to the generic elements of the product line. Software Engineering Institute (SEI) defines a product line as "a set of software-reliant systems that share a common, managed set of features satisfying a particular market or mission area, and are built from a common set of core assets in a prescribed way [9]." A software product line can also be described as a family of systems sharing "a common set of core technical assets, with preplanned extensions and variations to address the needs of specific customers or market segments [10]." In product line based reuse, the core products, including architecture, requirements, components, and models, are reused, with some level of customization.	Basic requirements,[a] use cases, architecture, models, test products, and code.

Continued

Table 1 Development Approach-Specific Systematic Reuse Strategies—cont'd

Development Approach	Definition	Reusable Assets
Ontology	A catalog of the basic capabilities that an organization is confident of delivering cross referenced to the locations of those capabilities. An ontology is a description of concepts and their relationships. "Ontology is the term referring to the shared understanding of some domains of interest, which is often conceived as a set of classes (concepts), relations, functions, axioms, and instances. Ontology organizes terms with a type of hierarchy and can be drawn upon to describe the different facets with domain-specific terms... [11]." Or, "An ontology is a formal, explicit specification of a shared conceptualization [12]."	Retrieval information, documentation, libraries, requirements, use cases, links to models, test products, and code artifacts.

[a]*Note:* In the aerospace industry, requirements are "shall" statements in a specification. Top level requirements are either provided by the customer or developed jointly by the customer and engineering team. Requirements become contractual, requiring proof of satisfaction in order for the product to be accepted for delivery. These requirements are often reused from project to project. See also Ref. [13] for reuse of requirements.

role in the specification, design, integration, validation, and operation of a system. For many organizations, this is a paradigm shift from traditional document-based and acquisition life cycle model approaches, many of which follow a waterfall model of system definition, system design, and design qualification [8]." MBSE reuses models as well as code.

Product Line Development. The Software Engineering Institute (SEI) defines a PL as "a set of software-reliant systems that share a common, managed set of features satisfying a particular market or mission area, and are built from a common set of core assets in a prescribed way [9]." A software PL is a family of systems sharing "a common set of core technical assets, with preplanned extensions and variations to address the needs of specific customers or market segments [10]." PL development reuses the core products, including architecture, requirements, components, and models, with some level of customization.

Ontology-Based Software Engineering. An ontology is a description of concepts and their relationships. "Ontology is the term referring to the shared understanding of some domains of interest, which is often conceived as a set of classes (concepts), relations, functions, axioms, and instances. Ontology organizes terms with a type of hierarchy and can be drawn upon to describe the different facets with domain-specific terms... [11]." In other words, an ontology is similar to a catalog that cross-classifies items based on different sets of relationships. In software engineering, the ontology becomes a catalog of software artifacts (capabilities, requirements, services, and components) that an architecture or developer can use in product development.

2.2. Embedded versus Nonembedded Systems

Our analysis distinguishes between embedded software systems and nonembedded software systems.

Embedded Software Systems. We use the terms embedded systems and cyber-physical systems interchangeably. ISO defines embedded systems as "a program which functions as part of a device. Often the software is burned into firmware instead of loaded from a storage device. It is usually a freestanding implementation rather than a hosted one with an operating system [15]." They are further defined as "CyberPhysical Systems (CPS)...integrations of computation with physical processes. Embedded computers and networks monitor and control the physical processes, usually with feedback loops where physical processes affect computations and vice versa [16]." Examples of embedded software include avionics, consumer electronics, motors, automobile safety systems, and robotics. *Nonembedded Software Systems.* For lack of another definition, nonembedded software is defined as software which is not embedded, that is, software not tied to the processors or inherently integrated with the physical system. Examples of nonembedded software include web-based systems applications (like the Global Information Grid (GIG)), desktop system test applications, ground systems, logistics systems, etc. Some of the empirical studies on reuse include both types of systems. These are classified as "both embedded and nonembedded."

2.3. Types of Empirical Studies

To identify, catalogue, and analyze empirical work assessing reuse, we follow [17, 18, 19, 20]. We classified empirical studies of reuse into the following categories:

Quasi-Experiment. In a quasi-experiment, one or more characteristics of a controlled experiment are missing, such as strict experimental control and/or randomization of treatments and subject selection. This is typical in industrial settings [21]. The researcher has to enumerate alternative explanations for observed effects one by one, decide which are plausible, and then use logic, design, and measurement to assess whether that might explain any observed effect [17].

Case Study. A case study is an empirical inquiry that investigates a contemporary phenomenon within its real-life context, especially when the boundaries between phenomenon and context are not clearly evident. In a case study, all of the following exist: research questions, propositions (hypotheses), units of analysis, logic linking the data to the propositions, and criteria for interpreting the findings [18]. Observational studies are either case studies or field studies. Case studies focus on a single project, while multiple projects are monitored in a field study, maybe with less depth. Case studies may also involve analysis of historical data [19].

Survey. A survey consists of structured or unstructured questions given to participants. The primary means of gathering qualitative or quantitative data in surveys are interviews or questionnaires [17]. Structured interviews (qualitative surveys) with an interview guide, investigate rather open, and qualitative research questions with some generalization potential. Quantitative surveys with a questionnaire contain mostly closed questions [22]. For purposes of this chapter, surveys are questions asked of individuals, such as engineers, rather than companies, the surveys of companies in industry are included under reviews of industry practice. *Review of Industry Practice.* Similar to a survey, a review of industry practice consists of discovering and analyzing the ways different companies in the industry perform their tasks. Often they share the same data collection techniques with a survey, but the questions focus on company practice.

Meta-Analysis. A meta-analysis consists of analyzing multiple studies on the topic in question. Meta-analysis covers a range of methods to generalize and compare results of a group of studies.

Experience Report. An experience report is similar to a case study, but it does not have the same level of controls or measures. It is retrospective, generally lacks propositions, may not answer how or why phenomena occurred, and often includes lessons learned [20]. In this chapter, we combine example applications with experience reports because most papers had features of both. An example application consists of "authors describing an application and providing an example to assist in the description, but the example is 'used to validate' or 'evaluate' as far as the authors suggest [20]," but without the rigor of a formal case study.

Expert Opinion. An expert opinion provides some qualitative, textual, opinion-oriented evaluation. It is "based on theory, laboratory research, or consensus [19]." These expert opinions assess processes, strategies, approaches, theoretical models, policies, curriculum, or technology, that may or may not allude to full-scale evaluation or empirical studies. Often such articles are based on experience, observations, and ideas proposed by the author(s).

3. REVIEW PROCESS AND INCLUSION CRITERIA

The search considered studies published in peer-reviewed journals and conferences, industry forums such as SEI, industry seminars, symposia and conferences, and industry- and government-funded studies. Industry sources were especially useful for PL development, since academic sources rarely have the need or ability to develop a PL for evaluation purposes. Additional sources were monographs and technical reports (for example, Ref. [23]).

We searched the ACM digital library and IEEE Xplore, Empirical Software Engineering Journal, Journal of Systems and Software, Journal of

Information Science, MIS Quarterly (MISQ), IEEE Transactions of Software Engineering (TSE), IT Professional, ACM Computing Surveys (CSUR), the Journal of Research and Practice in Information Technology, Springer Verlag, and Google Scholar. Keywords included "reuse," "reuse benefits," "reuse case study," "reuse empirical study," "product line," "component-based," and "model-based."

The articles were filtered by relevance based on titles. From relevance of titles alone, we reduced the search to about 400. Reading the abstract and conclusion reduced the number to 126, which were finally cut to 55 after reading the full article.

Once we had selected an initial set of articles, we considered works cited by the 55 papers, adding about 12. We also included newer works by researchers whose papers were relevant, adding 7. In addition, we added from gray literature articles such as case studies in industry published by the SEI. The final set of articles about development approaches and strategies came to 83. (This does not include basic background information about software development, research methods, etc.) Due to our primary interest on the impact of reuse mandates, since the software reuse initiative, we only considered papers published between 1992 and 2013.

The papers were classified by study type (Sections 4.1, 4.2, and 4.4), system type (Sections 4.1 and 4.2), and development approach (Section 4.3). Once the papers were classified, it became clear that many reported on a particular reuse strategy or method, but were not discussing the value of reuse per se, nor were they performing a comparison against other methods or between types of systems. Because these did not add to the analysis, a threshold was established requiring that at least 20% of the paper be devoted to a discussion of the merits of reuse itself or comparison with other methods. While Ref. [24] find that only papers that devote at least 30% of their content to empirical results contain adequate experimentation, we determined that setting the threshold this high would exclude important data. This criterion resulted in the removal of 16 papers since they discussed (similar to Ref. [25]) empirical results only peripherally. The removed papers [26, 27, 28, 11, 29, 22, 30, 31, 32, 33, 34, 35, 36, 37, 38, 39] were from the experience report and expert opinion categories. We also excluded textbooks (e.g., [40]), since their major purpose is to teach a methodology rather than to evaluate reuse success.

Finally, in 24 papers, we could not determine whether the systems were embedded or nonembedded. This was disappointing, because highly regarded papers about reuse did not identify the system type, and thus could not be used in our analysis. We had to exclude the following papers: Refs. [41, 42, 43, 44, 45, 46, 47, 48, 49, 14, 50, 51, 52, 53, 54, 54, 55, 22, 56, 6, 57, 58, 59, 60]. This was particularly unfortunate, since they contain some highly regarded work. The final paper count for analysis was 43.

Seventeen articles evaluated reuse in embedded systems only, 17 evaluated reuse in nonembedded systems only, and nine dealt with empirical results for reuse in both embedded and nonembedded software systems. We found 10 discussions of case studies, one quasi-experiment, three surveys, two meta-analyses, four reviews of practice, nine expert opinions, and 14 experience reports.

While some papers discussed various development strategies, and embedded systems and nonembedded systems, none compared development approaches with each other and none compared reuse in embedded systems against reuse in nonembedded systems. This study compares reuse outcomes from studies using different development strategies, and outcomes from studies using embedded and nonembedded systems. In the studies that covered both embedded and nonembedded systems, we collected the data from each for comparison.

4. REUSE AND DEVELOPMENT APPROACHES FOR EMBEDDED VERSUS NONEMBEDDED SYSTEMS

We classified papers by type of system (embedded and nonembedded), development approach, and type of empirical research.

Some empirical studies covered combinations of two or more approaches. While the academic definitions of some approaches subsume other approaches, it was not clear that this was happening. One argument against is that embedded systems tend to include performance and reliability models, MATLAB models, etc. Further, over time, some parts of the system may have switched development approaches. Additionally, some studies reported on multiple projects. If their development approaches were not the same, the study was classified in more than one category. Therefore, we counted each development approach separately. An example of multiple classification is [61]. We distinguished studies by whether they provided qualitative data (e.g., the paper reported success as high, medium, low, or reuse outcomes as better, worse, or reuse satisfaction as satisfied, dissatisfied) or quantitative data (e.g., percent improvements, or r-values, p-values in statistical analysis results).

4.1. Software Reuse in Embedded Systems

Seventeen empirical studies covered reuse in embedded software. These included empirical studies of reuse in industry and at government agencies. When more than one reuse development approach was involved, the study was counted in multiple categories. Table 2 shows the data by development approach and study type.

Of the four case studies covering development strategies in embedded systems exclusively, one was a combination of ontology- and model-based reuse [62], two were PL reuse [13, 63], and one did not specify development approach [64]. The empirical study evaluating the combination of ontology- and model-based reuse involved an Ericsson product. It was based on interviews of Ericsson senior modelers. The particular object of study was a subproject within the company focused on developing embedded software for part of a mobile-communications-network product. The study identified 26 areas for improvement in modeling content, activities, and management for large projects [62].

The one quasi-experiment on reuse in embedded systems studied both component-based (CB) and MB development approaches [65]. They developed a method (MARMOT) to analyze performance of MB, component-oriented development in a small system. The system was a control system for an exterior car mirror.

Four expert opinion papers covered reuse in embedded software. Dos Santos and Cunha discussed an embedded satellite system [66]. One discussed modeling interacting hybrid systems [67]. The other two articles examined reuse trends in embedded software in real-time signal processing systems: one considered application and architecture trends, the other considered design technologies [68, 69]. These articles dealt with architecting and designing a very large-scale integrated (VLSI) chip.

Eight experience reports evaluated reuse in embedded systems. For example, one was a DARPA analysis from MB designers working with robotics, including tools and techniques [70]. The combination PL/CB reuse study involved digital audio and video projects [71]. They developed a process for platform development, found core assets in the digital AV domain and legacy assets, designed a common architecture, and reported their experience with this approach. The report on CB reuse involved field devices, such as temperature, pressure and flow sensors, actuators and positioners, in other words, small, real-time embedded systems [72]. Two of the studies on MB reuse were about the TechSat21 program and appear

Table 2 Empirical Studies of Embedded Systems Studies Reuse by Development Approach

Embedded Systems	Case Study	Quasi-Experiment	Survey	Review of Practice	Meta-Analysis	Experience Report	Expert Opinion	Total
Ontology	1							1
Product line	2	1				2		5
Model based	1	1				3	2	7
Component based						2		2
Unspecified	1					1	2	4

Note: Some studies included more than one development approach due to reporting on multiple projects, hence 19, rather than 17 studies.
Note: There were no surveys, reviews of practice, or meta-analyses that dealt with reuse in embedded systems.

to be the same study [73, 74]. They created an agent-based software architecture for autonomous distributed systems. Through Matlab, they were able to model clusters in a way that enabled operators to command the cluster as a virtual satellite by decomposing goals into specific satellite commands.

4.2. Software Reuse in Nonembedded Systems

Seventeen studies involved reuse in nonembedded software in industry and at government agencies. Table 3 shows the studies by development approach and study type.

Seven reuse case studies addressed reuse in nonembedded software (since one covered two development strategies, it is reported twice). Two studies addressed MB reuse, two studies addressed CB reuse, one studied a combination of PL and CB reuse. Two did not specify the development approach. The following are examples of case studies in nonembedded systems. One study of an MB approach involved reducing interface incompatibilities via feature models [75]. The study on a combination of PL and CB reuse involved large telecommunications products. The components were built-in house and shared across PLs. Standardized processes and architectures enabled the reuse [76]. One study on CB reuse reported on an industrial case study in a large Norwegian Oil and Gas company, involving a reused Java class framework and two applications. It analyzes reasons for differences in defect profiles [77]. The other involved research performed by the National Aeronautics and Space Administration (NASA) Earth Science Data Systems (ESDS) Software Reuse Working Group (WG) that was "established in 2004 to promote the reuse of software and related artifacts among members of the ESDS data product and software development community." Artifacts were shared via a web portal [78].

There were two surveys that specifically addressed a CB development approach in nonembedded software [79]. A questionnaire (answered by 26 developers) covered areas dealing with the practice and challenges for what they called "development with reuse in the IT industry." They studied company reuse levels and factors leading to reuse of in-house components. The other addressed success factors in reuse investment [47].

One review of practice studied the use of ontologies [80], including ontology mapping categories and their characteristics. This included four different ways of merging ontologies into a single ontology from multiple sources.

Table 3 Empirical Studies of Nonembedded Systems Studies Reuse by Development Approach

Nonembedded Systems	Case Study	Quasi-Experiment	Survey	Review of Practice	Meta-Analysis	Experience Report	Expert Opinion	Total
Ontology				1		1	1	3
Product line	1						1	2
Model based	2					1	1	4
Component based	3		2			1		6
Unspecified	2						3	5

Note: Some studies included more than one development approach due to reporting on multiple projects, hence 20, rather than 17 studies.
Note: There were no quasi-experiments or meta-analyses that dealt with reuse in nonembedded systems.

Four expert opinion papers discussed nonembedded systems. One expert opinion paper on development strategies covered ontology, PL, and MB reuse [61]. It analyzed developing an ontology of models into a PL in the insurance domain. One discussed the difficulties of architectural mismatch [81]. One investigated reuse libraries and their contributions to reuse [46]. One discussed success factors across business domains [44].

Three experience reports addressed reuse in nonembedded systems. The ontology experience report addressed processes and product development using an ontology for the budget domain of the Public Sector in Australia [82]. The experience report on MB reuse covered domain-specific modeling [83]. It discussed stock trading tasks such as buying and selling stock and creating user account details. The experience report on CB reuse discussed the SMC satellite ground system framework [84].

Clearly, compared to embedded systems, we find more case studies, most of which are dealing with CBSE. All empirical studies relating to ontologies are qualitative (review of practice, expert opinion, and experience report), maybe reflecting that ontologies are still somewhat novel in industry. Reuse in PL development shows predominantly qualitative data as well (3:1). Even reuse in MB development shows more qualitative (expert opinion and experience report) than quantitative analysis (case study). Reuse in CBSE has more quantitative results in its case studies. This is matched by four qualitative studies (survey, review of practice, experience reports). Empirical studies of reuse that do not identify the development approach are also predominantly qualitative (4:1) with three expert opinion studies compared to one case study and a survey. Clearly, the goal to analyze and compare reuse outcomes in embedded versus nonembedded systems for different development approaches would have been helped greatly with more "hard" data.

4.3. Software Reuse in Embedded and Nonembedded Systems

Nine studies covered development strategies in both embedded and nonembedded systems. Table 4 shows the type of data collected by development approach and study type.

Two case studies examined both embedded and nonembedded software systems. It was is a side-by-side comparison of two very different systems, a pump controller versus web mail [85]. It did not specifically address reuse characteristics that may be nonembedded system . The other case study examined data from two reuse projects at Hewlett Packard (HP), one an embedded system that developed, enhanced, and maintained firmware for

Table 4 Empirical Studies of Embedded and Nonembedded Systems Studies Reuse by Development Approach

Both Embedded and Nonembedded Systems	Case Study	Quasi-Experiment	Survey	Review of Practice	Meta-Analysis	Experience Report	Expert Opinion	Total
Ontology								
Product line			1			2	1	4
Model based	1		1				1	3
Component based	1							1
Unspecified				1	2		1	4

Note: Some studies included more than one development approach due to reporting on multiple projects, hence 12, rather than 10 studies.
Note: There were no quasi-experiments that dealt with reuse in both types of systems.

printers and plotters, the other a nonembedded system producing large application software for manufacturing resource planning [86].

The reuse survey covering both embedded and nonembedded systems addressed PL/MB reuse for both types of systems. Its purpose was to identify some of the key factors in adopting or running a company-wide software reuse program. The key factors were derived from information gained from structured interviews dealing with reuse practices, based on projects for the introduction of reuse in European companies. Twenty-four projects from 1994 to 1997 were analyzed. The projects were from both large and small companies, a variety of business domains, using both object-oriented and procedural development [87].

The two meta-analyses studied reuse (without clearly specifying the development approach). One was a study of reuse literature published between 1994 and 2005 covering benefits derived from software developed for reuse and software developed with reuse [6]. The other discussed factors that could lead to reuse success [88].

Two expert opinion papers discussed reuse in both embedded and nonembedded software systems. One expert opinion dealt with adding an MB reuse to a PL reuse development approach, thus developing and documenting the product via a model [89]. It discussed the creation of a model that would allow firms to develop related lines on a common product platform. Thus, the purpose of this study was model building, rather than a development approach assessment.

There were two experience reports. One report on PL reuse compared two case studies producing very different products (factory automation and medical information) using the configurable software product family approach [53].

Similar to the previous two categories of analysis, qualitative studies outnumber quantitative ones (6:3). More recent development approaches either have no empirical studies (ontology) or the studies are more in the expert opinion or experience categories (PL). Reuse in MB development shows quantitative data through a case study and a survey. The most extensive analysis of reuse with meta-analysis was performed on systems for which the development approach was not specified. This does not help in evaluating where and how the development approach may or may not have contributed to success.

As can be expected, empirical studies of reuse with specific development approaches start (after their introduction) with experience reports and expert opinions, progressing to more in-depth case studies, quasi-experiments, and finally meta-analysis over time (see Appendix A).

4.4. Comparing Study Types

In total, seven types of empirical studies were represented in our review. Of these, three were of the more rigorous type (case study, quasi-experiment, survey), two were a less rigorous type (review of practice and meta-analysis), and two were the least rigorous (expert opinion and experience report). When we look at the numbers of papers in these categories, five studies of embedded systems, nine studies of nonembedded systems, and three of both embedded and nonembedded systems were of the most rigorous types. No studies of embedded systems, one of nonembedded systems, and two studies of both embedded and nonembedded systems were of the less rigorous types. Twelve studies of embedded systems, seven studies of nonembedded systems, and four studies of both embedded and nonembedded systems were of the least rigorous type of study.

Case studies, quasi-experiments, surveys, reviews of practice, and meta-analyses provided quantitative data. The expert opinion and experience reports offered mostly qualitative information. One experience report offered quantitative data.

Reuse with an ontology approach was only evaluated once with a case study including only qualitative data. Reuse in PL reported quantitative data in two studies (a case study and a quasi-experiment), the rest included qualitative data (a case study and experience reports). Reuse in MB development had quantitative data in three studies (a case study, a quasi-experiment, and an experience report), but there were four less rigorous expert opinions and experience reports (all with qualitative data). Reuse in CBSE only reported qualitative data in experience reports. The studies that did not identify the development approach also were predominantly qualitative.

5. METRICS REPORTED

Next, we turn to the papers' reporting of metrics. The types of metrics included size, reuse levels, quality, effort, performance, and programmatic (such as staff, institutionalized process, or schedule). We noticed that, while all of the metrics reported fit into these categories, the way the metrics were collected and reported differed. For example, size could mean the size of the project, the software size, the model size, the size of the system, the size of the software staff, or the size of the project. Reuse level could refer to reused elements (total number or percent of the project), frequency in which certain components were reused, phase of reused assets, and reused requirements. Quality referred to defects, faults, severity of defects, reliability, and aspects of errors. Effort was reported in terms of phase (development, design, simulation), productivity, and rework. Programmatic reported schedule, staff, process, and time to market.

Table 5 shows metrics reported in studies of reuse of embedded systems. They include size, amount of reuse, quality, effort, and performance. Only one study reported performance metrics, which was somewhat surprising, since many embedded systems have to meet real-time performance requirements or deal with limited storage capacity. Reuse studies on embedded systems did not report metrics related to process or programmatics. All size metrics were ratio, as were quality and effort. Reuse metrics were ratio except for needs versus needs met, which was ordinal.

Table 6 shows metrics reported in studies of reuse of nonembedded systems. Except for performance metrics, the same categories of outcomes are reported, but there is a larger variety of measures for several of the categories. We notice, for example, that nonembedded systems report the frequency with which assets were reused as a measure of reuse, not reported by embedded systems. In quality, nonembedded systems report severity of defects, changes to software products, and component understanding, which are also not reported by embedded systems. Nonembedded systems report on productivity, an effort metric not mentioned by embedded systems.

Nonembedded systems also had a greater division of the metric scale. While all of the size metrics were ratio, in reuse level four were ratio and three were ordinal. In quality, four were ratio to two ordinal, and in effort three were ratio and one ordinal. This limited the types of analysis that we could perform.

Table 7 shows metrics reported in studies of reuse in both embedded and nonembedded systems. Unlike studies of only embedded or only nonembedded systems, we see metrics related to programmatics. Also unlike studies of only embedded or only nonembedded systems, the only reuse metric was the phase of reuse, and only this category measured rework.

Table 8 summarizes the commonalities and differences of metrics collected for embedded systems and nonembedded systems as well as the metrics collected when both types of system were studied. It shows that in the subattributes, there was little commonality in the metrics reported. It is only at the generalized outcome level that the reported metrics become comparable.

In summary, metrics varied widely, ranging from nominal to ratio level of measurement, and metrics for the same attribute varied quite a bit among studies. This makes direct comparison difficult.

Table 5 Metrics Used in Studies of Reuse of Embedded Software Systems

Attribute	Definition	Scale	Explanation	Source
Size				
Model size: absolute	"The numbers of elements: the number of classes, the number of use cases, the number of sequence diagrams, or the number of classes in a diagram"	Ratio	"Absolute size 'length' can be measured by source code, it is organized as a sequence of characters and lines. UML models are not sequences and there exists no meaningful notion of length. So, we replace 'length' by 'absolute size.' Metrics that measure a model's absolute size are the numbers of elements."	[65, 90]
Model size: relative	"Ratios between absolute size metrics, such as number of sequence diagrams, number of objects; number of use cases, number of classes; number of state charts/ number of classes"	Ratio	"These metrics enable to compare the relative size (or proportions) of different models with each other and they give an indication about the completeness of models."	[65, 90]
System size	KBytes of the binary code	Ratio	Executable	[65]
Size	Terminal semicolons, delivered source instructions	Ratio	Source code	[64]
Reuse				
The amount of reused elements	"The proportion of the system which can be reused without any changes or with small adaptations."	Ratio	Measures taken at model and code level.	[65]
Reusable requirements	Reusable requirement unit	Ratio	Any prominent and distinctive concepts or characteristics that are visible to various stakeholders.	[13]
Needs versus needs met	Direct needs expressed by the informants, indirect needs inferred from descriptions of situations or problems	Ordinal	As defined by surveyed engineers	[62]
Quality				
Defect density	Defects per 100 LOC	Ratio	"Collected via inspection and testing activities."	[65]
Reliability	Reliability of the software		Assumed to be 100%	[73]

Continued

Table 5 Metrics Used in Studies of Reuse of Embedded Software Systems—cont'd

Attribute	Definition	Scale	Explanation	Source
Effort				
Development effort	Development time (h)	Ratio	Collected by daily effort sheets.	[65]
Simulation effort	Person weeks	Ratio	Time to develop simulation environment	[91]
Performance				
Performance	On board fuel consumption and time to perform simulation		"Because time for communication has greatest impact, only communication time included."	[73]
Computation	Current CPU workload and total workload	Ratio	Percent of maximum computational rate (comp/s) or percent of CPU time dedicated to a task	[73]

Note: Performance metrics reported only in embedded systems.

6. ANALYSIS OF OUTCOMES

Unlike other studies that analyzed papers reporting on multiple studies, but reported results as a single data point per paper (e.g., Ref. [6]), we scored each project individually. For example, one study included 27 different projects with different results for different projects [87]. These are scored as 27 individual data points. When a study reported on reuse in both embedded and nonembedded systems, we included the individual projects in both categories, as appropriate. The remainder of this chapter reports on analyzing empirical evidence of reuse by project rather than by paper (or study), in both embedded and nonembedded systems [87].

Comparing Development Approaches. Table 9 shows how many projects used a particular development approach. In comparison, there were fewer studies investigating reuse with a product-line approach for embedded systems than for nonembedded systems (20 vs. 23). Embedded system reuse was studied for MB development approaches 19 times, compared to 24 times for nonembedded systems. CBSE was studied more frequently for reuse in nonembedded systems than embedded systems (14 vs. 7). It appears that across the board, reuse was studied in fewer projects in embedded systems than nonembedded systems.

Table 6 Metrics Used in Studies of Reuse of Nonembedded Software Systems

Attribute	Definition	Scale	Explanation	Source
Size				
Software size	Noncommented source lines of code	Ratio	Source code	[77]
Module size	KLOC	Ratio	Source code	[92]
Size	KSLOC	Ratio	Source code	[76]
Reuse				
Reuse level	Ratio of different lower level items reused in higher level items to total lower level items used	Ratio	RL is based on counting item types rather than item tokens	[21]
	Developers assessments of reuse levels	Ordinal	Developers assessments of reuse levels	[79]
Reuse frequency	Frequency of references to reused items	Ratio	Percentage of references to lower level items reused verbatim inside a higher level item versus the total number of references	[21]
	Frequency of module reuse	Ratio	Ratio of the yearly sum of reuse frequencies to number of modules stored in the library	[92]
Active module ratio	Ratio of active modules	Ratio	Ratio of number of modules reused at least once each year to number of modules stored in the library	[92]
Component requirements (re)negotiation	Developers assessments of component-related requirements (re) negotiation	Ordinal		[79]
Repository value	Developers assessments of value of component repository	Ordinal		[79]
Quality				
Defect density	The NSLOC of each system divided by the number of defects based on trouble reports	Ratio		[77]
Fault density	The number of faults divided by the software size	Ratio	An error correction may affect more than one module. Each module affected is counted as having a fault	[76]

Continued

Table 6 Metrics Used in Studies of Reuse of Nonembedded Software Systems—cont'd

Attribute	Definition	Scale	Explanation	Source
Severity	The number of defects of different severities divided by the NSLOC	Ratio		[77]
Number of module deltas	A change to a software work product such as code	Ratio	Either an enhancement or a repair, and since they correlate well with faults, deltas are sometimes used for estimating error rates	[21]
Component understanding	Developers assessments of component understanding	Ordinal		[79]
Quality attributes of components	Developers assessments of component attribute definitions	Ordinal		[79, 21]
Effort				
Time to develop	Staff months	Ratio	Staff months	
Productivity	Number of NCSLs produced per person day	Ratio	Relies on the effectiveness of NCSL as a measure of product size	[21]
	Effort in person days spent per module	Ratio	Effort to develop unit of compilation and deployment. A higher effort/module, means lower productivity	[21]
Developer attitudes	How developers felt reuse process affected productivity and quality	Ordinal		[93]

Note: There were no performance metrics.

Comparing Software Size. We measured software size as in Ref. [94]: (size of the software project on which reuse was applied): Small = less than 10 KLOC and 10 person months effort; Medium = 10–100 KLOC and 10–100 person months; Large = more than 100 KLOC, more than 100 person months. Table 10 compares the sizes of the embedded systems projects by development approach. For each development approach, "NR" states the number of such projects reported and % compares the percentage of projects in each size category. Table 11 does the same for nonembedded systems. Where possible, we also used synonyms of the sizes reported in Table 8.

Table 7 Metrics Used in Studies of Reuse of Both Embedded and Nonembedded Systems

Attribute	Definition	Scale	Explanation	Source
Size				
Team size	Persons	Ratio	Number of persons on the reuse team	[87]
Program size	KSLOC	Ratio	Source code	[87]
Reuse				
Phase of reuse	Phase in which artifacts are reused	Nominal		[87]
Quality				
Defect density	Defects per KSLOC	Ratio		[2]
Error source	Source of error	Nominal	Where did the error originate	[6]
Type of error	Error type	Nominal	Level of severity of error	[6]
Error slippage	Error slippage	Ratio	Error slippage from unit test	[6]
Effort				
Development effort	Effort in person hours	Ratio	Effort per module, asset, or product in person hours, days, or months	[6]
Design effort	Percent of total effort	Ratio	Percent of development time spent in design	[6]
Effort	Person months	Ratio		[6]
Productivity	LOC/time	Ratio	Apparent and actual LOC per time unit, size of application divided by development effort	[6]
Rework	Person months	Ratio	Effort spent in isolating and correcting problems, difficulty in error isolation or correction	[6]
Programmatic				
Schedule	Months	Ratio	Calendar time to complete	[2]
Time to market	Percent	Ratio	Reduction in time to market	[6]
	Months	Ratio	Months to deliver	[87]
Staff	Persons	Ratio	Overall staff size, software staff size	[94]
	Years	Ratio	Overall staff experience, software staff experience	[94]
Process	Software process	Nominal	Presence of reuse process integrated into organization software development process	[87]

Note: There were no performance metrics reported in studies of both embedded and nonembedded systems.

Table 8 Comparing Metrics Used for Embedded Systems, Nonembedded Systems, and Both Types of Systems

Attribute	Embedded	Nonembedded	Both Types
Size			
Software size		X	
Model size: absolute	X	X	
Model size: relative	X		
System size	X		
Size	X	X	
Team size			X
Program size			X
Reuse			
The amount of reused elements	X		
Reusable requirements	X		
Needs versus needs met	X		
Reuse level		X	
Reuse frequency		X	
Active module ratio		X	
Component requirements r(e)negotiation		X	
Repository value		X	
Phase of reuse			X
Quality			
Defect density	X	X	X
Fault density		X	
Severity		X	
Number of module deltas		X	
Reliability	X		
Component understanding		X	
Quality attributes of components		X	
Error source			X
Type of error			X
Error slippage			X

Table 8 Comparing Metrics Used for Embedded Systems, Nonembedded Systems, and Both Types of Systems—cont'd

Attribute	Embedded	Nonembedded	Both Types
Effort			
Development effort	X		X
Design effort			X
Simulation effort	X		
Time to develop		X	
Productivity			
Effort			X
Rework			X
Developer attitudes		X	
Performance			
Performance	X		
Computation	X		
Programmatic			
Schedule			X
Time to market			X
Staff			X
Process			X

Note: The types of attributes studied were more programmatic when both embedded and nonembedded systems were studied.

Table 9 Number of Projects by Development Type

	Ontology	Product Line	Model Based	Component Based	Unspecified	Total
Embedded	0	20	19	7	10	56
Nonembedded	3	23	24	14	15	79
Total	3	43	43	21	25	135

Note: Does not count projects where system type could not be determined by context.

Because many empirical studies did not report system size, the numbers in the tables do not add up to the total number of projects.

Empirical studies of both PL and CB development strategies use a larger proportion of medium and large systems, while studies of MB and

Table 10 Size of Embedded Systems

Embedded	Product Line		Model Based		Component Based		Unspecified Reuse	
Project sizes	NR	%	NR	%	NR	%	NR	%
Large	4	40	2	14	2	67		
Medium	6	50	3	21				
Small	1	10	9	65	1	33	2	100

Note: Many papers did not report size.

Table 11 Size of Nonembedded Systems

Nonembedded	Product Line		Model Based		Component Based		Unspecified Reuse	
Project Sizes	NR	%	NR	%	NR	%	NR	%
Large	1	50			6	60		
Medium								
Small	1	50			4	40		

Note: Many papers did not report size.

unspecified development strategies tend to study small systems. Given that embedded systems cover small, medium and large systems, this represents a reasonable cross section.

Let us turn to outcomes next.

Comparing Outcomes. Given the diverse ways in which various system attributes and reuse variables were measured, as well as the lack of effect size in most studies, it was not possible to perform a meta-analysis that could quantitatively assess and compare similarities and differences between outcomes. In an effort to quantify and analyze the data, we include as "characteristics of events" the concepts of "better or worse." "Better" meant that the reuse outcome under study was considered to be an improvement over not reusing. Conversely, "worse" meant that the reuse outcome had negative results. We use the term "mixed" when there was in improvement in some aspects of the outcome and other aspects of the outcome were negative, or when there was no noticeable difference between reusing and not reusing assets. Thus, we are able to assign an ordinal measure to outcomes, i.e., 1 for better outcomes, −1 for worse outcomes, and 0 for either no change in outcomes or mixed results. We use the same outcome categories as in Table 5. Tables 12 and 13 list development approach as major column

Table 12 Frequencies of Outcomes

	Product Line		Model Based		Component Based		Unspecified		Total	
Outcome[a]	E	N	E	N	E	N	E	N	E	N
Reuse level										
1	7	15	10	13	1	6	0	1	18	35
− 1	4	2	0	4	0	0	1	4	5	10
0	0	0	3	3	0	0	1	0	4	3
Effort										
1	7	5	3	10	1	4	2	9	13	28
− 1	0	0	7	2	1	0	0	0	8	2
0	0	0	6	7	1	2	1	0	8	9
Quality										
1	4	2	2	4	1	6	0	9	7	21
− 1	0	0	5	1	0	1	3	0	8	2
0	0	0	6	7	1	2	1	0	8	9
General										
1	13	3	2	8	2	4	2	10	19	25
− 1	3	0	1	1	0	0	0	0	4	1
0	0	0	6	6	0	0	0	0	6	6

[a]Number of projects reporting the outcome. *Note*: Not all projects reported all outcomes.

headers like Tables 10 and 11. For each development approach, we list number of projects for embedded (E) and nonembedded (N) systems. Rows list outcome scores within each outcome category. While three nonembedded systems projects report using an ontology approach, there were no embedded system projects using an ontology. Hence, we could not compare them and left them out of Tables 12 and 13.

A relatively large number of papers only reported very high level results rather than results for specific attributes of reuse outcomes. These are scored similarly and shown in Tables 12 and 13 under "general." The "general" category reflects the developers' reported overall reuse experience.

Embedded Systems. For *reuse level* in embedded systems, most of the studies reported positive reuse results for PL, MB, and CB development. This was not the case for the two studies that did not specify development approach.

Table 13 Normalized of Frequencies Outcomes

Outcome[a]	Product Line		Model Based		Component Based		Unspecified		Total	
	E	N	E	N	E	N	E	N	E	N
Reuse level										
Total	11	17	13	20	1	6	2	5	27	48
+	64%	88%	77%	65%	100%	100%	0%	20%	67%	73%
−	36%	12%	0%	20%	0%	0%	50%	80%	19%	21%
M	0%	0%	23%	15%	0%	0%	50%	0%	15%	6%
Effort										
Total	7	5	16	19	3	6	3	9	29	39
1	100%	100%	19%	53%	33%	67%	67%	100%	45%	72%
− 1	0%	0%	44%	11%	33%	0%	0%	0%	28%	5%
0	0%	0%	38%	37%	33%	33%	33%	0%	28%	23%
Quality										
Total	4	2	13	12	2	9	4	9	23	32
1	100%	100%	15%	33%	50%	67%	0%	100%	30%	66%
− 1	0%	0%	38%	8%	0%	11%	75%	0%	35%	6%
0	0%	0%	46%	58%	50%	22%	25%	0%	35%	28%
General										
Total	16	3	9	15	2	4	2	10	29	32
1	81%	100%	22%	53%	100%	100%	100%	100%	66%	78%
− 1	19%	0%	11%	7%	0%	0%	0%	0%	14%	3%
0	0%	0%	67%	40%	0%	0%	0%	0%	21%	19%

[a]Percent of projects reporting the outcome.

One of them reported mixed, the other negative results. For PL reuse in embedded software systems, we identified three reasons for reuse failure: complex reuse repository, lack of management commitment, and changing of the hardware. With an MB development approach, the failure may have been due to lack of experience in modeling. Under unspecified development approach, we found that for embedded systems, the results were no better and possibly worse than if no reuse had been employed. However, there is no explanation in the studies as to why that would be the case.

While *effort* was reduced in all projects with PL development that reported effort, this was not the case for MB development, where the majority of studies reported negative (7) or mixed (6) results. Each of the three projects using CB development reported a different outcome with regard to effort. Finally, when development approach was not specified, two projects reported positive, one a mixed outcome. It appears that while the majority of projects report positive outcomes with regard to effort, some development approaches show more mixed and negative results. This would indicate that the type of development approach matters.

Improvements for *quality* do not always materialize, as eight negative results indicate. They are related to MB and unspecified development approaches (UA). By contrast, all four projects (that reported quality outcomes) that used a PL approach report positive outcomes for quality, as opposed to two for MB development (compared to five negative and six mixed results) and only one for CB development reported a positive outcome. Again, development approach matters.

Projects that only report *overall reuse success* are generally favorable (19), but again, MB development projects reported one negative result, six mixed results, and only two positive ones. In the MB reuse projects that reported mixed results, while problems were identified, only the factors leading to the success of the successful projects were discussed. In the MB reuse project that failed, it appeared that the model was incomplete. "Our implementation was not carried out through widespread modeling, and there are a few reasons for this:

- the diverse team of experts in robotics, computer vision, software, and control were not all familiar with software modeling techniques;
- the operating environment of real-time behaviors required many components to run on a real-time operating system with limited tool support;
- the behavior of many components is best specified using general-purpose techniques, especially the advanced control algorithms used."

Whether a more experienced modeling team could have been successful is not clear. It appears that reuse with MB development poses challenges for embedded systems.

Under PL development, three projects report a failure. In one, the analyst found that the reuse structure was too complex to encourage reuse of software. "Not modifying nonreuse processes, and insufficiently publicizing the repository and the reuse initiative, were the immediate causes of failure."

In the other two, the analyst found that the management was not committed to reuse and that a change in hardware made the software reuse unsuccessful. "As a result, reusable assets were produced, but could never be reused because of changes to requirements, both in functionality and hardware [94, pp. 349–351]."

Reuse in embedded systems was successful for both CB and UA. Overall, 19 successful projects compare to four failures and six mixed results.

Nonembedded Systems. Table 12 also shows the reuse outcomes for nonembedded systems. Outcomes related to *reuse level* are overwhelmingly positive: 35 projects report success versus 10 negative and three mixed outcomes. Lack of success was attributed to a loose development approach, only reusing design and code, no domain analysis, no configuration management, no top management commitment, lack of reuse processes, and key roles. In the successful projects, reuse processes, modifying nonreuse processes, management commitment, and human factors were all important for a successful reuse program [94, p. 347].

Similarly, *effort reduction* was judged positive by 28 projects. Only two reported a negative outcome and nine reported mixed outcomes. Two negative outcomes were for MB development, as were seven of the mixed outcomes. Two of the mixed outcomes were in CB development. No reasons were given for the negative or mixed outcomes.

Quality. Quality also improved for most nonembedded systems with 21 reporting positive results, nine mixed results, and only two negative results. However, as for embedded systems, using an MB development approach had more negative and mixed results $(1 + 7 = 8)$ than positive ones (4).

Nonembedded system projects that report *overall reuse success* dominate with positive outcomes (25) versus one with negative and six with mixed outcomes. There also were three positive results using an ontology-based approach. Table 12 does not list outcomes of projects using an ontology development approach, since embedded systems do not use this approach and hence a comparison is not possible.

The results for nonembedded systems showed predominantly improvement in all outcomes areas, except quality in MB reuse, where the majority of outcomes is mixed or negative.

It appears that positive outcomes are more frequent for nonembedded systems, but negative outcomes for all types of outcome variables still occur for MB development. Note also that PL development is not immune to negative reuse outcomes, specifically, two projects report negative outcomes for reuse level.

The data in Table 12 indicate that reuse in nonembedded systems is more likely to be successful for some outcomes, like effort and quality. Overall outcome variables tend to be more positive for nonembedded systems. Particularly, there is a smaller proportion of negative outcomes for MB development for reuse level and effort. This is also true for PL development for all outcome variables. Table 12 shows that reuse success differs some between embedded systems, not only overall (last columns) but also with regard to successful development approach.

Table 13 shows reuse outcomes as percentages for PL, MB, CB, and UA. For PL development, the reuse level improved in 88% of the projects in nonembedded systems, but only for 64% in embedded systems. Thirty-six percent of the embedded systems reported lower reuse levels as opposed to only 12% of the nonembedded systems. For both types of systems, 100% of the projects reported improvements in effort and quality. However, in the general impression of reuse experience, 100% of the nonembedded systems projects reported improvement, but only 81% of the embedded systems projects reported improvement and 19% reported negative results. While the reasons for these results were not reported, we posit that platform dependence and the performance requirements of the embedded systems may have precluded some reuse and that the reuse level and the general impressions may be related.

In MB development, we see that 77% of the embedded systems projects reported improved outcomes. There were no reports of negative outcomes and 23% of the outcomes were mixed. In nonembedded systems, 65% reported improved outcomes, 15% reported mixed outcomes, and 20% reported negative outcomes. However, we find that in effort and quality, the embedded systems projects reported far worse results than nonembedded systems (effort: 19% vs. 53% positive, 44% vs. 11% negative, and 38% vs. 37% mixed; quality: 15% vs. 33% positive, 38% vs. 8% negative, and 46% vs. 58% mixed). The general impression of reuse using MB development was also different, with only 22% positive results for embedded systems compared to 53% positive outcomes for nonembedded systems. Eleven percent negative outcomes compare to 7% for nonembedded systems; 67% mixed responses for embedded systems compared to 40% mixed responses for nonembedded systems. These appear to be important differences in reuse outcomes for MB development in embedded versus nonembedded systems.

The outcomes for CB development also differed for effort and quality, but the number of observations was too small to draw conclusions.

The overall outcomes regardless of development method is also telling. Overall, the percentage of projects experiencing an increase in reuse level was similar between embedded and nonembedded systems. However, the savings in effort were quite different. While the positive effort outcomes were nearly the same (20–21%), the difference in negative effort outcomes was sizeable (40% vs. 14%) as well as in mixed outcomes (40% vs. 64%). The difference in quality outcomes was also striking, with nonembedded systems reporting positive outcomes twice as often as embedded systems (66% vs. 30%) and embedded systems reporting negative outcomes nearly six times as much as nonembedded systems (35% vs. 6%). General reuse experience was also noticeably different between embedded systems and nonembedded systems, with embedded systems reporting a positive outcome for 66% of the projects and nonembedded systems reporting a positive outcome for 78% of the projects, while embedded systems reported negative outcomes in 14% of the projects. Nonembedded systems reported negative outcomes for only 3% of the projects. The reasons for this cumulative difference are not clear. However, one study reported one failure in quality differences between the ground system (nonembedded) and the flight system (embedded) that was related to the size, reliability, and complexity of the software. While there was no discussion about which, if any, of these contributed to the failure, the conclusion was, "We found that development strategies in general performed as well or better than drastic change strategies on ground software, but did worse than adopting no strategy in the case of flight software systems [2]."

Testing for Significance. Our next question was whether the differences we observed and analyzed above are strong enough to be statistically significant. We performed a Chi-square test on the outcome scores. Table 14 shows the results. This indicates that the differences in reuse success described above are strong enough to be statistically significant for two situations:

Table 14 Chi-Squared *p*-Values Embedded Systems versus Nonembedded Systems

Outcome	Product Line	Model Based	Component Based	Unspecified Approach
Reuse level	0.1213	0.2291	N/A	N/A
Effort	0.2609	**0.0292**	0.3779	0.0704
Quality	N/A	0.2138	0.2062	**0.0005**
General	0.3059	0.2583	N/A	N/A

1. savings in effort are less likely to be successful for embedded systems when an MB approach to reuse is employed.
2. quality improvements are less likely to be realized in embedded systems (in studies that did not report on the development approach used).

Unfortunately, the papers do not provide a solid chain of evidence to identify reasons.

Since we did not have performance scores for nonembedded systems, we had to eliminate this success factor from the analysis. For some combinations of criteria and development strategies, the sample size was too small; hence, the corresponding table entries are marked N/A.

7. THREATS TO VALIDITY

Since much of the analysis is better classified as qualitative, we assess the following types of validity: descriptive validity, interpretive validity, theoretical validity, generalizability, and evaluative validity [95].

Descriptive Validity. Descriptive validity relates to the quality of what the researcher reports having seen, heard, or observed. Because observations are important, we needed to include grey literature. Since these are not always peer reviewed, the rigor of data collection or reporting is uncertain. To alleviate this threat to validity, we used SEI sources. While not peer reviewed, it is highly respected in industry. However, even in peer-reviewed material, the reporting might be subject to misinterpretation of what was observed.

We investigated how the researchers handled information, including their presentation of data, method, hypothesis, analysis, threats to validity, and significance. Of the 84 initial papers, half of the studies did not include the data that was claimed to be analyzed. Only five had a hypothesis. Only nine discussed threats to validity. Many studies are reports on reuse efforts undertaken by industry in specific approaches or products they were marketing. Many of these studies contained few or no metrics and they did not use hypothesis tests, analysis of their results, or clues about validity issues that might have affected outcomes. There was a great deal of expert opinion not backed up by metrics. Even in the very complete discussions of developers' attitudes to reuse, there was no discussion as to whether the way the developers felt about their reuse experience was backed up by quantitative results.

An important weakness is the failure of many studies to include enough metrics of outcomes, leading, by necessity, to few projects that could be reported in Section 6. Another weakness is the failure to include performance metrics in studies of nonembedded systems. As a result of this, some of the key differences may not be discovered. While the absence of stringent performance requirements may not affect reuse success in nonembedded systems, it makes it difficult to study embedded systems versus nonembedded systems in terms of reuse.

Interpretive Validity. The second threat to validity is concerned with what objects, events, and observations mean to the experimenters.

The first challenge in conducting this research was understanding development strategies and system types as variables. It was important to identify where system types and development approaches overlapped. For instance, a system as an end product could be embedded, but the simulation software and many subsystems could be nonembedded software. This required the ability to determine if the empirical study focused on the embedded portion of the system or on a nonembedded portion. In addition, the development strategies overlapped. Where more than one development approach appeared to exist, a determination had to be made as to whether the development approach was truly a combination or if one or another development approach dominated or even if one development approach subsumed others.

We found no studies whose major focus was comparing reuse in embedded systems versus nonembedded systems. Even when reuse in both types of systems is studied, the authors aggregate the results. This may have skewed the results reported in these studies. To alleviate this threat, we analyze each project individually.

Another interpretive threat to validity is the lack of common, consistent definitions. This is especially true with MB development strategies. While there are many types of models, the empirical studies are not clear what types of models are being used, whether they are architectural models, design models, or behavioral/performance models. It is also unclear, in empirical studies of CB reuse, whether the term component means the software with the platform or the software alone. In the gray literature mentioned above, the impartiality of the reporting is also uncertain. The mitigation, again, was to use respected industry sources, even though they are not peer reviewed.

In order to analyze the data, it was important to find a way to convert opinions into analyzable data. This was because quantitative data was scarce. It was also important to determine reuse outcome categories, since every paper had its own perspective and thus identified its own metrics (insofar as they used metrics). Categorizing metrics based on similarity required careful reading of each paper. The different viewpoints of different studies may have affected data interpretation (lack of clarity for our purposes).

Due to lack of information about system types, we had to exclude a series of studies. Had we known the system type in the studies, we could have had more data.

Finally, there was the question of the validity of subjective opinion as data. In many of the experience reports and expert opinions, the objectivity of the author may come into question. A few were possibly marketing. Setting the threshold for inclusion at 20% empirical content may have led us to include too many empirical papers that lack rigor, but setting it any higher would have reduced available data even further.

Theoretical Validity. Theoretical validity refers to an account's validity as a theory of some phenomenon. It depends on the validity of the construct of the experiment and on the validity of the interpretation or explanation of the observations. It also depends on whether there is consensus within the community about terms used to describe context, events, and outcomes. With the number of similar but not identical metrics presented, and ways of measuring success, there is a threat to the validity concerning the similarity or difference of the perceived value of reuse. This was mitigated by using a common scoring system, resulting in ordinal rather than ratio metrics.

Generalizability. "Generalizability refers to the extent to which one can extend the account of a particular situation or population to other persons, times, or settings than those directly studied [95]." It is comparable to external validity used in quantitative studies. In this situation, the threat to validity consists of the access to research that has been performed. Corporations may be performing studies that they choose not to release to the public. This could be because of the proprietary nature of the information, or because publication is not a corporate focus. The information in those studies could reveal factors not uncovered in the published material. There is a tendency to publish successes and to keep working on or terminate efforts that have failed, leading to overreporting of success. This also leads to the low numbers of projects available for comparison.

In some cases, the reuse process was being applied for the first time. This could have been one reason there was so much evidence of success through reuse. In these cases, it is fair to ask how much of the improvement is because there is SOME process being followed as opposed to none at all (in other words, was reuse the reason for improvement or was it the existence of a process?).

Evaluative Validity. Evaluative validity refers to the evaluative framework in deciding whether the reuse was, in fact, successful or not, and if so how much. The frameworks were likely to have differed in the different studies because the contexts were different. This was mitigated by considering both the researchers' evaluation of reuse and the observations upon which the evaluations are based.

8. CONCLUSION AND FUTURE WORK

We analyzed empirical studies of reuse dating from the time of DoD's release of the DoD software reuse (1992). We considered five development approaches to reusing software in both embedded and nonembedded types of software systems: ontology, PL, MB, CB, and unspecified approach (where the development approach was unknown). We considered eight different study types. Out of 84 candidate papers, only 43 had enough usable empirical content to enable a comparison of reuse outcomes in embedded versus nonembedded systems.

Reported studies (experiments, case studies, surveys, etc.) from industry as well as academia are surprisingly few. While we found a wealth of papers describing reuse, we found few with hard evidence either to the benefits or lack of benefits from reuse addressing or distinguishing between reuse in embedded versus nonembedded systems. We also found a number of papers questioning whether the benefits exist.

We divided the reuse studies into categories of embedded, nonembedded, and both embedded and nonembedded systems. We grouped these into subcategories based on development approach. Finally, we grouped them by type of empirical study.

Having catalogued the empirical studies, we proceeded to analyze individual projects in these studies. This allowed a first set of comparative analyses. We analyzed what reuse outcomes were reported and how they were measured. We mapped reported outcomes into a three point Likert scale as success, failure, or mixed result for reuse outcomes related to amount of reuse, effort, quality, performance (where available), and general reuse success. We compared embedded and nonembedded systems with regard to the proportion of positive, negative, and mixed reuse outcomes for each of the different development approaches. We also performed an overall comparison between reuse in embedded and nonembedded systems.

We found that results from reuse studies of nonembedded systems were not necessarily extendable to embedded systems. For example, in an MB development approach, effort outcomes were significantly more positive for nonembedded projects than for embedded projects. In order to suggest that a development approach or method is generally effective, it needs to be studied in both types of software systems. This research casts doubt on whether it is wise to extend findings from reuse studies of nonembedded systems to embedded systems.

Limitations of existing studies point to a lack of solid metrics to underpin the many opinions about reuse. While we were able to translate qualitative responses to ordinal data for comparative analysis, the power of nonparametric tests is lower than for parametric ones and may have prevented us from finding more differences that are statistically significant. It would be helpful to have research with reuse outcome measures that allow statistical tests with a higher power against which to test the hypotheses.

In embedded systems, where the source code is optimized against a processor, the reuse of source code may not generate much savings, because when the processor is changed, the code must be reoptimized. We saw symptoms of this in reports of unsuccessful reuse levels (i.e., less reuse than expected) in some of our data. This could contribute to the lack of success of reuse as reported in the reuse outcomes for MB development.

Another weakness in existing studies is the failure to include performance metrics. While the absence of stringent performance requirements may not affect success in nonembedded systems, it makes it difficult to compare embedded systems with nonembedded systems in terms of reuse when performance requirements must be met.

Based on our analysis, we have the following recommendations:

- If a company is interested in reusing embedded software, the existing empirical evidence suggests that it would be prudent to proceed carefully, and treat initial reuse attempts as pilot studies, rather than presuming that reuse benefits are a foregone conclusion.
- The tight connection between hardware and software in embedded systems, taken with the lack of performance metrics in existing reuse studies relating to embedded systems, suggests that embedded software reuse is less risky when the hardware is identical, or has characteristics which will yield improved performance when hardware and software are taken together (for instance, faster processor speeds with fully instruction-compatible processors).

An area for potential research would be to study whether an ontology-based approach would be of value in embedded systems. More research on combinations of approaches is also useful. Yet another potential area of research could be which types of models work best for MB development strategies, and whether they are the same for embedded and nonembedded systems.

ACKNOWLEDGMENTS

This material is based upon work supported in part by the National Science Foundation under grant # 0934413 to the University of Denver.

APPENDIX A: YEARS OF PUBLICATION

One question was how empirical results on development strategies was evolving over time. Our study collected research since 1992. Empirical research on reuse increased since 2001 after a short spike in the late 1990s. Nineteen of the 24 case studies were conducted since 2002, as well as three of the five surveys. While in 1997 all of the empirical papers on development strategies were expert opinion, in 2007 and 2009 (the years with the most empirical papers on reuse) the types of studies were fairly well divided among case studies, experience reports and expert opinion with one each of review of practice, meta-analysis, and quasi-experiment. Even in 2010 and 2012, the studies were case studies and review of practice, with only one experience report and no expert opinions. The empirical studies have become more focused on data and less on opinion. Figure A.1 illustrates this trend.

Another question was whether the development approaches using reuse were changing, or at least whether studies of development strategies were evolving. Empirical studies on PL reuse have been steady at one or two papers a year since 2003. However, the number of papers analyzing component-based and model-based reuse increased to a total of nine in

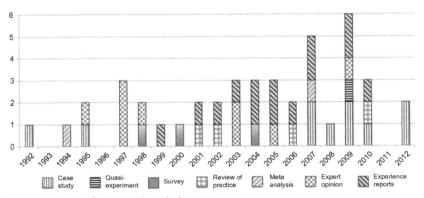

Figure A.1 Type of empirical study by year.

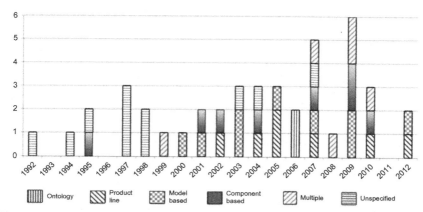

Figure A.2 Empirical studies of reuse by development approach by year.

2009. Research on PLs has been fairly steady since 2002. There have also been a number of studies that investigated multiple development approaches. Ontologies have begun to get attention lately as well. On the other hand, the number of empirical papers written on reuse where the development approach is unspecified has decreased to only one in each of 2008, 2009, and 2010. This shows that empirical research on reuse is beginning to focus on specific development strategies. Figure A.2 shows empirical studies on reuse by development approach by year.

REFERENCES

[1] C. Anderson, M. Dorfman, Aerospace software engineering: a collection of concepts, Progress in Astronautics and Aeronautics, American Institute of Aeronautics and Astronautics, 1991.

[2] A. Orrego, T. Menzies, O. El-Rawas, On the relative merits of software reuse, in: ICSP '09: Proceedings of the International Conference on Software Process, Springer-Verlag, 2009, pp. 186–197.

[3] L. Brown, DoD Software Reuse Initiative: Vision and Strategy, Technical report, Department of Defense, 1225 Jefferson Davis Highway, Suite 910, Arlington, VA 22202–4301, July 1992.

[4] T. Young, Report of the Defense Science Board/Air Force Scientific Advisory Board Joint Task Force on Acquisition of National Security Space Programs, Technical report, Office of the Under Secretary of Defense For Acquisition, Technology, and Logistics, Washington, D.C, May 2003, 20301-3140.

[5] M. Schwartz, The Nunn-McCurdy Act: Background, Analysis, and Issues for Congress, Technical report, Congressional Research Service, 2010.

[6] P. Mohagheghi, R. Conradi, Quality, productivity and economic benefits of software reuse: a review of industrial studies, Empirical Softw. Eng. 12 (5) (2007) 471–516.

[7] X. Cai, M.R. Lyu, K. Wong, R. Ko, Component-based software engineering: technologies, development frameworks, and quality assurance schemes, in: Proceedings of the Seventh Asia-Pacific APSEC, 2000, pp. 372–379.

[8] J. Estefan, Survey of candidate model-based engineering (MBSE) methodologies, in: INCOSE Survey of MBSE Methodologies, International Council on Systems Engineering (INCOSE), 2008, pp. 1–70.

[9] SEI, Software Product Lines, Technical report, Software Engineering Institute (SEI) (2010). URL http://www.sei.cmu.edu/productlines/.

[10] P.C. Clements, L. Northrop, Software Product Lines: Practices and Patterns, SEI Series in Software Engineering, Addison-Wesley, 2001.

[11] Y. Peng, C. Peng, J. Huang, K. Huang, An ontology-driven paradigm for component representation and retrieval, in: Ninth IEEE International Conference on Computer and Information TechnologyTechnology, 2009, CIT'09, 2009, pp. 187–192, vol. 2.

[12] R. Studer, V.R. Benjamins, D. Fensel, Knowledge engineering: principles and methods, IEEE Trans. Data Knowl. Eng. 25 (1998).

[13] S. Lee, H. Ko, M. Han, D. Jo, J. Jeong, K. Kim, Reusable software requirements development process: embedded software industry experiences, in: ASWEC '07: Proceedings of the 2007 Australian Software Engineering Conference, IEEE Computer Society, 2007, pp. 147–158.

[14] P.A.V. Hall, Architecture-driven component reuse, Inform. Softw. Technol. 41 (14) (1999) 963–968.

[15] International Organization for Standardization, Information Technology—Programming Languages, Their Environments and System Software Interfaces - Language-Independent Datatypes Technical Report on C++ Performance 2006, Technical report, ISO/IEC TR 18015:2006(E) (2006).

[16] E.A. Lee, CPS foundations, in: DAC '10: Proceedings of the 47th Design Automation Conference, ACM, 2010, pp. 737–742.

[17] C. Wohlin, P. Runeson, M. Höst, M.C. Ohlsson, B. Regnell, A. Wesslén, Experimentation in Software Engineering, Springer, 2012.

[18] R.K. Yin, Case Study Research Design and Methods, fourth ed., SAGE Publications, 2008.

[19] B.A. Kitchenham, Procedures for Performing Systematic Reviews, Technical report TR/SE-0401, Software Engineering Group, Department of Computer Science, Keele University, NSW 1430, 2004.

[20] C. Zannier, G. Melnik, F. Maurer, On the success of empirical studies in the international conference on software engineering, in: Proceedings of the 28th International Conference on Software Engineering, ACM, New York, NY, USA, 2006, pp. 341–350.

[21] W.B. Frakes, G. Succi, An industrial study of reuse, quality, and productivity, J. Syst. Softw. 57 (2) (2001) 99–106.

[22] E.K. Jackson, J. Sztipanovits, Towards a formal foundation for domain specific modeling languages, in: EMSOFT '06: Proceedings of the 6th ACM & IEEE International Conference on Embedded Software, ACM, 2006, pp. 53–62.

[23] S. Hallsteinsen, M. Paci, Experiences in Software Evolution and Reuse: Twelve Real World Projects, Springer, 1997, vol. 1.

[24] W.F. Tichy, P. Lukowicz, L. Prechelt, E.A. Heinz, Experimental evaluation in computer science: a quantitative study, J. Syst. Softw. 28 (1) (1995) 9–18.

[25] E. Heinz, P. Lukowicz, W.F. Tichy, L. Préchelt, Experimental evaluation in computer science: a quantitative study, J. Syst. Softw. 28–1 (1995) 9–18.

[26] J. Guojie, Y. Baolin, Z. Qiyang, Enhancing software reuse through application-level component approach, J. Softw. 6 (3) (2011) 374–385.

[27] N. Ilk, J. Zhao, P. Goes, P. Hofmann, Semantic Enrichment Process: An Approach to Software Component Reuse in Modernizing Enterprise Systems, Inform. Syst. Front. 13 (2011) 359–370.

[28] V. Koppen, N. Siegmund, M. Soffner, G. Saake, An architecture for interoperability of embedded systems and virtual reality, IETE Tech. Rev. 26 (2009) 350–356.

[29] C.A. Welty, D.A. Ferrucci, A formal ontology for re-use of software architecture documents, in: 14th IEEE International Conference on Automated Software Engineering, 1999, pp. 259–262.

[30] E.A. Lee, Embedded software, in: Advances in Computers, Academic Press, 2002, pp. 1–34.

[31] G.L. Zuniga, Ontology: its transformation from philosophy to information systems, in: FOIS '01: Proceedings of the International Conference on Formal Ontology in Information Systems, ACM, New York, NY, USA, 2001, pp. 187–197.

[32] A.M. de Cima, C.M.L. Werner, A.A.C. Cerqueira, The design of object-oriented software with domain architecture reuse, in: Proceedings of theThird International Conference on Software Reuse: Advances in Software Reusability, 1994, pp. 178–187.

[33] R. Kamalraj, D.K.A.R.P. Ranjani, Stability-based component clustering for designing software reuse repository, Int. J. Comput. Appl. 27 (3) (2011) 33–36, published by Foundation of Computer Science, New York, USA.

[34] D.H. Zhang, J.B.Z.M. Luo, Y. Tang, L.Q. Zhuang, A reference architecture and functional model for monitoring and diagnosis of large automated systems, vol. 2, in: Proceedings of the IEEE Conference on Emerging Technologies and Factory Automation, 2003, pp. 516–523.

[35] S. Henninger, An evolutionary approach to constructing effective software reuse repositories, ACM Trans. Softw. Eng. Methodol. 6 (2) (1997) 111–140.

[36] S. Winkler, J. Pilgrim, A survey of traceability in requirements engineering and model-driven development, Softw. Syst. Model. 9 (4) (2010) 529–565.

[37] S. Bhatia, C. Consel, C. Pu, Remote specialization for efficient embedded operating systems, ACM Trans. Program. Lang. Syst. 30 (4) (2008) 1–32.

[38] B. Graaf, H. Van Dijk, Evaluating an embedded software reference architecture—industrial experience report, in: Proceedings of the 9th European Conference on Software Maintenance and Reengineering (CSMR 2005), IEEE CS, 2005, pp. 354–363.

[39] R. Holmes, R.J. Walker, Systematizing pragmatic software reuse, ACM Trans. Softw. Eng. Methodol. 21 (4) (2013) 20:1–20:44.

[40] E.A. Karlsson (Ed.), Software Reuse: A Holistic Approach, John Wiley & Sons Inc., New York, NY, USA, 1995.

[41] Eichmann, Factors in Reuse and Reengineering of Legacy Software, Tech. rep., Repository Based Software Engineering Program Research Institute for Computing and Information Systems, University of Houston (1997).

[42] W.B. Frakes, C.J. Fox, Modeling reuse across the software life cycle, J. Syst. Softw. 30 (3) (1995) 295–301.

[43] P. Devanbu, S. Karstu, W. Melo, W. Thomas, Analytical and empirical evaluation of software reuse metrics, in: ICSE '96: Proceedings of the 18th International Conference on Software Engineering, IEEE Computer Society, 1996, pp. 189–199.

[44] D.C. Rine, Supporting reuse with object technology, Computer 30 (10) (1997) 43–45.

[45] I. Jacobson, M. Griss, P. Jonsson, Making the reuse business work, Computer 30 (10) (1997) 36–42.

[46] A. Mili, R. Mili, R.T. Mittermeir, A survey of software reuse libraries, Ann. Softw. Eng. 5 (1998) 349–414.

[47] D.C. Rine, R.M. Sonnemann, Investments in reusable software. A study of software reuse investment success factors, J. Syst. Softw. 41 (1) (1998) 17–32.

[48] Y. Kim, E.A. Stohr, Software reuse: survey and research directions, J. Manag. Inform. Syst. 14 (4) (1998) 113–147.

[49] M.A. Rothenberger, Systems Development with Systematic Software Reuse: An Empirical Analysis of Project Success Factors, 1999.

[50] M. Ezran, M. Morisio, C. Tully, Failure and success factors in reuse programs: a synthesis of industrial experiences, in: ICSE '99: Proceedings of the 21st International Conference on Software Engineering, ACM, 1999, pp. 681–682.

[51] W.B. Frakes, A case study of a reusable component collection, 2000, in: Proceedings of 3rd IEEE Symposium on Application-Specific Systems and Software Engineering Technology, 2000, pp. 79–84.

[52] M.A. Rothenberger, K.J. Dooley, U.R. Kulkarni, N. Nada, Strategies for software reuse: a principal component analysis of reuse practices, IEEE Trans. Softw. Eng. 29 (9) (2003) 825–837.

[53] M. Raatikainen, T. Soininen, T. Mannisto, A. Mattila, A case study of two configurable software product families, in: F. van der Linden (Ed.), Software Product-Family Engineering, vol. 3014 of Lecture Notes in Computer Science, Springer Berlin / Heidelberg, 2004, pp. 403–421.

[54] D.L. Nazareth, M.A. Rothenberger, Assessing the cost-effectiveness of software reuse: a model for planned reuse, J. Syst. Softw. 73 (2) (2004) 245–255.

[55] E.S. de Almeida, A. Alvaro, D. Lucredio, V.C. Garcia, S.R. de Lemos Meira, A survey on software reuse processes, in: IEEE International Conference on Information Reuse and Integration, 2005, pp. 66–71.

[56] J. Jiao, T. Simpson, Z. Siddique, Product family design and platform-based product development: a state-of-the-art review, J. Intell. Manuf. 18 (2007) 5–29.

[57] V.R. Basili, M.V. Zelkowitz, D.I. Sjoberg, P. Johnson, A.J. Cowling, Protocols in the use of empirical software engineering artifacts, Empirical Softw. Eng. 12 (1) (2007) 107–119.

[58] S.G. Shiva, L.A. Shala, Software reuse: research and practice, in: Fourth International Conference on Information Technology, ITNG '07, IEEE, 2007, pp. 603–609.

[59] H. Yan, W. Zhang, H. Zhao, H. Mei, An Optimization Strategy to Feature ModelsTM Verification by Eliminating Verification-Irrelevant Features and Constraints, in: S.H. Edwards, G. Kulczycki (Eds.), Formal Foundations of Reuse and Domain Engineering, vol. 5791 of Lecture Notes in Computer Science, Springer Berlin Heidelberg, 2009, pp. 65–75.

[60] R. Anguswamy, W.B. Frakes, A Study of Reusability, Complexity, and Reuse design Principles, in: Proceedings of the ACM-IEEE International Symposium on Empirical Software Engineering and Measurement, ESEM '12, ACM, New York, NY, USA, 2012, pp. 161–164.

[61] N. Ferreira, R.J. Machado, D. Gasevic, An ontology-based approach to model-driven software product lines, in: ICSEA '09: Proceedings of the 2009 Fourth International Conference on Software Engineering Advances, IEEE Computer Society, 2009, pp. 559–564.

[62] L. Pareto, M. Staron, P. Eriksson, Ontology guided evolution of complex embedded systems projects in the direction of MDA, in: Model Driven Engineering Languages and Systems, vol. 5301 of Lecture Notes in Computer Science, Springer Berlin / Heidelberg, 2010, pp. 874–888.

[63] W. Ha, H. Sun, M. Xie, Reuse of embedded software in small and medium enterprises, in: 2012 IEEE International Conference on Management of Innovation and Technology (ICMIT), 2012, pp. 394–399.

[64] B. Barlin, J.M. Lawler, Effective software reuse in an embedded real-time system, in: TRI-Ada '92: Proceedings of the Conference on TRI-Ada '92, ACM, 1992, pp. 281–287.

[65] C. Bunse, H. Gross, C. Peper, Embedded system construction—evaluation of model-driven and component-based development approaches, in: M.R. Chaudron (Ed.), Models in Software Engineering: Workshops and Symposia at MODELS 2008,

Toulouse, France, September 28–October 3, 2008. Reports and Revised Selected Papers, vol. 5421 of Lecture Notes in Computer Science, Springer, Berlin, Heidelberg, 2009, pp. 66–77.

[66] W.A. Dos Santos, A.M. da Cunha, An MDA approach for a multi-layered satellite on-board software architecture, in: 5th Working IEEE/IFIP Conference on Software Architecture, 2005, pp. 253–256.

[67] R. Alur, T. Dang, J. Esposito, Y. Hur, F. Ivancic, V. Kumar, P. Mishra, G.J. Pappas, O. Sokolsky, Hierarchical modeling and analysis of embedded systems, Proc. IEEE 91 (1) (2003) 11–28.

[68] P.G. Paulin, C. Liem, M. Cornero, F. Nacabal, G. Goossens, Embedded software in real-time signal processing systems: application and architecture trends, vol. 85, in: Proceedings of the IEEE, 1997, pp. 419–435.

[69] G. Goossens, J. Van Praet, D. Lanneer, W. Geurts, A. Kifli, C. Liem, P.G. Paulin, Embedded software in real-time signal processing systems: design technologies, Kluwer Academic Publishers, Norwell, MA, USA, 1997, pp. 433–451.

[70] J. Sprinkleand, J.M. Eklund, H. Gonzalez, E.I. Groetli, B. Upcroft, A. Makarenko, W. Uther, M. Moser, R. Fitch, H. Durrant-Whyte, S.S. Sastry, Model-based design: a report from the trenches of the DARPA urban challenge, Softw. Syst. Model. 8 (2009) 551–566.

[71] K. Kim, H. Kim, W. Kim, Building software product line from the legacy systems: experience in the digital audio and video domain, in: 11th International Software Product Line Conference, 2007, pp. 171–180.

[72] M. Winter, T. Genler, A. Christoph, O. Nierstrasz, S. Ducasse, R. Wuyts, G. Arevalo, P. Moeller, C. Stich, B. Schoenhage, Components for embedded software—the PECOS approach, in: CASES '02 Proceedings of the 2002 International Conference on Compilers, Architecture, and Synthesis for Embedded Systems, ACM Press, 2002, pp. 19–25.

[73] T. Schetter, M. Campbell, D. Surka, Comparison of multiple agent-based organisations for satellite constellations (TechSat21), Artif. Intell. 145 (1–2) (2003) 147–180.

[74] D.M. Surka, M.C. Brito, C.G. Harvey, The real-time object agent software architecture for distributed satellite systems, vol. 6, in: IEEE Proceedings of the Aerospace Conference, 2001, pp. 2731–2741.

[75] M. Kuhlemann, D. Batory, S. Apel, Refactoring feature modules, in: Proceedings of the 11th International Conference on Software Reuse: Formal Foundations of Reuse and Domain Engineering, ICSR '09, Springer-Verlag, Berlin, Heidelberg, 2009, pp. 106–115.

[76] P. Mohagheghi, R. Conradi, An empirical investigation of software reuse benefits in a large telecom product, ACM Trans. Softw. Eng. Methodol. 17 (3) (2008) 1–31.

[77] A. Gupta, J. Li, R. Conradi, H. Ronneberg, E. Landre, A case study comparing defect profiles of a reused framework and of applications reusing it, Empirical Softw. Eng. 14 (2) (2009) 227–255.

[78] R. Gerard, R.R. Downs, J.J. Marshall, R.E. Wolfe, The software reuse working group: a case study in fostering reuse, in: IEEE International Conference on Information Reuse and Integration, 2007, pp. 24–29.

[79] J. Li, R. Conradi, P. Mohagheghi, O.A. Saehle, O. Wang, E. Naalsund, O.A. Walseth, A study of developer attitudes to component reuse in three IT companies, in: Product Focused Software Process Improvement, vol. 3009 of Lecture Notes in Computer Science, Springer Berlin / Heidelberg, 2004, pp. 538–552.

[80] N. Choi, I. Song, H. Han, A survey on ontology mapping, SIGMOD Rec. 35 (3) (2006) 34–41.

[81] D. Garlan, R. Allen, J.M. Ockerbloom, Architectural mismatch: why reuse is still so hard, IEEE Softw. 26 (4) (2009) 66–69.

[82] G. Brusa, M.L. Caliusco, O. Chiotti, A process for building a domain ontology: an experience in developing a government budgetary ontology, in: AOW '06: Proceedings of the Second Australasian Workshop on Advances in Ontologies, Australian Computer Society, Inc., 2006, pp. 7–15.

[83] N.B. Bui, L. Zhu, I. Gorton, Y. Liu, Benchmark generation using domain specific modeling, in: 18th Australian Software Engineering Conference, ASWEC 2007 (2007) 169–180.

[84] T. Sullivan, D. Sather, R. Nishinaga, A flexible satellite command and control framework, Oct 27, 2009. @www.aero.org/publications/crosslink/summer2009/04.html.

[85] S. Uchitel, G. Brunet, M. Chechik, Synthesis of partial behavior models from properties and scenarios, IEEE Trans. Softw. Eng. 35 (3) (2009) 384–406.

[86] W.C. Lim, Effects of reuse on quality, productivity, and economics, IEEE Softw. 11 (5) (1994) 23–30.

[87] D.C. Rine, N. Nada, An empirical study of a software reuse reference model, Inform. Softw. Technol. 42 (1) (2000) 47–65.

[88] W.B. Frakes, S. Isoda, Success factors of systematic reuse, IEEE Softw. 11 (5) (1994) 14–19.

[89] V. Krishnan, R. Singh, D. Tirupati, A model-based approach for planning and developing a family of technology-based products, Manuf. Oper. Manag. 1 (2) (1999) 132–156.

[90] C.F.J. Lange, Model size matters, in: Proceedings of the 2006 International Conference on Models in Software Engineering, MoDELS'06, Springer-Verlag, Berlin, Heidelberg, 2006, pp. 211–216. http://dl.acm.org/citation.cfm?id=1762828.1762863.

[91] N.G. Leveson, K.A. Weiss, Making embedded software reuse practical and safe, SIGSOFT Softw. Eng. Notes 29 (6) (2004) 171–178.

[92] S. Isoda, Experiences of a software reuse project, J. Syst. Softw. 30 (3) (1995) 171–186.

[93] A. Gupta, The Profile of Software Changes in Reused vs. Non-Reused Industrial Software Systems, Ph.D. thesis, Norwegian University of Science and Technology (2009).

[94] M. Morisio, M. Ezran, C. Tully, Success and failure factors in software reuse, IEEE Trans. Softw. Eng. 28 (4) (2002) 340–357.

[95] J.A. Maxwell, Understanding and validity in qualitative research, Harvard Educ. Rev. 62 (3) (1992) 279–300.http://her.hepg.org/index/8323320856251826.pdf.

ABOUT THE AUTHORS

Julia Varnell-Sarjeant received a B.S. in Economics from University of Missouri, Columbia, her Masters in Computer Science from the University of Colorado, Denver, and her Ph.D. from the University of Denver, Denver, Colorado. She has worked in the aerospace industry since 1981. She has been involved with numerous aerospace projects, including the Hubble Space Telescope, Mars Observer, NPOESS, GOES, GPS, Orion, and many classified programs. In 2011, she was chief engineer on a reference architecture project for AFRL. She developed company-wide classes in architecture fundamentals and DoDAF.

Anneliese Amschler Andrews holds an M.S. and Ph.D. from Duke University and a Dipl.-Inf. from the Technical University of Karlsruhe. She served as Editor in Chief of the IEEE Transactions on Software

Engineering. She has also served on several other editorial boards including the IEEE Transactions on Reliability, the Empirical Software Engineering Journal, the Software Quality Journal, the Journal of Information Science and Technology, and the Journal of Software Maintenance. She is Professor of Computer Science at the University of Denver. Dr. Andrews is the author of a text book and over 200 articles in the area of Software and Systems Engineering, particularly software testing, system quality, and reliability.

CHAPTER TWO

Advances in Behavior Modeling

Ella Roubtsova

Open University of the Netherlands, Heerlen, The Netherlands

Contents

Abstract

This chapter provides a survey of existing approaches to discrete event behavior modeling. The comparison is based on the selected set of semantic elements useful for the major system life cycle activities, such as requirements engineering, analysis, system understanding, system design, and evolution. The semantic elements are identified in the observed approaches and illustrated with examples of models. The advantages of the semantic elements for the major system life cycle activities can be taken into account for the choice and for the design of behavior modeling approaches.

The survey is based on a series of successful international workshops on behavior modeling run by the author and is enriched by the results of her research experience.

Advances in Computers, Volume 97
ISSN 0065-2458
http://dx.doi.org/10.1016/bs.adcom.2014.10.003

1. INTRODUCTION

Modern software-based businesses are various and dynamic. E-commerce and E-procurement, Insurances, Mortgages, and E-education take a holistic approach, incorporate changeability of software to make a profit of it. As a result, the life cycle of businesses becomes similar to the software life cycle.

The users, being the parts of interactive business processes, always propose new requirements. Most often, the requirements deal with changes in the system behavior. Behavior models serve to clarify what is wanted and how it can be integrated into the existing system.

The competitors inspire analysis of success factors sometimes hidden in business processes. Analysis requires behavior models leading businesses to the business goals.

Optimization of expenses drives the search for collaboration and services that are capable of implementing auxiliary subprocesses. However, the orchestration and choreography of collaborative businesses are fulfilled based on behavior models.

With such tendencies, even daily business terminology, including key performance indicators and capability, cannot be fully understood without behavior models.

The question is whether the available behavior modeling techniques are good enough for the challenges of the support of all activities of the system life cycle from requirements engineering, analysis, implementation to model-based testing (MBT), simulation, and reengineering?

In order to answer this question in this chapter, we

- formulate the properties of behavior modeling semantics needed for the major activities of the system life cycle support;
- define common elements for separation of behavior models from other types of models, and the properties associated with combinations of elements with different semantics;
- analyze the behavior modeling approaches inside the Unified Modeling Language (UML) and outside the UML and summarize the analysis in a table that relates the combinations of modeling semantics to the properties of behavior modeling approaches needed for the system life cycle support.

The goal of the survey is to provide the semantic help for the choice or design of behavior modeling techniques for different activities of the system life cycle support.

2. PROPERTIES OF THE MODELING SEMANTICS NEEDED FOR SYSTEM LIFE CYCLE SUPPORT

Any system, whether it be a business system or a software system or a combination of both, lives a spiral life cycle. Each turn of the spiral goes through the same stages of goal definitions, requirements gathering, design, analysis (simulation), implementation, and testing. After that, the system is maintained. When the new goals and requirements appear, the cycle is repeated.

1. *Requirements engineering* is a process of collecting of descriptions of desired system behavior. A requirement item always presents a part of behavior observed by a stakeholder from the stakeholder's perspective. Some of the requirements concern a localized domain; others crosscut many domains like the plumbing in a building across all its flats. In any case, a requirement represents a part of system behavior. The ability of the modeling technique to separate modeling of partial behavior simplifies interaction of stakeholders during modeling.

    *Therefore, the desired property of the modeling technique is the ability to **separate the modeling of partial behavior both for the localized and cross-cutting concerns**.*

2. The *design* process is aimed to combine all partial descriptions and produce a system that meets the requirements.

    An ideal modeling method for design should allow ***composition of all the behavior models of requirements*** into the system model.

3. The *analysis* phase is aimed to validate the completeness of the design against the requirements. The adequate completeness can be validated by the execution of the model on different data. The result of the model execution is compared with the requirements.

    *For this stage, the ideal behavior modeling method should be **executable** or, in other words, work with data. The semantics of the modeling techniques at the design phase should be comparable or easy transformable to the semantics of the modeling techniques used for the requirements engineering.*

    During the comparison of the design model with the model of requirements, the tacit knowledge [1], hidden in the heads of users, often triggers new requirements so that the design is repeated until no more requirements are produced or until the deadline. If the semantics of the modeling techniques used for the requirements specification and the design are comparable, such a repetition of the design cycle demands less effort and time.

4. The *implementation* phase demands the modeling methods which reflect the restrictions of implementation platforms. Modern implementation platforms often do not support separation of concerns and their composition. The discrete event behavior modeling techniques used for modeling of the implementation reflect the implementation restrictions. The practice to apply the behavior modeling techniques reflecting implementation restrictions for modeling of business results in complex and not easily changeable models.

The implementation platforms evolve, and they will inevitably evolve to support smooth transformation of business models to implementation. Nowadays, however, the behavior modeling approaches need to propose *traceable transformation to implementation models*. The traceable transformation of executable behavior models to implementation leaves less room for errors because the models and implementation can be tested against requirements.

5. The *testing* phase is meant to check that the implementation corresponds to the requirements. The design level model is a very useful artifact for testing. It can even become the basis for the model-based automated testing. However, if the design phase produces a model with implementation details, then the model can cause error propagation in models both in the code and in the tests [2]. This means again that the *traceability between the implementation model and the requirements models should be maintained*. As we mentioned earlier, this activity has more precision when the model is executable.

6. *The maintenance and evolution* are also the activities of any system life cycle. These activities may be seen as analyses, requirements engineering, and design within the existing system. The composition property of behavior models eases the maintenance and evolution.

If we summarize the **requirements for the modeling techniques coming from all activities of the system life cycle support**, we can make the following conclusion: the behavior modeling techniques supporting the whole system life cycle should enable

1. separation of modeling concerns gathered at the requirement phase;
2. composition of concerns modeled from requirements;
3. execution of the model of requirements for establishing relations between the model and the requirements and between the model and the implementation.

In this survey, we analyze the semantic elements of behavior modeling approaches aiming to find how the semantic elements contribute to meeting the formulated above requirements.

3. EVENTS, STATES, TRANSITIONS, AND COMMUNICATION–COMPOSITION

Discrete event behavior modeling techniques are all descendants of the finite-state machines (FSMs) (or finite-state automata) [3].

A finite-state machine $FSM = (E, S, T)$ is an abstract machine, where

- E is a finite set of recognized event types. Instances of events $e \in E$ often called *actions*.
- S is a finite set of states. The initial state $s_0 \in S$ and the set of final states $F \in S$ are optionally specified in the set of states. A machine is situated in one state $s \in S$ at a time.
- T is a finite set of transitions. Any state can be an input state or an output state of a transition or both:

$$T \subseteq S \times E \times S; \quad t \subseteq T; \quad t = (s_i, e, s_j), \quad s_i, s_j \in S$$

The set of transitions is a subset of the Cartesian product of sets of input states, events, and output states.

An FSM can be depicted as a graph, where the states are the nodes and the transitions are the arcs labeled with the corresponding events. Figure 1 shows an example of an FSM presenting behavior of a *Door*.

- Its initial state is shown by the black ellipse.
- It states **Closed**, **Open**, **Locked** are the nodes.
- **Install, Open, Close, Lock**, and **Unlock** are the names of event types labeling the arcs presenting transitions.
- FSM **Door** does not have the final state.

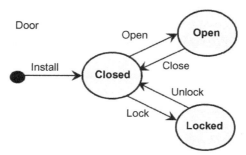

Figure 1 Graphical presentation of finite-state machine Door [4].

The behavior of an FSM is a set of sequences of transitions (*si*, *e*, *sj*). A sequence is also called a trace or a path from the initial state to a "target" state. An example of a trace is

(*Initial state*, *Install*, *Closed*), (*Closed*, *Open*, *Open*), (*Open*, *Close*, *Closed*),
  (*Closed*, *Lock*, *Locked*).

FSMs can be deterministic and nondeterministic. Each state of a deterministic state machine has exactly one transition labeled with a possible event. From a state of a nondeterministic state machine can be more than one different transitions labeled with the same event. The FSM in Fig. 1 is deterministic.

The concept of an FSM proved to be very productive. It is the basis for design and analysis of computer programs and sequential logic circuits. It is used to model behavior of many hardware systems like traffic lights, elevators to business processes, patterns of searching documents, and computer applications for speech and language processing.

However, the FSM model has its expressivity limitations. In particular, the memory of an FSM is limited by the number of states, and the events are abstract triggers of transitions.

In order to overcome the limitation in expressivity, the semantics of FSMs was extended in many ways. The extensions gave rise to a family of *Labeled Transition Systems* (*LTSs*).

An LTS is also a tuple of states, events, and transitions, $LTS = (E, S, T)$. The extensions are concerned with the semantics of events, states, and transitions. As the events are the means of communication of machines with each other and also with the environment, the extensions use different semantics for communication mechanisms of machines and the environment and, correspondingly, different composition techniques.

We define all these extensions separately. In Sections 4 and 5, we give examples of approaches that use the combinations of those extensions.

3.1. Events

3.1.1 Abstract Events Versus Structured Messages

One group of LTSs considers an event as an elementary trigger (*its name is a string*) coming from the environment. An event presents an event type, i.e., an infinite set of event instances. Each event instance is identical with another event instance [5]. For example, an event type is "*Open Door.*" The instances of event "*Open Door*" may be submitted to the model infinite number of times.

Another group of LTSs treats an event as a *message of a given structure* [6,7]. An event instance in this case also belongs to a certain event type. All instances of this type have one common type name and may have different values of all elements of the message structure.

For example, an event type "***Open Door number XXX***" may open an infinite set of doors with different numbers because the message type structure element "Door number XXX" may have an infinite set of values.

3.1.2 Events as Inputs Versus Inputs and Outputs

The set of events can be seen as a *set of inputs*. The machines with this property are called *acceptors* [3].

The set of events can be split into the *set of inputs and outputs*. The machines with such a split are called *transducers* [3].

As we will show later, the choice between acceptors and transducers defines the possible composition of behavior specified by LTSs.

3.2. States

3.2.1 Abstract States Versus States with Variables

States represent the memory space in an FSM (Fig. 1). State can be seen as an enumerated variable. The set of state names forms its set of values.

The state space **S** is often extended with a set of variables **V** of different types used in programming (integer, string, enumerated, lists, arrays, and types of LTSs). The variables are called attributes.

As a result of such an extension, the set of states **S** can be seen as a set of variables of an enumerated type and defined state types. Each value of state $s \in S$ in the pair (**S**, **V**) can define an (often infinite) set of state instances.

For example, the state of the ***Door*** can contain variable ***Number: Integer***. This number gets its value when event ***Install*** happens. The value of ***Number*** will allow distinguishing different instances of the ***Door*** model representing different doors and relate the events addressed to a given instance.

3.2.2 State Localized Versus Distributed

State of an LTS can be localized or distributed in the model. In the case of the distributed state, a tuple of values of places ($s1, s2, s3, ..., sn$) represents a model state. The variables may extend the distributed state as global variables. In Sections 4 and 5 we will give examples of semantics with localized and distributed states.

3.3. Transitions

The definition of a transition depends on the definition of states and events.

If the events and states are abstract, then a transition is a triple (s_i, e, s_j) $\in S \times E \times S$.

For an acceptor LTS (the events are only the inputs), the transition means that if the machine accepts even e, it *can* transit from state s_i, to state s_j.

For a transmitter LTS, the transition may mean two things:

(1) if the machine **receives** event e, it transits from state s_i to state s_j;

(2) if the machine **sends** event e to environment, it transits from state s_i to state s_j.

3.3.1 Transitions with Can, Must, Motivate Semantics

In most approaches, only the *"can-semantics"* is used: the machine *can-transit* from one state to another.

Not all systems are adequately modeled with the *can-semantics*. There is also semantics of *must-transit* or a combination of the *can- and must-transit semantics*.

The *can- and must-transit semantics* are often insufficient for business systems. There are attempts to introduce elements of motivation into semantics of transitions. The examples will be described in the next section.

3.3.2 Transitions That Update States Versus Transition That Update States and Variables

If the events of LTSs are structured messages and the states include memory variables, then a transition is accompanied with a function that makes calculations of new values for the state variables, memory variables, and/or events. States can be defined by a transition or derived from the other states and variables as a result of the transition.

3.4. Communication of LTSs and Composition

The composition is often understood only as composition of classes [8] in the sense of set theory. In order to avoid confusion, we need to mention that we refer here to the composition of behaviors constructed from transitions and modeled as LTSs with different semantics.

LTSs may present the behaviors of system parts (or processes taking place in system parts) and then be composed to the behavior of the complete system. The behaviors of system parts can take place sequentially or concurrently. In the latter case, they can potentially interact with each other.

The composition of LTSs presenting behaviors or processes is studied by algebraic approaches called process algebras. They formulate the rules of composition that need to be implemented in order to achieve the desired behavior properties of a system of concurrent LTSs. The main algebraic approaches to concurrency are the *Calculus of Communicating Systems* (CCSs) by Milner [9] and *Calculus of Communicating Sequential Processes* (CSPs) by Hoare [10]. In order to manipulate the processes in an algebraic way, that is, with formulas, the elements of LTSs use algebraic presentation.

The states in process algebra are abstract begins and ends of an event. The basic element of formulas in process algebra is an event or action.

- Any event is identified by a small letter: $a, b, \ldots$ or by its name. It is assumed that any event can execute itself and terminate.
- A sequence of events in the process is expressed using the dot symbol $a \cdot b$.
- An alternative choice between two actions is expressed with the plus symbol $a + b$.
- A repetition of a process is shown with the star symbol a^*.
- Round brackets are used to combine event expressions.
- Symbol $\sqrt{}$ expresses termination.

The axioms of the basic process algebra are used for proofs of process properties [5].

- $A1 : a + b = b + a$;
- $A2 : (a + b) + c = a + (b + c)$;
- $A3 : a + a = a$;
- $A4 : (a + b) \cdot c = a \cdot c + b \cdot c$;
- $A5 : (a \cdot b) \cdot c = a \cdot (b \cdot c)$.

For example, the LTS from the Fig. 1 can be presented as the following process:

$$Install \cdot ((Open \cdot Close)^* + (Lock \cdot Unlock)^*).$$

The basic rules tell us that

- In the sequence of events, only the first event can execute itself and enable another event or terminate. For example, only **Lock** can take place in the sequence **Lock · Unlock**.
- An alternative does not influence the execution and termination of the event of another branch. For example, the branch **Lock · Unlock** does not change the execution and termination of the event **Open**.

In this work, we use the process algebra axioms to explain the results of composition of behaviors. The sequence, alternative, and repetition are the basic forms of behavior composition. However, the modeling of many systems cannot be done without composition of concurrent processes that take place simultaneously and potentially interact with each other.

3.4.1 CCS Composition

For modeling of concurrent systems, Milner [9] introduced a binary operator. This operator presents parallel composition of two processes (or behaviors). That is, $a \cdot P1 \| b \cdot P2$ can choose to execute an initial transition a of $P1$ or an initial transition b of $P2$ in the interleaving manner, i.e., one after another. If the processes do not interact, they do not influence each other

$$a \cdot P1 \| b \cdot P2 = P1 \| b \cdot P2 \ \ or$$
$$a \cdot P1 \| b \cdot P2 = a \cdot P1 \| P2.$$

Moller [11] proved that the complete finite axiomatization of this composition needs the left merge operator. Left merge operator takes its initial transition from the process $P1$ and then behaves like merge.

If the concurrent processes interact, then the *send-receive semantics is used for process merging or composition*. The interaction takes place if two things take place: the sender can send event e and the receiver is in a state to receive the event. The sent event is often labeled with the exclamation symbol $!e$. The received event is labeled with the question mark $?e$. One LTS instance sends an event, and another LTS instance receives it. The send-receive composition takes place if the send event of the same name is followed by the receive event with the same name: $(!e \cdot ?e)$. Bergstra and Klop [12] introduced a communication merge that combines the send and receive in one action. The state of both processes is updated in the case of communication:

$$a \cdot P1 \| b \cdot P2 = P1 \| P2; \ where \ a = !e; \ b = ?e.$$

The consequence of this semantics is the race conditions between two events sent to the same receiver. Which of the events will arrive first depends on the factors that do not belong to the LTS model. These factors are: the time needed for the signal transfer; the path chosen for the signal transfer, etc.

In the case of *the send-receive composition*, the notion of environment does not exist in the model. The relevant elements of environment are modeled as LTSs sending events. The LTSs communicate in this case via messages. In order to use this composition, the LTSs should be transducers (be able to send outputs).

The popularity of this model is explained with its closeness to the implementation platforms and programming languages that use the send–receive semantics for communication of objects, both local and distributed.

The send–receive composition semantics often demands an existence of buffers (queues) in the behavior model. Events may arrive to the system when the system is not ready to accept them. In this case, the events are kept in buffers. The events in buffers contribute to nondeterminism of the model as the events from buffers compete with the arriving events for handling by the model. The examples of approaches with the send–receive semantics will be given in the next section.

3.4.2 CSP Composition

If the LTSs present the systems parts that are separated virtually and not distributed in space, the LTSs may interact by reading state of each other. The composition semantics in this case is the **synchronous composition**. This semantics is known as the operator of parallel synchronous composition described in the *Calculus of Communicating Sequential Processes* by Hoare [8].

The main idea is that an event can be accepted by several LTSs which are ready to accept it. The synchronization means that an event is accepted only if all the LTSs that recognize this event are ready to accept it. If at least one such an LTS is not ready to accept, the system refuses the event.

Symbol $\|$ is also traditionally used to represent CSP parallel composition in process algebraic expressions:

$$a \cdot P1 \| a \cdot P2; \text{ where } a \equiv a.$$

Two processes are executed in parallel and able to accept the same event $a\|a$. There is no difference in the events at all. The event a is an input. The LTSs are acceptors.

The models that use parallel synchronous composition semantics have such a property as *observational consistency* of the trace behaviors of parts in the behavior of the whole [13]. This property is very useful for relating requirements and design models. In the next section, we will give an example of LTS semantics that possesses the observational consistency. In the case of *the synchronous composition*, the environment is an element of the system, which can only send events. The output of the LTSs in this case is their state.

3.4.3 Combined Composition Semantics

As we write about the advances in behavior modeling, we have to mention the new ideas about combination of two composition semantics.

There is a possibility to combine the synchronous and asynchronous communication semantics [14,15]. In the case of ***the combined communication semantics***, the environment and the LTSs may produce events for the model:

$$Message\,"a"\,contains\,the\,direction\,symbols\ (!,?);$$
$$Event\,"b"\,is\,an\,internal\,event\,of\,P1\,and\,P2\ (labeled\,only\,by\,symbol\ !):$$
$$CCS: (!a \cdot !b \cdot P1) || (?a \cdot !b \cdot P2);\ b = \gamma(a)$$
$$CSP: !b \cdot P1 || !b \cdot P2 = P1 || P2$$

We will present an example that demonstrates a great potential of the combined semantics in modeling of interacting services.

3.5. Choice of a Behavior Modeling Semantics

*A **behavior model*** in our definition is a concept that is described by events, states, transitions, and the communication–composition mechanism. We have specified variations of semantics for events, states, transitions, and communication–compositions.

The Cartesian product of all the semantics for events, states, transitions, and the communication–compositions gives all the variety of semantic combinations for the LTS-based modeling techniques. We will classify each approach summarizing all the described semantic dimensions and use two tables (Figs. 25 and 26) to present the existing behavior modeling approaches. The practice of the semantic choice often depends on the familiarity with semantic elements and properties guaranteed by the semantics. This chapter may contribute to familiarity with different behavior semantics and may help to make the right choose of the behavior modeling technique.

It is practical to choose the behavior semantics that meets the requirements of the life cycle support activity (Fig. 26). Perhaps, one reason for combining the behavior modeling semantics into the UML [8] was to give the developers a possibility to choose from a set of modeling semantics. Section 4 will answer the question if the set of semantics combined in the UML meets the requirements for the activities of the system life cycle support.

4. BEHAVIOR SEMANTICS IN UML

Let us begin our survey with the groups of behavior modeling semantics defined in the UML being the OMG modeling standard for more than a decade now. The groups of approaches presented in the UML are wisely chosen, no doubts about this. The semantics of approaches in each group suits to selected activities of the life cycle. However, the semantics chosen for some of the groups in the UML waits for improvement.

By supporting the UML, the Object Management Group (OMG) promotes modeling to a central role in the development and management of application systems. The document [16] suggests that "fully specified platform-independent models (including behavior) can enable intellectual property to move away from technology-specific code, helping to insulate business applications from technology evolution and further enable interoperability." In the view of Richard Soley, CEO of OMG "Models are **testable** and **simulatable**" [17].

Testable and simulatable models are only possible if behavior is fully represented. Therefore, the semantics of the techniques available for modeling behavior is the key to achieving the Model Driven Software Development. While there is a general understanding that behavior modeling is essential and the models should be executable, we can show that the behavior modeling techniques collected in the UML mostly provide means for modeling of internal behavior of systems. They do not contain the semantics supporting the spectrum of human involving activities, from requirements engineering and testing of external behavior. The transformation from one sort of UML diagrams to another is needed for each stage of the development life cycle. The transformation results in inconsistency and the corresponding complexity of development methods that need validation of any transformation.

Figure 2 [18] shows the family of behavior diagrams combined in the UML: use cases, interaction diagrams, activities, and state machines.

4.1. Use Cases

Use Cases describe scenarios, or episodes, of the use of a system by specifying the set of interactions between the system and the domain in which it is embedded.

Figure 3 shows an example of a use case *Buyer–Seller* inspired by Ref. [19]. The use case presents the actors (dolls and system) participating in the modeled case: *Buyer*, *Seller*, and *Generic User*. Ellipses are the activities of actors, for example, activities *Purchases Item*, *Places Bid*. An activity may be seen as another use case and can be presented in detail on another diagram.

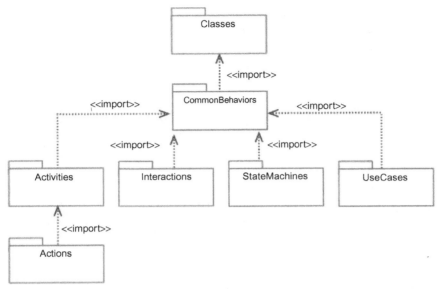

Figure 2 UML behavior diagrams [8].

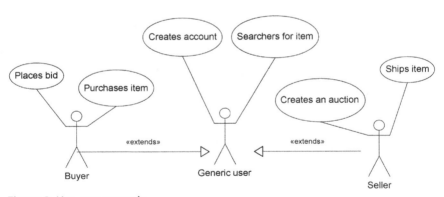

Figure 3 Use case example.

The communication of actors and the system and the transitions and events causing the start and finish of activities are not presented. Use case-based models involve neither detailed data nor message exchanges. The behavior is presented partially, which is acceptable to early require-ments engineering. However, the partial nature does not make the use case-based approaches expressive enough for needs of design, analyses, implementation, testing. While an "animation" (like playing a movie) of a use case may be possible, the "execution" in the sense of interactive behavior is not [18].

Use cases are described using a combination of natural language and informal diagrams. Use cases do not contain the elements of the notion behavior model (events, states, transitions, and compassion). Figure 25 shows that use cases cannot be even classified as LTSs.

4.2. Sequence Diagrams

A sequence diagram expresses a sequence of interactions of communicating objects. Normally, it presents one scenario of interaction or, with the use of decision and loop constructs, a limited set of related scenarios.

One scenario cannot represent the complete behavior. Sequence diagrams can be defined as a very limited case of LTS:

- Events are presented as directed arcs between the object lifelines (vertical lines). The states of an LTS can be recognized as points of intersection between events and object lifelines. These points can be named [20].
- There are no semantics of data, composition model, communication model, and variables or buffers for the events that arrive but not consumed.
- The composition techniques, used in sequence diagrams, are restricted with the sequence, fork, and cycle of actions. The join of actions is not defined.
- The communication mechanisms are not used for composition of sequences. In order to present an interaction, an event often has a respond (in implementation models, an event is a method call; a respond is a method return).

This summary of semantic elements of sequence diagrams and the properties of models rendered in sequences diagrams are shown in Figs. 25 and 26.

Figure 4 [21] shows a sequence diagram that presents the communication of a user with a program. The program draws graphs from the data series, chosen by the user. Three objects of classes *User*, *Graph Maker*, and *Graph Drawer* interact in the sequence. Events (operation calls and returns) are presented as strings (or symbols): *IGetGraph*, *IGetGraph:true*, etc.

Sequence diagrams do not have the join semantics. In order to combine scenarios and enable reasoning about the behavior represented by sequence diagrams, the "mechanical" composition approaches that join the repeated heads of sequences were suggested in Refs. [21–25]. However, the proposed join semantics is not generally used.

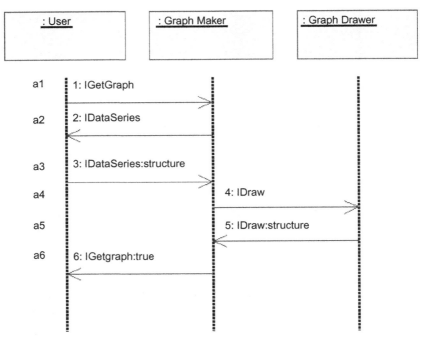

Figure 4 Sequence diagram [21].

Figure 5 shows an example of "mechanical" composition of sequence diagrams [21] into a process p. Events (operation calls and returns) are labeled with letters $a_1, a_2, \ldots, a_7$. The points between events mean sequential composition, and the summation symbol means an alternative. The *start* and the *final* events are used to start and finish the process.

Sequence diagrams are very useful not only for requirements gathering but also as abstract descriptions of test cases. They provide a flexible presentation of sequential fragments of crosscutting behavior in those aspect-oriented system development approaches [24,26] that identify the aspects of system behavior with scenarios.

4.3. Activity Diagrams

Activity diagrams are used to show "the sequence and conditions for *coordinating* lower-level behaviors, rather than the behavior of classes" [8]. As coordinating diagrams, activity diagrams replace the composition of object's behaviors. That is why activity diagrams are often used to orchestrate behaviors of objects and specify global contracts of choreography of communicating services.

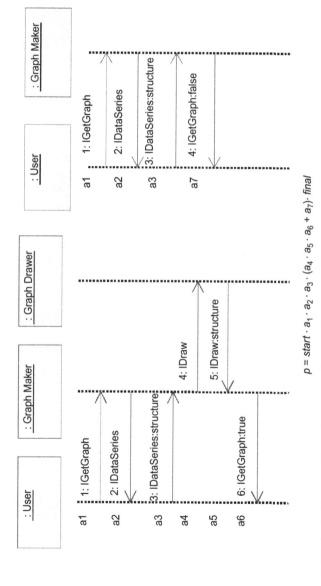

Figure 5 "Mechanical" composition of sequence diagrams into process [21].

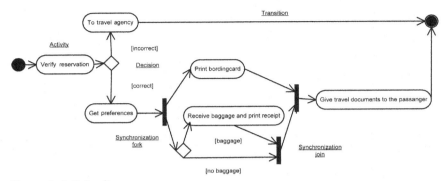

Figure 6 Activity diagram.

Figure 6 gives an example of activity diagram inspired by Ref. [27]. It presents a procedure of *Check-In* at the airport.

Activity diagrams can be seen as LTSs.

- The initial and the final states are shown as black circles.
- Rounded rectangles depict activities, both elementary events (inputs and outputs) and complex activities. The states are hidden in activities as the starts and ends of activities.
- An arrow from the end of one activity toward the start of another activity represents the order in which activities happen.
- The composition techniques are the sequence, fork, and cycle of activities and the split and join for concurrent activities. The diamonds represent forks. Bars represent the start (*split*) or end (*join*) of concurrent activities. The semantics of the transition from one activity to another is the "can-transit" semantics.
- Transitions show the flow of activities. This type of transition can be referred to as a completion transition. It does not require an explicit trigger event; it is triggered by the completion of the previous activities.
- *Decisions* have their guard conditions. These guard conditions control which transition of a set of alternative transitions follows once the activity has been completed.
- Synchronization bars allow one to show *concurrent threads* in the workflow [27].
- An activity state can be refined as a new activity diagram. Such a refining activity is called nested.
- While activity diagrams can be executed (see, for example, Engels *et al.* [28]), the execution is fulfilled at the level of a single flow and does not include the behavior of objects.

The activity diagrams contain many semantic elements of Petri Nets. The family of Petri Nets is not included in the UML. In the next section, we describe the family of Petri Nets in more detail.

4.4. State Machines (UML)

State machines exist in the UML in two variants:
- Behavior State Machines (BSMs) and
- Protocol State Machines (PSMs).

While there is some lack of clarity in their definitions (see, for example, Fecher *et al.* [29]), state machines do provide complete behavior descriptions and can be used for model-based execution [8].

4.4.1 UML Behavior State Machines

A BSM or statechart presents the behavior of one class.

"Behavior is modeled as a traversal of a graph of state nodes interconnected by one or more joined transition arcs that are triggered by the dispatching of series of (event) occurrences" [8]. The attributes of the class are updated when an event is accepted.

The semantics of the UML BSMs is relatively complex. There is an ongoing research about the metrics of their complexity [30]. Let us describe the semantics.

A state diagram is an LTS presented as a tuple of the set of initial states S_0, the set of states S ($S_0 \subseteq S$), and the set of relation R among states $SchD = (S_0, S, R)$.

S is a tree of states. In general, a state $s \in S$ is marked by (*Name, In, Out, History*) labels. The labels *History, In, Out* can be empty. There are states of three types in this tree: $\{AND, XOR, simple\}$. One of hierarchical states (AND or XOR) is a root of the tree of states. We shall name this state M (main). The states are depicted in the statechart diagrams by boxes with round corners. Nodes of XOR or AND state are drawn inside of this state (Fig. 7).

The state diagram in Fig. 7 illustrates an AND state without history. An AND state is divided into regions. Each region contains a BSM. In order to understand and explain the semantics of UML BSMs a transformation was proposed in Refs. [31–33]. The hierarchical states are flattered using the CCS composition. The parallel composition of two flat statecharts is a flat statechart such that the set of its transitions is defined by the rules of the CCS parallel composition.

Figure 7 shows the hidden elements of the CCS composition activating and finalizing the internal BSMs A and B. Each of them is activated with one

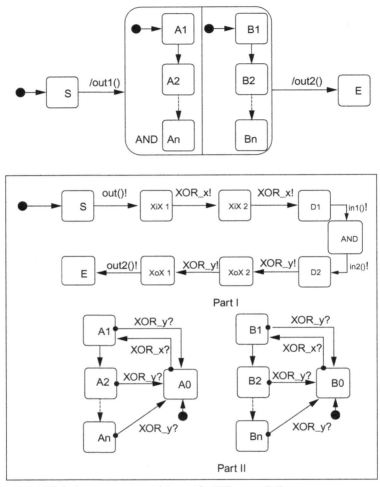

Figure 7 A UML behavior state machine with AND state [31].

of internal events *XOR_x!*. Each of them receives *XOR_x?*. Depending on the visible operation calls and the run of the processes *A* and *B*, each of them can be finished in any state when the event *out2()* will happen and the synchronization *XOR_y!*, *XOR_y?* will be sent and received. An XOR state is a case of AND state with one internal BSM in the hierarchical state.

Moreover, the set of relations among states includes not only transitions TR *but* also the *Join-Fork* connector and the *synchronization* construction from two *Join-Fork* connectors *R = { TR, Join-Fork, Synch}*. The *Join-Fork* constructors also have hidden semantics. Figure 8 shows this hidden

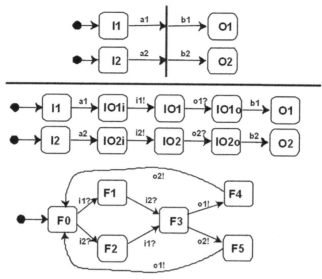

Figure 8 Join-Fork constructor [31].

semantics. The graph with states *F* (*Fork*) shows the asynchronous arrival of the joint processes. *I1* may send the action first and then *I2* or other way around.

The semantics of one transition $t \in TR$ depends on the transition label. A transition label is of the form: *event* [*guard*]/*action* where *event* specifies the event that triggers the transition, *guard* defines a condition that can restrict firing of the transition, and *action* is the action that happens when the transition fires.

The composition semantics for BSMs defines that state machines are executed asynchronously and communicate using events. The events are created as a result of actions within the system or within the environment. An event instance is queued until dispatched, at which point it is conveyed to one or more BMSs. An event dispatcher mechanism selects and dequeues event instances and an event processor handles the firing of state machine transitions and execution of consequent activity defined by the machines [8].

The consumption of events depends on the active state of a state machine. If an event triggers a transition in the current state of the machine, for which it is queued, it is dispatched and consumed, and this involves the firing of one or more transitions. If an event can cause two (or more) transitions to fire, which transition is chosen is not defined. If no transition is triggered then either the event is discarded, or it may be held (deferred) for later processing. "A state may specify a set of event types that may be deferred in the state. An event instance that does not trigger any transition in the current state will not be dispatched if its type matches with the type of one of the deferred events. Instead it remains in the event queue while another not deferred message is dispatched instead." [8]

In other words:

- if an event enables a transition in the current state of the machine then it can be dispatched and consumed;
- if an event does not enable a transition in the current state of the machine, but is listed as a deferrable event for this state, it is kept in a queue for later processing [18].

The resulting behavior of a population of state machines is, in general, asynchronous and nondeterministic.

The semantic model used for BSM execution in UML2 (which was first included in UML at version 1.5) is based on the "Recursive Design" method of Shlaer and Mellor [26] whose work has been mainly in the real-time and embedded systems domain. Following the adoption of Shlaer and Mellor semantics into UML the MDA approach based on their ideas has been rebranded as "Executable UML" [34]. The approach is based on using BSMs to model so-called "active objects": objects whose instances execute autonomously and asynchronously (i.e., as if executing on independent threads) resulting in system behavior that is inherently nondeterministic [35].

It is very hard to accommodate this semantic basis with the characteristics of the business information systems domain, where behavioral issues are related to transactional integrity and business rules, and strictly deterministic behavior of business logic is important to ensure repeatability, auditability, and testability [18]. The commercial tools that support Executable UML (such as those from Telelogic, Kennedy Carter and Mentor Graphics) are not well adapted for use in the business information systems domain and are positioned by their vendors to target the real time and embedded market.

The complex composition semantics cumbers the reasoning about behavior. Complete analysis of the behavior of the model must allow, in general, for arbitrary queuing of events between objects and for the accumulation of deferred events. If a model comprises a number of communicating objects, this results in a large number of possible execution states for the system as a whole, and reasoning on models is impossible without model checking algorithms. Model checking slows down the interactive process of model development and frequent changes. As described in Ref. [26] a single object class is modeled with a single state machine, and only concrete classes are modeled. This also means that crosscutting behaviors (aspects) have to be addressed by other means, potentially further complicating the model analysis [18].

4.4.2 UML Protocol State Machines

The UML Protocol State Machines (PSMs) are used to express the legal transitions that a class can trigger [18]. A PSM is a way to define a life cycle for objects, or an order of the invocation of its operations. The effect actions of transitions are not specified in a PSM transition as the trigger itself is the operation. However, pre- and postconditions are specified so that the label of a transition is of the form:

[pre-condition]/event/[post-condition].

The occurrence of an event that a PSM cannot handle is viewed as a precondition violation, but the consequent behavior is left open. "The interpretation of the reception of an event in an unexpected situation (current state, state invariant and pre-condition) is a semantic variation point: the event can be ignored, rejected, or deferred; an exception can be raised; or the application can stop on an error. It corresponds semantically to a pre-condition violation, for which no predefined behavior is defined in UML" [8].

Unlike BSMs, PSMs can (to a limited extent) be composed. "A classifier may have several protocol state machines. This happens frequently, for example, when a class inherits several parent classes having protocol state machine, when the protocols are orthogonal" [8]. In this context, "orthogonal machines" have a disjoint set of events.

PSM semantics is simpler and more abstract than the BSM semantics, however, as evidenced by the language used to describe them, PSMs are clearly positioned in UML as *contracts of legal usage* [18], and this gives PSM a role and meaning different from that of BSMs. While a contract must specify what is legal, it is not concerned with the mechanism by which nonlegal behavior is avoided, nor is it required to specify the effect of violation.

In other words: "*a contract cannot be used as the instrument that guarantees its own satisfaction*" [18]. It would therefore be a logical error to execute PSMs directly or to generate code from them, and other devices must be used in order to ensure that the software that is built complies with the contract PSMs that have been defined for it. To use PSMs as executable models would be inconsistent with this semantic positioning as contracts.

Summarizing, Figs. 25 and 26 show that the BSMs are the most advanced technique from the UML behavior modeling techniques. However, because of the complex semantics, it is not practical to use BSMs at all stages of the system development life cycle.

The idea to use different modeling semantics at different phases of the system development life cycle proposed in the UML has shown the problems of inconsistency [36]. The inconsistencies have their principal roots in the mismatch between the expression of requirements as visible system states and the modeling semantics with hidden states, queues, and the asynchronous CCS composition of models.

The complexity of BSMs and the roots of inconsistency built into semantics of the UML behavior modeling techniques drive the search of other practical approaches for system modeling outside the UML. The goal of the search is to find a technique that can be used on different stages of the system life cycle to avoid inconsistencies. It needs to be executable and can incorporate changes without remodeling the unchanged parts of the model.

In the next section, we present two families of techniques.

One family of techniques called Colored Petri Nets (CPNs) is advanced in the sense that it is executable and can support many stages of the life cycle of the nondeterministic systems. However, this technique has difficulties with incorporating model changes.

Another family is called Protocol Modeling. Protocol models are executable and can support many stages of the life cycle of deterministic systems. The semantic elements of Protocol Machines allow one to easily incorporate model changes.

5. OUTSIDE UML

5.1. Classical Petri Nets

In parallel with UML, there is a family of modeling techniques extending Classical Petri Nets.

Classical Petri Nets exist since 1962 [37]. Petri Nets and their extensions are used for design of distributed systems, business application logic, and information systems with web services.

5.1.1 Classical Petri Nets Semantics

A classical Petri Net is a tuple $N = (P; T; F; M0)$, where
- P is a finite set of places;
- T is a finite set of transitions;

- $F \subseteq (P \times T) \cup (T \times P)$ is the set of arcs, called a flow relation;
- M_0 is the initial marking being a vector of places with the corresponding tokens [37]. A token abstractly represents an instance of a concept flowing thorough the Petri net.

Each place initially has a bag of tokens. A bag of a selected place can be empty. M_0 is a vector of all places with their tokens. A marking distinguishes places with tokens and places without tokens and presents any current state of a Petri Net.

5.1.2 A Petri Net of a Web Service

In order to illustrate Petri Nets, let us show different concerns of a model of a web service (Fig. 9). The client-related concern of this service recognizes the following functionality.

A client

- looks for a specific product (transition *look* represented with box),
- makes a choice of a product (place *choice depicted as an ellipse*),
- then he/she can repeat searching and choosing (transition *more*).
- or pay (transition *pay* and leave the web service).

For any client, an instance of this service is created. Therefore, the client can use the service if there is a token in the place *Instance* and in the place *Client*.

The most popular interpretation of Petri Nets is based on the concepts of conditions and events [39–41]. Transitions are depicted by boxes and usually used to model events (Fig. 9). Places are drawn as ellipses (or circles) and represent conditions. A transition has a certain number of preconditions, modeled by places connected to the transition with input arcs. A transition has also a number of postconditions, modeled by places connected to the transition with output arcs. For example, transition *look* at Fig. 9 possesses two preconditions *client* and *instance* and one postcondition *choice*.

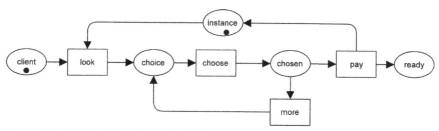

Figure 9 Petri Net of a web service [38].

A precondition becomes *true* if the place that models this precondition contains at least one token. If all preconditions of an event are true, i.e., each of their places contains at least one token, then the transition modeling this event becomes *enabled*, i.e., gets a chance to occur. If it occurs, then the postconditions of this event become *true* and the places modeling such post-conditions get tokens in them.

The *tokens flow* through the net. Each moment, the state is presented with a marking, being a snapshot of a Petri Net. We can name the set of places that contain tokens and indicate the number of tokens in each of the places. This snapshot of places with tokens is called the *current marking*.

A Petri Net is an executable model. The tokens are propagated by firing transitions. This is called execution. In the initial marking shown in Fig. 9, transition *look* is enabled. If this transition fires, place *choice* gets one token and transition **chosen** can fire. If it fires, two transitions *pay* and *more* become enabled. One of them will happen and we do not know which one. Petri Net is a nondeterministic model. If transition **more** happens, then the *choice* can be repeated. If transition **pay** happens, then the client is *ready* with the purchase and the *instance* of this service is released for another client (token goes to the place *instance*).

5.1.3 Model Changes

The aim of this chapter is identification of advanced modeling techniques that support different stages of the system development life cycle and incorporate changes without remodeling the unchanged parts of the model. Systems are designed to meet some specific requirements of society, users, environment, and other systems. There is no ready recipe telling us how to start designing a system or a system model. What usually given is a set of already existing systems or their models and the basic ideas of what the system have to fulfill and how the system should do this. The answer on the what-question can be named the functional or basic concern. The answer on the how-question provides other concerns like security, logging, cancelation, and garbage collection.

The decomposition in any system results in appearance of main classes and so-called *crosscutting concerns or aspects* [42]. The users and designers think in terms of concerns. So, decomposing the system, it would be wise to keep concerns in the design logic. Aspects cross or scatter the main functionality and complicate the model understanding. There is a need to model each aspect separately and then compose them in the predefined points of the model automatically.

There are the established basic dimensions of aspect-oriented approach: a join point model and an aspect quantification mechanism [42]. A choice of a join point model defines the elements in a model where aspects can be attached. The choice depends on the form of event and state presentation in the chosen notation. The chosen join point model restricts the allowed quantification, i.e., the types of predicates that a designer can use to attach aspects to each other.

A concern is represented by an aspect together with its quantification expression. The main principle of aspect-oriented approach is the principle of obliviousness of an aspect specification. The *obliviousness* of a concern specification means that the concern on which we quantify "should not know" about joining of other concerns and the mechanisms used for their quantification. Obliviousness allows designers to produce independent specifications of concerns.

As well as the UML behavior modeling approaches, Petri Nets also cannot separate aspects and automatically compose them. Figure 10 illustrates a change of the web service from Fig. 9 by extending it with the secure access to the service and to the payment.

The security extension demands two cuts of the Petri Net between place **client** and transition **look** and place **chosen** and transition **pay**. Then the security checks are inserted: **check1**, **check2**, and the places with two alternative output transitions: **checked1** and **checked 2**. One of alternative outputs is the transitions denying the access: **deny1**, **deny2**. The other alternative transition is the transition of the web service: **look, pay**.

Classical Petri Nets do not allow to separate modeling the crosscutting model extension. Figure 10 shows that the repeated functionality of the security checks is scattered through the model. The ways of separation in

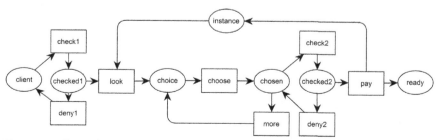

Figure 10 Classical Petri Net: web service with security checks [38].

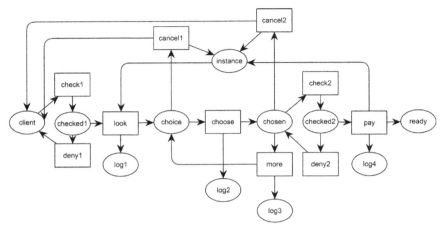

Figure 11 Classical Petri Nets with security checks, logs, and canceling [38].

Petri Nets are restricted with sequential composition, alternative and parallel split. As a result, any change in the model demands remodeling of the complete model. Adding nonlocalizable concerns usually results in repeated subnets and spaghetti-like Petri Nets.

Figure 11 shows a Classical Petri Net of the same web services with the security checks, logs, and canceling functionality.

The UML Activity Diagrams include many features of Classical Petri Nets. Both the Petri Nets and the Activity Diagrams are used to specify a single overall flow often called orchestration (of services). They do not separate the behavior of objects or other components.

There are many attempts to extend behavior modeling semantics with aspects. The examples of them are reviewed in Ref. [43]. There are aspect-oriented modeling extensions for sequence diagrams [44] and attempts of extension of activity diagrams [45]. However, the composition semantics is not generic. The composition is specified as rules of concatenation of fragments or hierarchical insertion.

Classical Petri Nets also do not work with data variables. For the system life cycle, they provide an abstract perspective useful for early stages of system requirements engineering.

5.2. Colored Petri Nets

There are many attempts to extend expressivity of Classical Petri Nets to support different design stages further than earlier requirements engineering.

The classification of Petri Nets was proposed by Monika Trompedeller in 1995 based on the survey [41]. We do not repeat the classification and focus on the advances.

The most practical extension of Petri Nets is called Colored Petri Nets (CPNs) [46]. The CPN development and execution are supported with CPN tools [47].

5.2.1 Colored Petri Nets Semantics

A CPN is a tuple $CPN = (C; B, P; T; V, F)$, where

- C is a finite set of color sets (colsets), being finite and nonempty types. They define the functions that can be used in the CPN description.
- B is a bag of tokens (values) of colors $c \in C$.
- P is a finite set of places $\{p1, ..., pm\} \in P$, depicted by ellipses (Fig. 12). Each place p possesses a color $c\_p \in C$ and a bag $b\_p \subseteq B$ of tokens of color c_p. We represent bag b_p of place p using the dot-notation $p.b\_p$ and name it **place-marking**. By default bag b_p is empty. A vector of place markings is the CPN marking.
- T is a finite set of transitions.
- V is a finite set of variables $v \in V$ of colors $c \in C$. Arc expressions and guards contain variables $v \in V$ of the suitable types.
- F is a finite set of functions. The functions are used as arc expressions, guards, and constants.

A state of a CPNet is **distributed** and presented by the bags in all its places, i.e., by the CPN marking. An execution of a CPNs is a propagation of tokens from input places (Fig.12) by calculation guards allowing or denying transitions and if the transition is enabled, then calculation of new tokens of the output places.

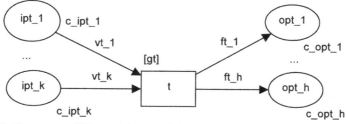

Figure 12 Shows one CPN transition **t** with its input places **ipt_1,...,ipt_k** and output places **opt_1...opt_h**. Each place has own color **c_ipt_1,...,c_ipt_k; c_opt_1,..., c_opt_h**. The transition has its guard **[gt]**. An input arc is labeled with a variable **v∈V**. The type of the variable is the color of the input place of the arc. An output arc is labeled with a function **f∈F** depending on variables on input arcs. The type of the function is the color of the output place of the arc.

A bag of a place may contain several tokens. The choice of the token from any bag is random. Therefore, *the behavior of a CPN is nondeterministic.*

CPNs can be seen as one of the most advanced behavior modeling techniques. They are able to support the system life cycle from requirements to implementation. There are published case studies that use CPNs in all stages of development for flexible manufacturing [48], industrial applications [49], business processes [50], and embedded systems [51]. Execution, simulation, and analysis of CPNs are supported by the CPN tool [47].

The applicability of CPN models for generation the tests for MBT needs further research. One group of research questions is related to the level of model abstraction needed for the MBT as the model should not contain implementation details. Another group of research questions concerns with the nondeterminism of CPN models and the selection of tests with suitable coverage behaviors from the infinite set of scenarios.

What remains problematic and error prone in CPN is the modification and evolution with or without crosscutting concerns. A CPN is a coordination model; it mixes (does not separate) behavior of classes. Any modification usually demands dissecting of transitions of the existing CPNet and then coordination of the existing parts of the model with the new parts.

5.2.2 Colored Petri Net of a Mobile Phone with Phone Book

Let us illustrate the problems of modification and evolution of the CPN models with a simplified case study of a mobile phone with a phone book that can save names and associated numbers. In this section, we render this case using CPN. In the next section, we present a Protocol Model of the same system. The reader will be able to compare the ability of modeling semantics to localize concerns and support model evolution.

Figures 13 and 14 [51] show the CPN model of a mobile phone with a phone book. Figure 13 contains the declarations of the variables and functions. The functions are written using the functional programming language ML. This model represents the mobile phone software as a single CPN per phone. The mobile phone model can be initialized (transition *INITIALISE*) and switched on (transition ON). Switching On enables both the call and the phone book functionality (place *Call and Phone Book enabled*).

The initialization means that a token (an empty list) is set into place *Phone Book*. This place contains tokens of the type *color BOOK=list RECORD*, where *color RECORD=product NAME*NUMBER*.

Declarations
```
colset E = with e;
var u:E;
colset INT = int;
colset BOOL = bool;
colset STRING = string;
colset ON = STRING;
colset INITIALISE = STRING;
colset OFF = STRING;
colset ENDTALKING = STRING;
colset ENDCALLING = STRING;
colset CALL = product STRING*INT;
colset RECEIVE = product STRING*INT;
colset FINDCALL = product STRING*STRING;
colset ENDCALLINGSAVE = product STRING*STRING;
colset RECORD = product STRING*INT;
colset BOOK = list RECORD;
colset INSERT = product STRING*STRING*INT;
colset DELETE = product STRING*STRING*INT;
colset UPDATE = product STRING*STRING*INT;
fun insert (z:RECORD,[]) = [z] | insert (z:RECORD,h::t:BOOK) = if (z=h) then (h::t) else (h:: insert (z,t));
fun delete(z:RECORD,[]) = [] | delete(z:RECORD,h::t:BOOK) = if (z=h) then (t) else (h::delete(z,t));
fun find (m:STRING,[]) = 0 | find(m:STRING,(a,b)::t:BOOK) = if (m=a) then b else find(m,t);
fun update((y,z) :RECORD,[]) = [(y,z)] | update(y,z):RECORD,(a,b)::t:BOOK) = if (y=a) then (y,z)::t else ((a,b))::update((y,z):RECORD,t:BOOK));
var s,v:STRING;
var l:BOOK;
var n:INT;
var m:STRING;
```

Figure 13 Declarations of the CPN model of the mobile phone [51].

If the call functionality is enabled, a call can be made (transition *CALL*). There are two options to end the call. The call can be ended without saving the number (transition *END1*). The call can be ended with saving the number in the phone book as a record (*name, number*) (transition *END CALL SAVE*).

If the user wants to call someone but has forgotten the number, an attempt can be made to find the name in the phone book. If the name is found, a call is initiated (transition *FIND CALL*). In this case, the number is already in the phone book, so the call is ended without saving the number (transition *END2*).

While no call is active, new records (*name, number*) can be inserted in the "phone book" and the existing records can be updated or deleted (transitions *INSERT, UPDATE, DELETE*):

The CPN in Fig. 14 contains one token *1'e* in place *Call enabled* (*Call enabled, 1'e*), one token *123* in place *Call* (*Call,("call",123)*), and two tokens "ecs" and "Ann" in place *End Call Save* (*End Call Save,("ecs","Ann")*). In this marking transition *CALL* can fire, then the transition *END CALL SAVE* can fire and the record ("*Ann*", *123*) will be saved in the phone book.

5.2.3 Model Changes

If we extend the phone book with a game functionality, both functionalities are wired in the same CPN. It is possible to use hierarchical transitions to replace the call and game functionality; however, the functionalities remain

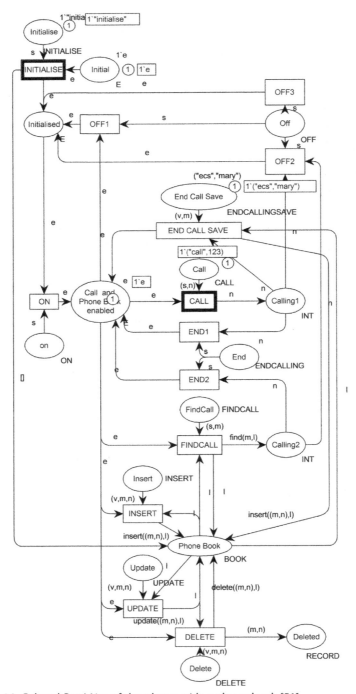

Figure 14 Colored Petri Net of the phone with a phone book [51].

hardwired and the understandability of the model decreases. Figure 15 renders the extended model in CPN without hierarchical transitions.

It is required that

- when the initialized phone switched On, the play is enabled;
- when the phone switched Off, the play is disabled;
- the playing may be interrupted by the events **Call** and **Find Call**. In this case, the interrupted state of the game is saved and the play can be resumed or stopped.

Transition **On** makes the **Play Enabled**. A play can be started and stopped. **Playing** can be interrupted. The interrupted token may come from transition **Call** or transition **FindCall**.

As we see, the functionalities of **Phone Book**, **Phone**, and **Game** are mixed together.

Petri Nets do not support keeping separation of concerns and track of modifications. This shortcoming makes it difficult to reuse models, because models do not allow tracing design decisions without additional documentation.

All attempts to solve the problem with separation of concerns in CPN by hierarchy [52 and 63], when one transition includes a subnet, work only for sequential concerns. Hierarchies hide concerns inside functions or hierarchical transitions and make the separation of concerns even more difficult. A rule-based composition of CPN fragments was proposed [38,45], but the rules were found not generic. In the next section, we present the composition semantics that may be also applied in different modeling notations, including for CPN to make them compositional [62].

5.3. Protocol Modeling

"The composition techniques developed in process algebras such as Hoare's CSP [10] and Milner's CCS [9] have not made their way into the UML, perhaps because the domain of algebraic processes (CSP and CCS) and software models (UML) have been viewed as too different" [18]. However, research work into behavior specification techniques, such as those by McNeile *et al.* [7] and Grieskamp *et al.* [52], has shown that CSP parallel composition transplants successfully into software modeling. Other recent work in the context of collaborative service behavior and service choreography specification is making use of CCS and pi-calculus, such as the work of Carbone *et al.* [53].

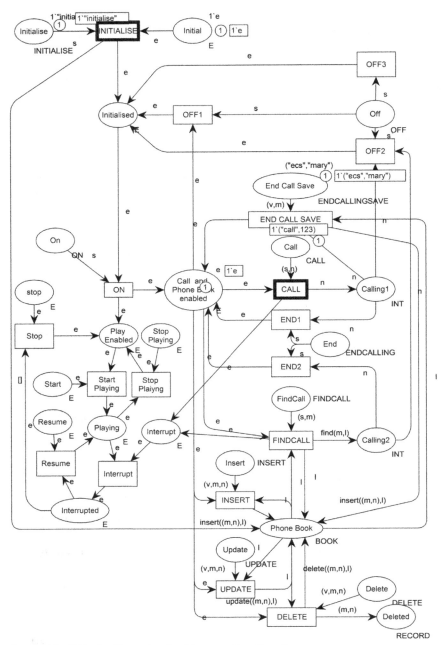

Figure 15 CPN of a Phone book with game functionality.

One of the most advanced behavior modeling semantics nowadays is the Protocol Modeling semantics [7] that combines the findings of the process algebras on behavior composition and the modeling of the data abstractions: both objects and aspects. This semantics supports all stages of system life cycle including system evolution and has a broad domain of application.

This section presents the Protocol Modeling semantics, explains its properties, and gives the examples of models in different domains supporting all stages of the life cycle.

5.3.1 Protocol Modeling Semantics

An object protocol machine is a tuple of following elements:

PM_OBJECT = (NAME, INCLUDES, ATTRIBUTES, STATES, TRANSITIONS, CALLBACK)

The set of types used for specification of elements of events and protocol machines includes traditional programming types: *String, Integer, Boolean, Currency.*

- *NAME: String;*
- *INCLUDE∈ INCLUDES. INCLUDE: PM_BEHAVIOR.*

PM_BEHAVIOR = (INCLUDES,   ATTRIBUTES,   STATES, TRANSITIONS, CALLBACK)

Unlike PM_OBJECT, PM_BEHAVIOR does not have a unique identifier-NAME.

- *ATTRIBUTES, ATTRIBUTE: TYPE.*
- *STATES, STATE: String,*
- *TRANSITIONS. TRANSITION = (S1, E, S2), where S1, S2 are states.*

E is an event coming from environment.

E = (NAME, ATTRIBUTES, CALLBACK).

The events that appear in transitions of a protocol machine are recognized by this protocol machine.

- *CALLBACK (PM1,. . .,PMn, E1,. . .,Em) = (PM1,. . .,PMn,E1,. . .,Em).*

A *CALLBACK* is a function that generates new values of the protocol model elements: attributes, states, events. A callback may be associated with a protocol machine or with an event.

The extreme cases of protocol machines are

- a passive protocol machine that contains only attributes (like a data structure). The set of transitions is empty. The set of states contains only the initial states. Such a protocol machine can be included in other protocol machines.
- a protocol machine without attributes and callbacks. This protocol machine is an LTS.

A Protocol Model (*PMD*) is a set of protocol machines *PM* (both *PM_OBJECT* and *PM_BEHAVIOR*) $PMD = PM1 \, || \, PM2 || \ldots || PMn, n \in N$ that
- exist in the environments that generate events and
- are synchronized by the rules of allowing, rejecting, and ignoring of events.

If an event is recognized by the Protocol model, it can be allowed or refused depending on the state of Protocol Machines *PM1, ..., PMn* of the Protocol model *PMD*.

In a given state, a *PMD*
- *ignores* any action that is not in its alphabet;
- depending on its state, either *allows* or *refuses* an action that is in its alphabet;
- if it engages in an action, it moves to a new state [18].

Informally, *ignoring* an action means that a machine "does not know this action." *Refusing* an action by a machine means that the machine knows this action and knows that it cannot happen in its current state. The distinction between these two, which is not made at all in the semantics of UML state machines, is the basis for parallel composition of protocol machines.

The composition can be seen as an external coordinator executing the generic composition rules. **The rules of the CSP parallel composition** say that if all protocol machines, recognizing an event, are in a state to allow the event, the event is allowed by the protocol model. If at least one of all protocol machines recognizing the event refuses it, the event is refused by the protocol model.

The CSP parallel composition of two protocol machines is another protocol machine [7]. In particular, it is also deterministic and quiescent.
- **Quiescence.** If it is starved actions, a protocol machine is bound to reach *quiescence*, and only at quiescence is its state well defined. A machine with this property is sometimes called *reactive*. This means that a protocol machine cannot engage in an action that results in a computation that does not terminate.
- **Determinism.** A protocol machine is deterministic, so the new state it moves to when it allows an action is dependent only on the old state and the action in which it engages.

Because the rules of CSP parallel composition synchronize protocol machines of a protocol model, a protocol model possesses the properties of quiescence and determinism. This form of composition does not have the restriction present in the UML for composition of PSMs that the composed machines are "orthogonal" (independent, concurrently active). It is the ability to compose **nonorthogonal** machines that gives the Protocol Machines its expressivity [18].

5.3.2 Protocol Model of a Mobile Phone with Phone Book

Figure 16 presents a protocol model of a mobile phone with a phone book. It is the same system that was rendered as a CPN model in Fig. 14. The protocol model is the CSP parallel composition of three protocol machines: *Calling Machine, Singleton,* and *Save Number*.

The graphical form of the protocol model is not expressive enough to include all elements of the model. (Analogously, the graphical presentation of a CPN is not expressive enough and needs declarations and the CPN tool.)

First, the CSP parallel composition is the same for all protocol models. It belongs to the middleware that executes protocol models. An example of such middleware is the Modelscope tool [54].

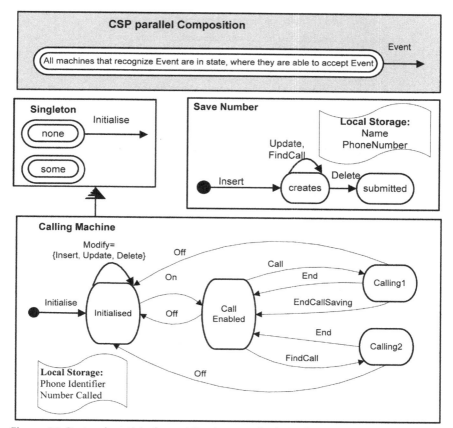

Figure 16 Protocol model of a mobile phone with phone book [51].

Second, the callback updating the model local storage cannot be presented in the graphical form.

The textual form of the protocol model presented below is able to express both the graphical information and the callbacks.

```
OBJECT Calling Machine
    NAME Phone name
    INCLUDES Singleton
    ATTRIBUTES Phone name: String,
                !Status: String,
                Calling: String
    STATES Initialised, Call enabled, Calling1, Calling2
    TRANSITIONS@new*Initialise=Initialised,
                Initialised*On=Call enabled,
                Call enabled*!Call=Calling1,
                Calling1*!End=Call enabled,
                Calling1*End Call Saving=Call enabled,
                Call enabled*!Find Call=Calling2,
                Calling2*!End=Call enabled,
                @any*!Off=Initialised,
                Call enabled*Insert=Call enabled,
                Call enabled*Update=Call enabled,
                Call enabled*Delete=Call enabled
BEHAVIOR!Singleton
    STATES none, some
    TRANSITIONS none*Initialise=@any
OBJECT Saved Number Machine
    NAME Person name
    ATTRIBUTES Person name: String, Phone number: String
    STATES Saved, Deleted
    TRANSITIONS@new*Insert=Saved,
                @new*End Call Saving=Saved,
                Saved*Update=Saved,
                Saved*Delete=Deleted,
                Saved*Find Call=Saved
EVENT Initialise
    ATTRIBUTES Phone: Calling Machine, Phone name: String
EVENT On
    ATTRIBUTES Phone: Calling Machine
EVENT Off
    ATTRIBUTES Phone: Calling Machine
```

```
EVENT Call
    ATTRIBUTES Phone: Calling Machine, Phone number: String
EVENT End
    ATTRIBUTES Phone: Calling Machine
EVENT Find Call
    ATTRIBUTES Phone: Calling Machine, Saved Number: Saved Number
                Machine
EVENT Insert
    ATTRIBUTES Phone: Calling Machine, Saved Number: Saved Number
                Machine, Person name: String, Phone number: String
EVENT Update
    ATTRIBUTES Phone: Calling Machine, Saved Number: Saved Number
                Machine, Person name: String, Phone number: String
EVENT Delete
    ATTRIBUTES Phone: Calling Machine, Saved Number: Saved Number
                Machine
EVENT !End Call Saving
    ATTRIBUTES Phone: Calling Machine, Saved Number: Saved Number
                Machine, Person name: String
CALLBACKES
public class CallingMachine extends Behavior {
    public String getStatus() {
    // Current status of the phone
        return this.getState("Calling Machine");
    }
public void processCall (Event event, String subscript) {
        // Sets up the Calling attribute when a call starts with Call
        this.setString("Calling", event.getString("Phone number"));
    }
public void processFindCall (Event event, String subscript) {
        // Sets up the Calling attribute when a call starts with
        // Find Call
        this.setString("Calling", event.getInstance("Saved
        Number").getString("Phone number"));
    }
public void processEnd (Event event, String subscript) {
        // Blanks out the Number attribute when a call finishes
        this.setString("Calling", "");
    }
```

```
public void processOff(Event event, String subscript){
    // Blanks out the Number attribute when the 'phone is
    // switched off
    this.setString("Calling","");
}
public class EndCallSaving extends Event {
    public void handleEvent(){
    Event insertName=this.createEvent("Insert");
    insertName.setString("Phone number",this.getInstance("
        Phone").getString("Calling"));
    this.createEvent("End").submitToModel();
    insertName.submitToModel();
    }
}
public class Singleton extends Behavior {
    public String getState(){
    // The state is calculated to be "none" if no instances of this object
    // type currently exist.
    // The "selectInState" looks for instances of this object type in any
    // state.
    return this.selectInState(this.getObjectType(),"@any").
    length==0 ? "none" : "some";
}
```

Let us recognize all elements of this protocol model in this textual form. Each event is specified with the key word *EVENT*: *Initialise, On, Off, Call*, etc. There are two *OBJECT* Protocol Machines: *Saved Number* and *Calling Machine*. The machines contain states, transitions, and attributes in their specifications.

Saved Number Machine models the phone book.

- An instance of the *Save Number machine* is created for each saved number with accepting event *Insert*.
- *The ATTRIBUTES Person name: String, Phone number: String* are storages of the information about the saved number.
- The number can be updated accepting event *Update*, deleted *with* event *Delete* or found with event *FindCall*.

Calling Machine models the phone functionality.

This model permits only one instance of the *Calling Machine*. In order to restrict the number of instances of the phone by one, we use the behavior protocol machine *Singleton* included into the *Calling Machine*.

The *Calling Machine* can be in states *Initialised, Call enabled, Calling1* corresponding to the calls to not yet saved numbers and *Calling2* corresponding to the saved numbers. Event *Initialise* being accepted transits the phone to state *Initialised*. The phone can be switched *On* and *Off*. Event *On* enables calls (state *Call enabled*).

Singleton machine represents a uniqueness aspect.

In the CPN model, the singleton functionality is not separated and can be seen as place *Initial* containing one token before firing transition *Initialise*. Transition *Initialise* is enabled only if there is a token in place *Initial* and *Initialise*.

The protocol machine BEHAVIOR Protocol Machine *Singleton* presents the enabling condition separately. *Singleton* is included into *Calling Machine*. This is shown with an arrow with the half-dashed end. *Singleton* can be reused in other models.

The BEHAVIOR Protocol Machine *Singleton* illustrates the semantics of derived states. A derived state is analogous to the familiar concept of a derived (or calculated) attribute, in that its value is calculated "on the fly" by a function when required. A machine may use its own attributes and/or those of other, composed, machines to derive its state. In the graphical form, the state icons for derived state machine are given a double outline. The *BEHAVIOR* Protocol Machine *Singleton* has two derived states: *none* and *some*. State *none* is calculated by the callback *public class Singleton extends Behavior* {...} if there are no instantiation *Calling Machine*. The state is *some*, if it is instantiated. The derived state machine does not has to be "topologically connected," because the state update is not driven by transitions. The graphical presentation of the *transition (None, Initialise, @any)* does not need the resulting state. The state of the model is defined by other protocol machines after transition *(None, Initialise, @any)*.

All protocol machines are CSP parallel composed. This means that if all machines recognizing an event are able to accept the event, it is accepted, otherwise it is refused.

For example, when the *Calling Machine* in state *Call enabled, events Call* or *Insert[New Number], Delete[Existing Number], Update[Existing Number]* can be accepted. Also event *Find Call* is enabled. If the number is in the phone book, then the phone transits to state *Calling2*. If the number of the call is new, then the phone transits into state *Calling1*. From state *Calling1* event *EndCallSaving* is enabled. This event generates internal event Insert and creates the new *Saved Number* protocol machine.

The behavior of the CSP parallel composition of protocol machines is the set of sequences of accepted events with the corresponding updates of the states and attributes.

An example of such sequences for the mobile phone with the phone book is the following:

Initialise, On, Call [Number], End Call Saving [Number, Person Name], Find Call [Person Name], End, Off

The generation of these sequences is not obvious as the rules of composition need to be applied. However, the Modelscope tool [54] allows to submit events to the model and execute the sequences. As the CSP procedure is a generic algorithm, the sequences can be generated. The data of events are inserted interactively by the model user.

5.3.3 Model Changes

The CSP parallel composition allows one to model the concerns gathered at the requirements engineering phase separately and then compose them. The flexibility provided by this composition separates both objects (Object Protocol Machines) and aspects (Behavior Protocol Machines).

Let us extend the Protocol Model of the mobile phone with a game. We remind the requirements:

- when the initialized phone switched On, the play is enabled;
- when the phone switched Off, the play is disabled;
- the playing may be interrupted by the events **Call** and **Find Call**. In this case, the interrupted state of the game is saved and the play can be resumed or stopped.

We can localize the game functionality in an *OBJECT Game Machine* with states *Off, Play enabled, Playing, and Interrupted*. The description of events also changed as many events are recognized by the *Game Machine*. The event *Interrupt* is matched with events *Call* and *Find Call*. The *Call Machine* and *Save Number Machine* are not changed.

```
OBJECT Game Machine
    NAME Game name
    ATTRIBUTES Game name : String
    STATES Off, Play enabled, Playing, Interrupted
    TRANSITIONS @new*Initialise=Off, Off*On=Play enabled,
                Play enabled*Off=Off,
                Play enabled*Interrupt=Play enabled,
                Play enabled*Start=Playing,
                Playing*Stop=Play enabled,
```

```
                        Playing*Interrupt=Interrupted,
                        Interrupted*Interrupt=Interrupted,
                        Interrupted*Resume=Playing,
                        Interrupted*Stop=Play enabled
#EVENT definitions
EVENT Initialise
    ATTRIBUTES Phone: Calling Machine, Phone name : String,
    Game: Game Machine
EVENT On
    ATTRIBUTES Phone: Calling Machine, Game: Game Machine
EVENT Off
    ATTRIBUTES Phone: Calling Machine, Game: Game Machine
EVENT Call
    ATTRIBUTES Phone: Calling Machine, Phone number: String,
    Game: Game Machine
EVENT End
    ATTRIBUTES Phone: Calling Machine
EVENT Find Call
    ATTRIBUTES Phone: Calling Machine, Saved Number: Saved Number
    Machine, Game: Game Machine
EVENT Insert
    ATTRIBUTES Phone: Calling Machine, Saved Number: Saved Number
    Machine, Person name: String, Phone number: String
EVENT Update
    ATTRIBUTES Phone: Calling Machine, Saved Number: Saved Number
    Machine, Person name: String, Phone number: String
EVENT Delete
    ATTRIBUTES  Phone:Calling  Machine, Saved  Number: Saved  Number
    Machine
EVENT !End Call Saving
    ATTRIBUTES Phone: Calling Machine, Saved Number: Saved Number
    Machine, Person name: String
EVENT Start
    ATTRIBUTES Game: Game Machine
EVENT Stop
    ATTRIBUTES Game: Game Machine
EVENT Resume
    ATTRIBUTES Game: Game Machine
GENERIC Interrupt
    MATCHES Call, Find Call
```

All protocol machines are CSP parallel composed. The model is shown graphically in Fig. 17.

The advantageous features of the model for requirements engineering is locality of changes and executability. Locality of changes simplifies modeling.

The executability of Protocol Models is used for communication with customers and revealing possible tacit requirements. Generic events are used for composition of crosscutting concerns (aspects) [4,55].

The CSP parallel composition technique has the property of Observational Consistency (as defined by Ebert and Engels [56]) when applied to protocol machines. This property, as discussed in Ref. [55], gives the ability to perform local reasoning on models, whereby conclusions about system behavior as a whole can be based on examining single machines in isolation. Indeed, we can design and discuss behavior of the game independent from the call and vice versa. This is essentially because CSP parallel composition preserves the trace behavior of the composed machines. The ability to perform local reasoning is crucial if intellectual control is to be maintained over a complex model as it grows [4]. The state-transition models in other modeling approaches techniques do not possess the property of local reasoning. They need to be analyzed using standard model checking algorithms and tools, and this is important in complex cases where true concurrency is involved.

We also need to mention two other semantic advances of protocol modeling:

- the ability to vary the semantics of transitions from the "can" semantics to "must" and "motivate" and
- the ability to combine CCS and CSP parallel composition techniques.

5.3.4 Can and Must Semantics

The conventional semantics for enabled transitions in LTSs is the *"Can"* semantics: an enabled transition *can fire*. This is an indication of the fact that any model is an abstraction from reality; it does not present all factors that influence the firing of a transition.

There are, however, the situations, when the system is designed protectively insensitive to any events that are not recognized by the model, so that there is functional dependency between a state, an event, and its firing. In such a case, the *"Must"* semantics is employed. In Protocol Modeling, the events can be generated by the callbacks and these events *must fire*.

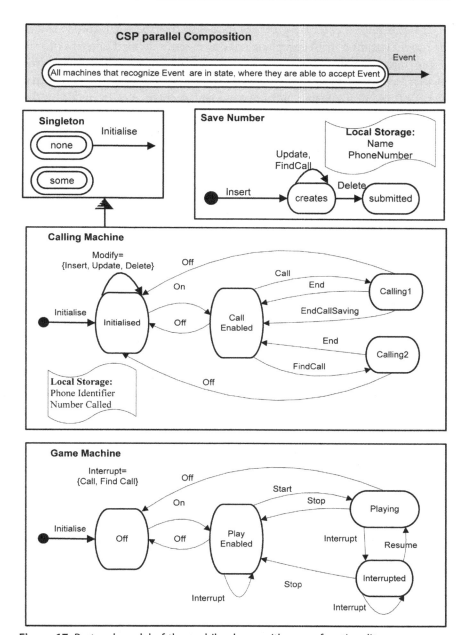

Figure 17 Protocol model of the mobile phone with game functionality.

It is possible to extend a protocol model so that the total stored state of the model resulting from acceptance of one event is defined in terms of a set of generated events. These generated events present so-called "*inter-object behavior*" contrasted with "*intra-object behavior*" [57]. Figure 18 shows that events *e3*, *e4* are generated as a response on acceptance of event *e2* by the model. Callback is specific to an event type and is used for every instance of that event type presented to *PM2*. It is generated for every instance of event by a machine with must semantics. When an event is presented to it, it *must* accept it. The machine with "*must*" semantics has access to the attributes of *e2* and to the interim stable states that *PM1* reached between the presentations of successive generated events.

An example of the *must*-semantic is generating events *Insert* and *End* as a "must" after appearance of event *EndCallSaving*.

```
package PhoneBook;
import com.metamaxim.modelscope.callbacks.*;
public class EndCallSaving extends Event {
        public void handleEvent() {
        Event insertName=this.createEvent("Insert");
        insertName.setString("Phone number",
            this.getInstance("Phone").getString("Calling"));
                InsertName.submitToModel();
                        this.createEvent("End").submitToModel();
```

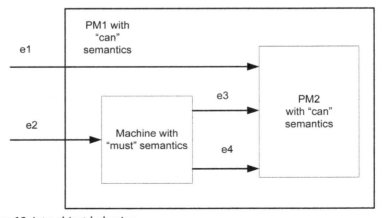

Figure 18 Intraobject behavior.

5.3.5 Motivation Semantics

Systems are created to achieve given goals. The goals define priorities on acceptance of events. Acceptance of some of events leads to achieving the goals.

In order to introduce motivation of events, that lead to goals, the set of transitions may be presented as a set of two relations $T = \{C, U\}$ [58,59]:

- $C = A \times S$ is a binary relation, where $(a, s) \in C$ means that action A is a possible action for LTS when in states. C is called the can-model because it models the actions that LTS "can do" in each state.
- U is a total mapping $C \to S$ that defines for each member of C the new state adopts as a result of the action. $U(a; si) = sj$ means that if LTS engages in action a when in state si, it will then adopt state sj. U is called the update-model.

With separation of the can- and update-models, an LTS is a tuple: $LTS = (S, A, C, U)$. This is the same process; it does not contain motivation yet.

There is always a set of states in the process where a particular goal is achieved. Let us name the states from this set of states **goal states**. From the goal perspective, the actions leading to a goal state are the priority actions or wanted actions in the states preceding the goal state. So, a state preceding a goal state and the action that may lead to the goal state, form a new binary relation:

In order to model motivation, the motivation relation should be added to the model.

$$M \subseteq (A \times S), (a; s) \in M$$

The motivation relation means that event a is a motivated action for LTS when in state s. In order to model motivation, M is added to the process:

$$LTS_M = (S, A, C, U, M).$$

The can- and motivation-models of a process are independent of each other, so when a process is in a given state, an action can have different combinations of can- and motivation-alternatives:

{**can happen**; **cannot happen**} × {**motivated**; **not motivated**}

The motivation models do not contribute to behavior of the systems but motivate the human communication with the service and communication with other services. The simplest application of motivation models is the justified design of human–computer interface.

Usually relation $M \subseteq C$ and in this case the semantics of M means highlighting the transitions that lead to the goals state. The semantics of the Protocol Modeling approach offers an easy and practical way to model motivation separately from the can–update–model of the process.

Our example [58] is a *Pay by Credit Card* web service that can be seen in many electronic booking systems. The user instantiates the service. The user is asked to fill in his credit card number and read the privacy conditions of the service. The user may fill in the credit card number without reading the privacy conditions and after reading and accepting the privacy conditions. When the user has accepted the privacy conditions, he can rethink and read the statement again. The service can always be canceled before the credit card number is filled in.

We model the can–update process as a CSP composition of protocol machines *Input*, *Decision*, and *Cancelation* (Fig. 19). Protocol machines *Motivate Insert* and *Motivate Accept* are the motivation modules.

```
MODEL InsertCreditCardNumber
OBJECT Input
    NAME Session
    INCLUDES Decision,Cancellation,Motivate Insert,Motivate Accept
        ATTRIBUTES Session:String,Card Number:Integer
    STATES instantiated,inserted
    TRANSITIONS@new*Instantiate=instantiated,
            instantiated*Insert=inserted
BEHAVIOR Decision
    STATES instantiated,not accepted,accepted,final
```

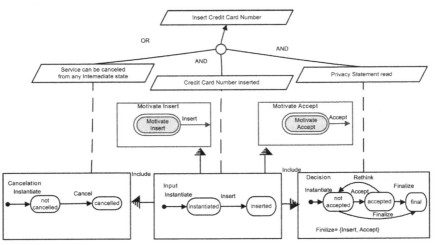

Figure 19 A protocol model with motivation models [58].

```
        TRANSITIONS@new*Instantiate=not accepted,
                not accepted*Accept=accepted,
                accepted*Rethink=not accepted,
                accepted*Finalize=final,
                not accepted*Finalize=final
BEHAVIOR Cancellation
   STATES not cancelled, cancelled
   TRANSITIONS@new*Instantiate=not cancelled,
                not cancelled*Cancel=cancelled
BEHAVIOR!Motivate Insert
TYPE DESIRED
   STATES motivate insert, other
   TRANSITIONS motivate insert*Insert=@any
BEHAVIOR!Motivate Accept
TYPE DESIRED
   STATES motivate accept, other
   TRANSITIONS motivate accept*Accept=@any
EVENT Instantiate
   ATTRIBUTES Input:Input, Session:String,
EVENT Insert
   ATTRIBUTES Input:Input, Credit Card Number:Integer,
EVENT Accept
   ATTRIBUTES Input:Input,
EVENT Rethink
   ATTRIBUTES Input:Input,
EVENT Cancel
   ATTRIBUTES Input:Input,
GENERIC Finalize
MATCHES Insert, Cancel
```

```
CALLBACKS
public class MotivateAccept extends Behavior {
    public String getState() {
        String x=this.getState("Decision");
            if(x.equals("not accepted")
            ) return "motivate accept"; else return "other";
            }
    }
```

```
public class MotivateInsert extends Behavior {
```

```
public String getState(){
   String x = this.getState("Decision");
      if(x.equals("accepted")
      ) return "motivate insert"; else return "other";
      }
}
```

The motivation models have TYPE DESIRED. This is recognized by the Modelscope tool, and the motivated events are highlighted green (Fig. 20) in the user interface to motivate the choice of these events. However, the user can choose other enabled events as well.

5.3.6 Combining the CCS and CSP Parallel Composition in Protocol Models

The advantages of Protocol Modeling are achieved by using the CSP parallel composition when it is possible. This gives the power to separate objects and aspects.

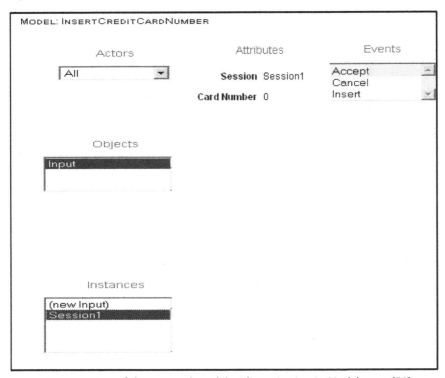

Figure 20 Execution of the protocol model with motivation in Modelscope [58].

An ***Object Abstraction*** is an abstraction that uses own state and can read (but cannot change) the local storage of other, composed objects and aspects deciding on how to react on events.

An ***Aspect Abstraction*** is an ***Object Abstraction*** that abstracts over the events and states of other objects and aspects using generalized events and generalized states [15].

Objects and aspects are the abstractions that can read (not change) the state of each other.

There is another abstraction called ***Service*** that cannot read state of other abstractions. A service has private data and state (do not share data). Services communicate with each other by message passing that is modeled using CCS composition style,

- one constituent is able to **send** (engage in !*a*) and
- another is able to receive (engage in ?*a*),
- there is a reaction whereby the corresponding message of type *a* passes from sender to receiver and the states of the sender and receiver are changed according to their respective process definitions.

Inside, any service may contain objects and aspects, but the communication between services does not allow state access (Fig. 21). The rules of such communication are known as CCS composition by Milner [9].

Unlike other modeling semantics, Protocol Modeling is able to use both CCS and CSP parallel composition. Figure 22 shows the different domains for application of composition forms.

- If a stand along service reacts on events, it may react by presenting state. The CSP parallel composition is used inside of the service.
- If the system consists of communicating services, then the CCS composition rules need to be applied.

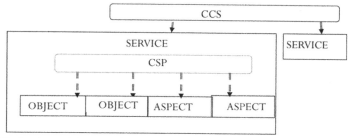

Figure 21 Services, objects, and aspects [15].

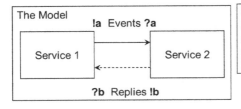

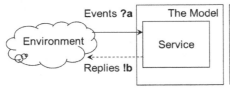

Figure 22 CCS and CSP composition [15].

Figure 23 presents a protocol model of a *Public Information System* [15]. It consists of two services *Publisher* and *Notifier*. Service *Publisher* provides information about existing educations and exemptions. The service *Publisher* contains objects and aspects. There are objects of classes *Education* and *Exemption*. The information to the service is provided by the clerk with a password. The aspect *Password Management and Control* implements the rules of password setting. The aspect *Password Handler* demands the password for any event of objects *Education* and *Exemption*. Objects and aspects are composed using the CSP parallel composition (all events are received with sigh "?").

Services *Publisher* and *Notifier* are composed using CCS parallel composition. Any event accepted by object *Education* and *Exemption* causes a message *of type* ?*Information* sent from the *Publisher* to the *Notifier*. The *Notifier* should be able to receive it !*Information*.

6. SUMMARY OF SEMANTIC ELEMENTS OF BEHAVIOR MODELING APPROACHES AND THEIR PROPERTIES

In this survey, we deliberately included only the system behavior modeling approaches and left out the models of programs and parallel programs. Only the approaches that have all the elements of a behavior model: events, states, transitions, and communication–composition mechanism were the target of this survey. The aim of the survey was to show how a set of semantic elements makes a behavior modeling technique capable of meeting the requirements for models at different stages of the system development life cycle.

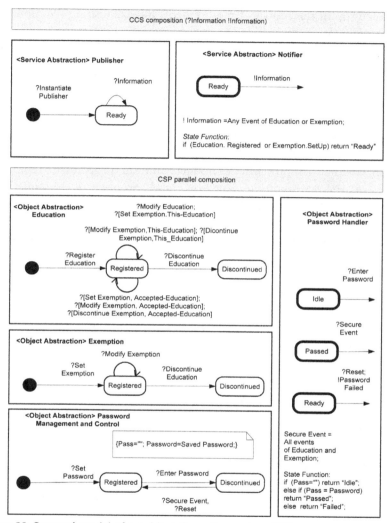

Figure 23 Protocol model of a public information system [15].

In the begin of this chapter, we formulated requirements to the behavior modeling techniques for support the activities of the system life cycle. The modeling approaches should enable:

1. separate modeling of concerns gathered at the requirement phase;
2. composition of concerns modeled from requirements:
   2.1 composition of classes;
   2.2 composition of crosscutting concerns;

3. Execution of the model of requirements for establishing traceability of requirements in models and models in implementations.

Figure 24 compares semantic elements (Events, States, Transition, and Communication–Composition mechanism) of behavior modeling approaches. Figure 25 indicates the properties of behavior modeling techniques.

The combination of semantic elements of a behavior modeling approach defines the properties of this approach. For example, the Activity Diagrams consider events as inputs and outputs and use the control flow communication–composition mechanism (sequences, forks, join). These semantic elements define such properties as nondeterminism, problematic separation of classes and crosscutting concerns, and problematic modifiability. Although the CPNs have addition semantics to work with data associated with events and states, the properties of nondeterminism, problematic separation of classes and crosscutting concerns, and problematic modifiability remain.

BSMs support separation of classes, but the CCS composition semantics with buffers results in the properties of nondeterminism and problematic separation of crosscutting concerns.

The Protocol Modeling [7] approach demonstrates advances when the abstractions are not distributed. The CSP parallel communication–composition is accompanied with the CCS mechanism for the system of distributed services. Protocol models have the most advanced semantics of states. States are used to present the output and keep internal state. In order to move to different abstractions, the derived states are used. The semantics used in Protocol Modeling can enrich other approaches as well.

The knowledge of the properties of behavior modeling approaches and the semantic elements that cause these properties is the basis for active use of models at different stages of a system life cycle. Figure 26 summarizes the abilities of modeling approaches to support one or another system life cycle activity.

The application of models for different activities of the system life cycle is inevitable.

The experience of the author, however, is that the models are usually not immediately applicable for requirements engineering, MBT, simulation, and system evolution. For application of modeling techniques to one or another activity of the system life cycle,

- *the elements of the modeling semantics should be made visible* and
- *a method relating the modeling to the human activities should be proposed.*

Dimensions of Behavior Modeling Semantics			Use Cases (UML)	Sequence Diagrams (UML)	Activity Diagrams (UML)	Behavior State Machines (UML)	Protocol State Machines (UML)	Protocol Models
Events	Only inputs	Enumerated						
		Message (data structure)						v
	Inputs and outputs	Enumerated		v	v	v	v	
		Message (data structure)				v	v	v
States	Enumerated				v	v	v	v
	Derived states							v
	Set of variables					v		v
Transitions	accept	can			v	v	v	v
		must						v
		motivate						v
	send-receive	can		v		v	v	v
		must						v
		motivate						v
Comminication-composition	sequence, fork			v	v	v	v	v
	join				v	v	v	
	CCS				v	v	v	v
	CSP							v

Figure 24 Semantics elements of modeling approaches.

Requirements for Behavior Modeling Semantics	Use cases (UML)	Sequence Diagrams (UML)	Activity Diagrams (UML)	Behavior State Machines (UML)	Protocol State Machines (UML)	Colored Petri Nets	Protocol Models
1. Separate modeling of concerns gathered at the requirement phase;		v		v	v		
2..1 Composition of classes modeled from requirements				v	v		v
2.2. Composition of crosscutting concerns modeled from requirements							v
3.Execution of the model of requirements for establishing of relations between the model and the requirements and between the model and the implementation			v	v		v	v
Property 1 : Determinism							v
Property 2: Observational consistency							v
Property 3: Model completeness			v	v		v	v

Figure 25 Properties of modeling approaches.

Activities of a System Life Cycle	Use Cases (UML)	Sequence Diagrams (UML)	Activity Diagrams (UML)	Behavior State Machines (UML)	Protocol State Machines (UML)	Colored Petri Nets	Protocol Models
Requirements engineering	v	v	v	v	v	v	v
Analysis		v	v	v		v	v
Design				v			v
Implementation				Possible		Possible	Possible
Integration			v	v	v	v	v
Testing		v		v		Possible	Possible
Evolution							v

Figure 26 Support by modeling approaches system life cycle activities.

That is why this survey was focused on semantic elements of behavior modeling approaches. The author hopes that the knowledge of semantic elements will serve as a guidance for development of model application methods. An example of a method for application of protocol modeling to requirements engineering can be found in Ref. [60]. Another method under development is for application of protocol modeling for MBT [61]. The model application methods for different domains may promote the adoption of modeling in practice.

ACKNOWLEDGMENTS

The author thanks all participants of six international workshops on Behavior Modeling—Foundation and Application (BM-FA 2009–2014) for fruitful discussions of behavior modeling approaches. In particular, the author thanks Ashley McNeile for several years of collaboration and sharing thoughts and insights and Serguei Roubtsov for sharing interest to the field and collaboration on several related topics.

REFERENCES

[1] H. Collins, Tacit and Explicit Knowledge, The University of Chicago Press, Chicago and London, 2010.
[2] I. Schieferdecker, Model based testing, IEEE Softw. 29 (1) (2012) 14–18.
[3] J. Belzer, A.G. Holzman, K. Allen, Encyclopedia of Computer Science and Technology, vol. 25, CRC Press, USA, 1975, p. 73.
[4] A. McNeile, E. Roubtsova, CSP parallel composition of aspect models, in: Proceedings of the 2008 AOSD Workshop on Aspect-Oriented Modeling (AOM '08), ACM, New York, NY, USA, 2008, pp. 13–18, http://dx.doi.org/10.1145/1404920. 1404923, http://doi.acm.org/10.1145/1404920.1404923.
[5] W. Fokkink, Introduction to Process Algebra, first ed., New York, Inc., Secaucus, NJ, 2000.
[6] M. Jackson, System Development, Prentice Hall, Englewood Cliffs, New Jersey, 1983.
[7] A. McNeile, N. Simons, Protocol modelling. A modelling approach that supports reusable behavioural abstractions, Softw. Syst. Model. 5 (1), Springer-Verlag, Heidelberg, Germany, 91–107, 2006.
[8] OMG, Unified Modeling Language: Superstructure Version 2.1.1 formal/2007-02-03, 2003.
[9] R. Milner, A Calculus of Communicating Systems, Springer-Verlag New York, Inc., Secaucus, NJ, USA, 1982.
[10] C.A.R. Hoare, Communicating Sequential Processes, Prentice-Hall, Inc., Upper Saddle River, NJ, USA, 1985.
[11] F. Moller, The importance of the left merge operator in process algebras, in: M.S. Paterson (Ed.), Proceedings of the 17th Colloquium on Automata, Languages and Programming (ICALP'90), Warwick, in: LNCS, vol. 443, Springer-Verlag, Heidelberg, Germany, 1990, pp. 752–764.
[12] J.A. Bergstra, J.W. Klop, Process algebra for synchronous communication, Inf. Control 60 (1/3) (1984) 109–137.
[13] J. Ebert, G. Engels, Dynamic models and behavioural views, in: LNCS, vol. 858, 1994.

[14] A.T. McNeile, Protocol contracts with application to choreographed multiparty collaborations, Serv. Orient. Comput. Appl. 4 (2) (2010) 109–136.

[15] E.E. Roubtsova, A.T. McNeile, Abstractions, composition and reasoning, in: Proceedings of the 13th International Workshop on Aspect-Oriented Modeling, ACM DL, Charlottesville, VA, 2009, pp. 19–24.

[16] OMG, Model Driven Architecture: How Systems Will Be Built, Object Management Group website: www.omg.org/mda/, 1997.

[17] R. Soley, Presentation: MDA: An Introduction, 2009), Object Management Group website.

[18] A.T. McNeile, E.E. Roubtsova, Composition semantics for executable and evolvable behavioral modeling in MDA, in: Proceedings of the 1st Workshop on Behaviour Modelling in Model-Driven Architecture (BM-MDA'09), ACM DL, New York, 2009.

[19] D. Levy, Use Case Examples—Effective Samples and Tips, http://www.gatherspace.com/static/use_case_example.html, 2014.

[20] M. Gogolla, L. Hamann, F. Hilken, M. Sedlmeier, Q. Dung Nguyen, Behavior modeling with interaction diagrams in a UML and OCL tool, in: Proceedings of the 2014 Workshop on Behaviour Modelling-Foundations and Applications (BM-FA '14), ACM, New York, NY, USA, 2014, 12 pages, http://dx.doi.org/10.1145/2630768.2630772. Article 4, http://doi.acm.org/10.1145/2630768.2630772.

[21] E.E. Roubtsova, S.A. Roubtsov, UML-based tool for constructing component systems via component behaviour inheritance, Elsevier, Electron. Notes Theor. Comput. Sci. 80 (2003) 141–156.

[22] E. Roubtsova, R. Kuiper, Process semantics for UML component specifications to assess inheritance, Elsevier, Electron. Notes Theor. Comput. Sci. 72 (3), 145–159, 2003.

[23] J. Greenyer, J. Rieke, O. Travkin, E. Kindler, TGGs for Transforming UML to CSP: Contribution to the ACTIVE 2007 Graph Transformation Tools Contest. University of Paderborn: Technical report tr-ri-08–28, 2008.

[24] S. Hanenberg, D. Stein, R. Unland, From aspect-oriented design to aspect oriented programs: tool-supported translation of JPDDs into code, in: AOSD, 2007, pp. 49–62.

[25] E.E. Roubtsova, S.A. Roubtsov, Behavioural inheritance in the UML to model software product lines, Springer-Verlag, Berlin, Heidelberg, Germany, Sci. Comput. Program 53 (3) (2004) 409–434.

[26] S. Shlaer, S.J. Mellor, Object Lifecycles: Modeling the World in States, Yourdon Press, 1991, ISBN: 0-13-629940-7, http://www.ooatool.com/References.html.

[27] M. Ericsson, Activity Diagrams: What They Are and How to Use Them, IBM, Software Group, 2004), http://www.ibm.com/developerworks/rational/library/2802.html.

[28] G. Engels, A. Kleppe, A. Rensink, M. Semenyak, C. Soltenborn, H. Wehrheim, From UML activities to TAAL—towards behaviour-preserving model transformations, in: ECMDA-FA, 2008, pp. 94–109.

[29] H. Fecher, J. Sch¨onborn, M. Kyas, W. de Roever, New unclarities in the semantics of UML 2.0 StateMachines, in: ICFEM, 2005, pp. 52–65.

[30] G. Zhang, M. Hölzl, A set of metrics for states and transitions in UML state machines, in: Proceedings of the 2014 Workshop on Behaviour Modelling-Foundations and Applications (BM-FA '14), ACM, New York, NY, USA, 2014, p. 6 pages, http://dx.doi.org/10.1145/2630768.2630770. Article 2, http://doi.acm.org/10.1145/2630768.2630770.

[31] H. Toetenel, E. Roubtsova, J. van Katwijk, A timed automata semantics for real-time UML specifications, in: Proceedings of the IEEE Symposia on Human-Centric Computing Languages and Environments (HCC'01), Visual Languages and Formal Methods (VLFM'01), IEEE Computer Society Catalog No. PE00474, pp. 88–95, Proceedings of the IEEE Symposia on Human-Centric Computing Languages and Environments (HCC'01), Visual Languages and Form Stresa, Italy, 2001.

[32] E.E. Roubtsova, J. van Katwijk, W.J. Toetenel, C. Pronk, R.C.M. de Rooij, Elsevier, Electron. Notes Theor. Comput. Sci. 39 (3) 293–305.

[33] E.E. Roubtsova, J. van Katwijk, R.C.M. de Rooij, H. Toetenel, Transformation of UML specification to XTG, in: D. Bjørner, M. Broy, A.V. Zamulin (Eds.), Revised Papers from the 4th International Andrei Ershov Memorial Conference on Perspectives of System Informatics: Akademgorodok, Novosibirsk, Russia (PSI '02), Springer-Verlag, London, UK, 2001, pp. 247–254.

[34] S. Mellor, M. Balce, Executable UML: A Foundation for Model Driven Architecture, Addison Wesley, MA, USA, Reading, 2002.

[35] T. Santen, D. Seifert, Executing UML State Machines: Technical report 2006–04, Fakultät für Elektrotechnik und Informatik, Technische Universität Berlin, Berlin, 2006.

[36] E.E. Roubtsova, L.C.M. van Gool, R. Kuiper, H.M. Jonkers, Consistent specification of interface suites in UML, J. Softw. Syst. Model. 1 (2) (2002) 98–112.

[37] T. Murata, Petri Nets: properties, analysis and applications, Proc. IEEE 77 (4) (1989) 541–580.

[38] E.E. Roubtsova, M. Aksit, Extension of Petri Nets by aspects to apply the model driven architecture approach, in: Preliminary Proceedings of the First International Workshop on Aspect-Based and Model-Based Separation of Concerns in Software Systems (ABMB), Nuremberg, 2005, Report TR-CTIT-05-56.

[39] W. Reisig, G. Rozenberg (Eds.), Lectures on Petri Nets I: Basic Models: Advances in Petri Nets, vol. 149, Springer-Verlag, Berlin Heidelberg, Germany, 1998.

[40] G. Rozenberg, P.S. Thiagarajan, Petri Nets: basic notions, structure, behaviour, in: J.W. de Bakker, W.-P. de Roever, G. Rozenberg (Eds.), Current Trends in Concurrency, Lecture Notes in Computer Science, vol. 224, Springer, Berlin Heidelberg, 1986, pp. 585–668.

[41] L. Bernardinello, F. De Cindio, A survey of basic net models and modular net classes, in: LNCS, vol. 609, Springer-Verlag, Berlin, Heidelberg, Germany, 1992.

[42] R. Filman, T. Elrad, S. Clarke, M. Aksit, Aspect-Oriented Software Development, Addison Wesley, 2004.

[43] M. Alférez, N. Amálio, S. Ciraci, F. Fleurey, J. Kienzle, J. Klein, M.E. Kramer, S. Mosser, G. Mussbacher, E.E. Roubtsova, G. Zhang, Aspect-oriented model development at different levels of abstraction, in: R.B. France et al., (Ed.), ECMFA 2011, in: LNCS, vol. 6698, Springer-Verlag, Berlin, Heidelberg, Germany, 2011, pp. 361–376.

[44] D. Stein, S. Hanenberg, R. Unland, Expressing different conceptual models of join point selections in aspect-oriented design, in: Proceedings of AOSD 2006, 2006, pp. 15–26.

[45] S. Mosser, M. Blay-Fornarino, R. France, Workflow design using fragment composition, in: Transactions on Aspect-Oriented Software Development, vol. VII, Springer Berlin Heidelberg, 2010, pp. 200–233.

[46] K. Jensen, Coloured Petri Nets: Basic Concepts, Analysis Methods and Practical Use, vol. 1, Springer-Verlag, Berlin, Heidelberg, Germany, 1997.

[47] K. Jensen, L.M. Kristensen, L. Wells, Coloured Petri Nets and CPN tools for modelling and validation of concurrent systems, Int. J. Softw. Tools Technol. Transfer 9 (3–4) (2007) 213–254.

[48] M. Silva, R. Valette, Petri Nets and flexible manufacturing, in: Advances in Petri Nets, Springer-Verlag, Berlin, Heidelberg, Germany, 1990, pp. 374–417.

[49] R. Zurawski, M. Zhou, Petri Nets and industrial applications: a tutorial, IEEE Trans. Ind. Electron. 41 (6) (1994) 567–583.

[50] W. van der Aalst, C. Stahl, Modeling Business Processes: A Petri Net-Oriented Approach, MIT press, Cambridge, MA, 2011.

[51] A.T. McNeile, E.E. Roubtsova, Protocol modelling semantics for embedded systems, in: Proceedings of the Special Session on Behavioural Models for Embedded Systems at the International Symposium on Industrial Embedded Systems, SIES'2007, ISBN: 1-4244-0840-7, 2007, IEEE Catalog 07EX1633C, Library of Congress 2006937976, Lisbon, Portugal.

[52] W. Grieskamp, F. Kicillof, N. Tillmann, Action Machines: A Framework for Encoding and Composing Partial Behaviours: Microsoft technical report MSR-TR-2006-11, 2006.

[53] M. Carbone, K. Honda, N. Yoshida, R. Milner, G. Brown, S. Ross-Talbot, A Theoretical Basis of Communication-Centered Concurrent Programming, www. w3.org/2002/ws/chor/edcopies/theory/note.pdf, 2002.

[54] A. McNeile, N. Simons, Modelscope Tool, http://www.metamaxim.com/, 2014.

[55] A. McNeile, E. Roubtsova, Aspect-oriented development using protocol modeling, in: S. Katz, M. Mezini (Eds.), Transactions on Aspect-Oriented Software Development VII, Springer-Verlag, Berlin, Heidelberg, 2010, pp. 115–150.

[56] J. Ebert, G. Engels, Observable or Invocable Behaviour—You Have to Choose: Technical report, Universitat Koblenz, Koblenz, 1994.

[57] D. Harel, R. Marelly, Come, Let's Play, Springer-Verlag, Berlin, Heidelberg, Germany, 2003.

[58] E. Roubtsova, Motivation modelling for human-service interaction, in: Proceedings of the Fourth Workshop on Behaviour Modelling - Foundations and Applications (BM-FA '12), ACM, New York, NY, USA, 2012, 8 pages, Article 4.

[59] A. McNeile, E. Roubtsova, Motivation and guaranteed completion in workflow, in: BMSD, LNBIP, vol. 142, Springer-Verlag, Berlin, Heidelberg, Germany, 2013, pp. 16–42.

[60] E. Roubtsova, EXTREME: EXecuTable requirements engineering, management and evolution, in: V.G. Diaz, J.M.C. Lovelle (Eds.), Progressions and Innovations in Model-Driven Software Engineering, IGI Global, 2013.

[61] E. Roubtsova, S. Roubtsov, A test generator for model based testing, in: BMSD, Luxembourg, ISBN: 978-989-758-032-1, 2014, pp. 103–112.

[62] E.E. Roubtsova, A.T. McNeile, Coloured Petri Nets with parallel composition to separate concerns, in: ICEIS 2010 - Proceedings of the 12th International Conference on Enterprise Information Systems, vol. 3, ISAS, Funchal, Madeira, Portugal, June 8–12, 2010, pp. 501–504.

[63] P. Huber, K. Jensen, R.M. Shapiro, Hierarchies in coloured Petri Nets, in: Advances in Petri Nets, Springer-Verlag, Berlin, Heidelberg, Germany, 1991, pp. 313–341.

ABOUT THE AUTHOR

Dr. Ella Roubtsova is a dedicated researcher and professor of technical sciences with over 20 years of academic instructional experience; skilled and highly regarded writer with works in over 90 scientific publications; and efficient and systematic instructor and lecturer with proven problem-solving skills, experienced with Computer Science, Business Intelligence, and Information Technology course development and delivery.

CHAPTER THREE

Overview of Computational Approaches for Inference of MicroRNA-Mediated and Gene Regulatory Networks

Blagoj Ristevski[1]

Faculty of Information and Communication Technologies—Bitola, St. Kliment Ohridski University, Bitola, Macedonia
[1]Corresponding author: e-mail address: blagoj.ristevski@uklo.edu.mk

Contents

Abstract

This chapter describes biological backgrounds of regulatory relationships in living cells, high-throughput experimental technologies, and application of computational approaches in reverse engineering of microRNA (miRNA)-mediated and gene regulatory networks (GRNs). The most commonly used models for GRNs inference based on Boolean networks, Bayesian networks, dynamic Bayesian networks, association networks, novel two-stage model using integration of *a priori* biological knowledge, differential and difference equations models are detailed and their inference capabilities are compared. The regulatory role of miRNAs and transcription factors (TFs) in miRNAs-mediated regulatory networks is described as well. Additionally, commonly used methods for target prediction of miRNAs and TFs are described as well as most commonly used biological regulatory relationships databases and tools are listed. The mainly validation criteria used for assessment of inferred regulatory networks are explained. Finally, concluding remarks and further directions for miRNA-mediated and GRNs inference are given.

1. INTRODUCTION

Many biological, physiological, and biochemical molecular processes occur simultaneously in living cells. Regulation of these processes is conducting by inherited information contained in the organisms' genome. Inference of the mutual interactions between numerous components of biological systems based on available experimental data for interactions between DNAs, RNAs, proteins, and metabolites is needed to clarify and represent existing regulatory mechanisms. These components and their mutual interactions compose complex networks named as gene regulatory networks (GRNs) [1]. Generally speaking, there are two approaches for inferring of GRNs [2]:

- Mechanistic (or physical) networks that employ protein–DNA and protein–protein interactions (PPIs) data are usually named as transcription or protein networks. The aim of this static networks modeling is to reveal regulatory interactions on physical level, and
- Influence networksthat refer to the reverse engineering of GRNs based on gene expression data and the inferred networks regard to gene–gene interactions.

The GRNs structure is depicted by a graph consisted of *nodes* representing the genes, proteins, metabolites, their complexes or even modules, and *edges* that represent direct or indirect interactions between nodes. In the influence GRNs, proteins and metabolites appear as hidden variables in GRNs, while the only observable variables are gene expression data. These hidden variables might cover unobserved results that are not measured. Figure 1 illustrates the projection of interactions from the space of metabolites and proteins into the space of genes. Dashed lines represent gene regulatory

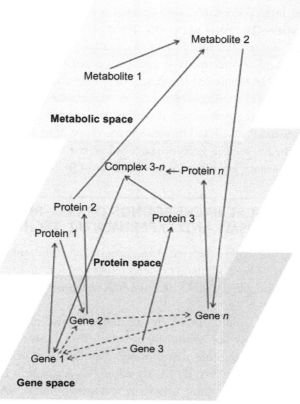

Figure 1 Projection of GRNs in different spaces: gene, protein, and metabolic space.

relationships, whereas the full lines depict the interactions among genes, proteins, metabolites, and their complexes [3].

This chapter systematizes the different models for GRNs inference such as Boolean, Bayesian, dynamic Bayesian, association networks, and other models comparing their advantages and shortcomings. In addition, the role of microRNAs (miRNAs) in posttranscriptional regulation and computational approaches for reconstruction of miRNA–mediated regulatory networks are explained. In addition, network topology and network validation of the inferred regulatory networks are depicted.

This chapter is organized as follows. In Section 2, the biological and experimental backgrounds of the cells' regulatory mechanisms are presented. Section 3 describes the computational backgrounds of the inference of miRNA-mediated and GRNs. The following section provides more detail description of most commonly used models for GRNs inference such as Boolean networks, Bayesian networks (BNs) and dynamic Bayesian networks (DBNs), differential and difference equations system model, association networks, and several other models. Computational approaches for inference of miRNA-mediated regulatory networks and miRNA and transcription factors (TFs) target prediction algorithms are depicted in Section 4.5. The subsequent section describes the commonly used validation criteria for assessment of applied models for inference of regulatory relationships. Finally, the last section gives the concluding remarks and further directions toward inference of miRNA-mediated and GRNs.

2. BIOLOGICAL BACKGROUNDS OF CELL REGULATORY MECHANISMS AND EXPERIMENTAL TECHNOLOGIES

Genes are fundamental physical and functional inheritance units of all living organisms. The coding genes are templates for protein synthesis. Other genes might specify RNA templates as machines for production of different types of RNAs.

The process in which DNA is transcribed into messenger RNA (mRNA) and proteins are produced by translation represents the well-known central dogma in molecular biology. The first stage of gene expression is DNA transcription into RNA. Resulted RNA can be mRNA, if the expressed gene is protein coding, otherwise it is noncoding RNA. Then the second stage follows, in which mRNA translates into a sequence of amino acids that composes a protein. When a protein is synthesized, the matching protein-coding gene is expressed.

Only a small part of RNAs is coding RNAs, whereas the bigger part from the genome of eukaryotes transcribes into noncoding RNAs. In the last decade, several small noncoding RNAs such as miRNAs and small inferring RNAs (siRNAs) are revealed [4]. The length of miRNAs is about 18–25 nucleotides [5]. To date, there are more than 1800 human miRNAs listed in the miRBase database [6].

A regulatory relationship between a miRNA and an mRNA denotes that a change in the miRNA expression level will effect a change in the expression level of the target mRNA. Each of these miRNAs might regulate expression of hundreds or even thousands of target mRNAs. MiRNAs regulate expression by more than 30% of coding genes [7,8]. MiRNAs cause transcription cleavage or translation repression by connecting to their target mRNA [9]. MiRNAs regulate gene expression by inhibiting mRNA translation and/or lightening mRNA degradation. Recent *in vitro* and *in vivo* studies have shown that miRNAs can inhibit translation initiation and support decay of target mRNAs. There are three different potentials not mutually exclusive manners of miRNA-mediated repression by destabilization of target mRNAs, inhibition of translation initiation, or blocking of translation after initiation.

The gene expression regulation on the posttranscriptional level taking place by mRNA cleavage or translation repression with binding of miRNAs to the 3'-untranslated regions (3'-UTRs) of target mRNA [10]. To identify mRNAs regulated by silencing or overexpression of a specific miRNA, quantitative real-time polymerase chain reaction is used [11].

Recent studies have shown that miRNAs are one of the key participants of regulation in many biological processes in metabolism, proliferation, differentiation, development, apoptosis, cellular signaling, cancer development, and metastasis. MiRNAs are involved in cancer, rheumatic, infectious cardiovascular and neuronal diseases, metabolic disorders (glucose and lipid metabolisms), epigenetics (mitotically and meiotically heritable gene expression changes not involving a change in the DNA sequence) [7,8,12,13].

One of the most important regulatory functions of proteins is transcription regulation. Proteins, which bind to DNA sequences and regulate the transcription of DNAs and hence gene expression, are called TFs. TFs can inhibit or activate gene expression of the target genes [14].

The gene expression levels indicate the approximate number of produced RNA copies from the corresponding gene, which means that gene expression level corresponds to the amount of synthesized proteins. To obtain gene expression data experimentally of many genes in a sample, high-throughput technologies are used, such as DNA microarray, serial analysis of gene expression (SAGE), quantitative polymerase chain reaction (qPCR), as well as next-generation sequencing technology like RNA-Sequencing (RNA-Seq).

The essential basis of DNA microarrays is hybridization between two strands of DNA. This technology is used to measure the expression levels of large numbers of genes simultaneously or to determine genotype of multiple regions of a genome. It is known as DNA chip or biochip used for DNA detection, or to detect RNA that may or may not be translated into proteins. SAGE technology produces a snapshot of the mRNA population in a sample of interest. SAGE sampling is based on sequencing mRNA output, not on hybridization of mRNA output to probes, so transcription levels are measured more quantitatively than using DNA microarray. qPCR technology amplifies and quantifies a targeted DNA simultaneously, whereas RNA-Seq is able to identify and quantify transcripts, perform robust whole-transcriptome analysis on a wide range of samples at a given time moment.

Besides gene expression data, other data types such as protein–DNA, PPIs data, and miRNAs targets are needed to reveal regulatory relationships.

Experimentally, identifying of TF binding sites (TFBSs) on the genome for particular proteins and to reveal protein–DNA interactions, chromatin immunoprecipitation (ChIP)-based methods are used [15]. ChIP-chip technology uses ChIP with hybridization microarrays (chips) to identify the protein binding sites and their locations throughout the genome. ChIP-chip technology uses short DNA sequences as probes. A population of immunoprecipitation-enriched DNA fragments is produced and enrichment of each probe from produced population is measured [16]. Differently, ChIP-Sequencing (ChIP-Seq) technology uses secondary sequencing of DNA instead of microarray [15]. The sequencing technology such as ChIP-Seq, RNA-Seq, and miRNA-Seq are very well-established technologies.

TFs and miRNAs are in mutual interaction with more *cis*-regulatory elements. Similarly to TFs, genes also contain binding sides for other TFs that may be targeted by miRNAs. Thus, the mutual interactions between miRNAs and TFs make miRNAs very important factors in the gene regulation.

High-throughput techniques and data such as proteomics, transcriptomics, and miRNAomics lighten inference of large-scale miRNA-mediated and GRNs. Integration of these different types of biological data can significantly improve the accuracy and the reliability of the inferred miRNA-mediated and GRNs [17].

3. COMPUTATIONAL BACKGROUNDS OF THE INFERENCE OF MiRNA-MEDIATED AND GRNs

Theoretical studies of GRNs have started in the 1960s. The emergence of experimental high technologies for discovering regulatory mechanisms such as DNA microarrays, ChIP-chip, ChIP-Seq, RNA-Seq, and qPCR has provided huge amounts of gene expression, protein–protein, and protein–DNA interactions data. Because the experimental wet lab technologies cannot measure mutual influences among all genes from one organism's genome simultaneously, computational methods are needed to infer and reveal regulatory interactions between genes, miRNAs, TFs, and other constituents that compose complex regulatory networks.

GRNs reconstruction is useful to elucidate disease-causing perturbations in two different manners: changes in the interactions of the component genes and changes in the cell type in which a gene is expressed, the magnitude of gene expression, the beginning time and time span of the transcriptional activity [18].

Several models for GRNs inference have been developed, which are based on the basic reverse engineering methods. However, these models handle with only certain data types and inferred networks do not largely match the real regulatory mechanisms. The reverse engineered networks might contain many erroneous regulatory relationships. This shortcoming is a motivation for developing of new models that can include *a priori* knowledge and could be able to integrate heterogeneous data. Such inferred GRNs should elucidate gene regulatory mechanisms more correctly and more reliably.

Finding more accurate and reliable structures of GRNs from gene expression data is a problem of machine learning known as structure learning, while the parameter learning aims to find parameters of inferred networks that match best to the true regulatory relationships. Both structure and parameter learning of the reconstructed networks are challenging topics that bring together learning techniques from artificial intelligence with bioinformatics, functional genomics, and biostatistics [1].

In miRNA-mediated regulatory networks, TFs and miRNAs have very important role. Determination of the TFs of the given genes is by using TF binding matrix (motif)-based methods. TFBSs are usually short (around 5–15 basepairs) and regularly degenerate sequences. The sequence pattern is presented by a matrix (motif), whose entries give the probability distribution of DNA nucleobases adenine (A), cytosine (C), thymine (T), and guanine (G) at each site. The motifs of TFs are concluded from known TFBSs determined experimentally [19]. TRANSFAC [20] and JASPAR [21] provide major collections of currently annotated TF binding motifs. Predicted TF targets can be determined by scanning promoter regions of given genes with motifs.

In order to understand the multiple functions of miRNAs in biological processes, it is crucial to determine their targets. Prediction of miRNA targets by using computational methods is often imprecise because the miRNA–mRNA interactions are relied on a limited sequence length of the miRNAs seed region. Additionally, mRNA recognition is affected by the sequence context around the target as well by factors that might halt miRNA binding.

By inference of miRNAs-mediated and GRNs, several networks' properties should be taken in consideration such as sparseness, scale-free topology, modularity, and structure of the inferred networks [2].

The inferred regulatory networks should be sparse. It means that a limited number of nodes regulate the other nodes. Some nodes in the network called hubs can have regulatory relationships to many targets, i.e., the out-degree of the nodes is not limited.

Another important feature of the inferred regulatory networks is their topology, which should be scale free. Scale-free networks have the power distribution function of the nodes connectivity degrees [22]. This property provides the robustness of the inferred networks considering the random topology perturbations.

Structures with small connectivity follow the regulatory hierarchy. The networks structure allows decomposition of a network into basic modular units composed of several nodes, called network motifs [2]. Modularity of the networks regards to the presence of clusters of highly coexpressed genes/miRNAs and/or genes/miRNAs with similar function.

4. MODELS FOR GRNs INFERENCE

A plethora of models such as Boolean networks, BNs, DBNs, Petri nets, graphical Gaussian models (GGMs), linear and nonlinear differential and difference equations, information theory approach, state space models, fuzzy logic models, two-stage model that integrates biological *a priori* knowledge, and many other models are utilized to reverse engineer GRNs. GRN models extend from maps of genetics interactions, physical interaction graphs to models that cover the gene expression kinetics, and hence network dynamics.

4.1 Boolean Networks

The model based on Boolean networks is one of the simplest models for GRNs inference. A Boolean network is presented by graph whose nodes present the genes and the edges between nodes represent the regulatory interactions between genes. In this model, gene expression data are discretized and presented by two values: 1 or 0. If the gene expression is above a set threshold, the corresponding state is 1, otherwise 0.

The network diagram shown in Fig. 2A is not sufficient to understand logical dependencies between genes. The aim of the reverse engineering in Boolean networks is to find Boolean functions of every gene in the network, so discretized values of gene expression can be explained by the model as shown in Fig. 2B. Alternatively, Boolean networks can be represented by state transitions table presented in Fig. 2C.

The small changes in gene expression time series data cannot be encompassed by two-level discretization, because it leads to information loss. Thus, inferred regulatory networks can be unrealistic and with erroneous interactions between nodes. Another weakness of Boolean networks is the super-exponential number of all possible networks. If n is the number of genes, then the number of all Boolean functions depends on n super-exponentially and it is equal to 2^{2^n}.

Several extended models based on Boolean networks have been proposed. A REVerse Engineering ALgorithm (REVEAL) constructs a Boolean network of given gene expression data by setting the genes in-degree values to k[23]. This algorithm derives minimal network structures from the state transition tables of the Boolean network by using the mutual information approach. If n is the number of nodes, the number of all possible networks is given by:

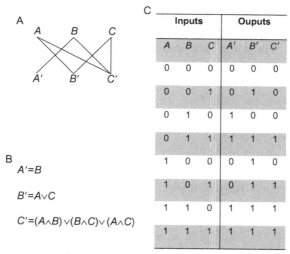

Figure 2 A Boolean network presented by (A) a wiring diagram, (B) Boolean functions, and (C) a state transition table.

$$\left(2^{2^k}\frac{n!}{(n-k)!}\right)^n \tag{1}$$

REVEAL can be applied on gene expression data discretized on multiple-value levels. On the other hand, multiple discretization levels increase the number of potential state transitions. Thus, the number of all possible networks is significantly greater than the number of networks derived from two-level Boolean networks. REVEAL has better inference capabilities for smaller in-degree value k. For greater in-degree k, parallel processing and efficiency increasing of the search space of all possible networks are needed [23].

The models based on Boolean network simplify the structure and dynamics of gene regulatory relationships. They are deterministic, i.e., the state space is restricted and these networks reach the steady state or fall into dynamic attractor [24]. The inferred networks provide only a quantitative measure of gene regulatory relationships.

Probabilistic Boolean networks model is another model composed of several Boolean networks that work simultaneously [25]. All networks share information about the states of whole system. When a network transits in next state, the remaining networks are synchronized.

4.2 Bayesian Networks

BNs are among the most effective models for GRNs inference. A BN is special type of graph defined as a triple (G, F, q), where G denotes the graph structure, F is the set of probability distributions, and q is the set of parameters for F[26]. The graph structure G includes a set of n nodes $X_1, X_2, \ldots, X_n$ and a set of directed edges between nodes. The nodes correspond to the random variables while directed edges show the conditional dependences between the random variables.

A directed edge from the node X to node Y is denoted as $X \rightarrow Y$, which means that X is a parent node of Y, denoted as pa(Y), and Y is a child node of X. If the node Z can be attained by following a directed path starting from node X, then the node Z is a descendant of X, and X is ancestor of Z. Nodes and edges together have to make a directed acyclic graph (DAG). One directed graph is acyclic if there is no directed path $X_1 \rightarrow X_2 \rightarrow \ldots \rightarrow X_n$ such as $X_1 = X_n$, i.e., there is no pathway starting and ending at the same node.

The joint probability distribution of all network nodes is calculated by the following equation:

$$P(X_1, X_2, \ldots, X_n) = \prod_{i=1}^{n} P(X_i | \mathrm{pa}(X_i)) \qquad (2)$$

where multipliers are local probability distributions. This factorization of the joint probability distribution on multipliers facilitates its computing as a product of simpler conditional probability distributions.

GRNs inference using BNs is accompanied by structure and parameter learning. Structure learning aims to find network structure that fits best the real regulatory relationships. Similar to Boolean networks, the number of possible DAGs also super-exponentially depends on the number of nodes of the BNs. For a given network structure, the parameter learning includes estimation of the unknown model parameters for each gene. Parameter learning determines conditional dependencies between network nodes. Because the network inference using BNs is an NP-hard problem, BNs are the most suitable when they are applied to small-scale networks composed of tens to hundred genes [27].

It is possible to infer GRNs by BNs based on static, dynamic, discrete, or continuous gene expression data. If the node variables are continuous, then network inference is more complicated to perform because of the additional complex computations concerning learning of BNs.

BNs are able to deal with stochastic nature of gene expression profiles as well as with their incompleteness and noise. The main difficulty in BNs learning is the higher number of genes compared to the number of conditions and incapability to handle feedback loops that exist in the real GRNs.

Friedman et al. [28] have introduced a framework for discovering interactions between genes based on microarray data using BNs by modeling of each variable with conditional probability distribution function related to other variables. In the proposed approach, two comparative experiments are conducted for different probability distributions: multinomial distribution and linear Gaussian distribution. The main shortcomings of this model are nonconstraints search heuristics on the search space and nonusing a priori biological knowledge.

4.3 Dynamic Bayesian Networks

BNs can represent probabilistic relations between variables without considering time lags and they cannot deal with time series data [29]. However, regulatory interactions in the real GRNs do not occur simultaneously, so there is a particular time lagging. Another disadvantage of BNs is that they cannot represent real biological systems in which exist mutual interactions between entities of biological systems such as feedback loops [30].

These shortcomings make BNs inappropriate for GRNs inference from time series gene expression data, because it is necessary to include dynamic (temporal) features of gene regulatory relationships. Thus, BNs are extended to cover temporal features by introduction of DBNs. Supposing that the changes in time series gene expression data occur in a limited number of discrete time intervals T. Let $X = \{X_1, X_2, \ldots, X_n\}$ is a set of time-dependent variables, where $X_i[t]$ is a random variable representing the value of X_i at the time point t and $0 \leq t \leq T$. A DBN is a BN that contains the T random vectors $X_i[t]$ [31], an initial BN, a transitional BN consisted of transition DAG $G_{\rightarrow}$, and transitional probability distribution $P_{\rightarrow}$:

$$P_{\rightarrow}(X[t+1] = x[t+1]|X[t] = x[t]) \tag{3}$$

Then, joint probability distribution of the DBN is computed by:

$$P(x[0], \ldots, x[T]) = P_0(x[0]) \prod_{t=0}^{T-1} P_{\rightarrow}(x[t+1]|x[t]) \tag{4}$$

From Eq. (4), for each x at each time point t, the following is obtained:

$$P(x[t+1]|x[0], \ldots, x[t]) = P(x[t+1]|x[t]) \tag{5}$$

Equation (5) denotes that the variables values at time point t depend on the values of variables at the previous time point $t-1$ and no other information is required, i.e., DBNs have Markov property [32].

For probabilistic inference of DBNs, the standard algorithms used in BNs inference can be used, too. However, in the case of large-scale networks, learning of DBNs becomes too complex.

DBNs are effective for GRNs inference when they combine other types of biological data. An example for that is the proposed method that integrates gene expression data with *a priori* biologic knowledge about TFBSs using DBNs and structural expectation–maximization algorithm [33].

Daly *et al.* had used high-order DBNs to model time lag gene regulatory interactions based on time series gene expression data [34].

Figure 3 illustrates a DBN that describes cyclic regulation between gene 1 and gene 2 in different time points (red arrow lines; dark gray in the print version), although the graph does not contain obviously cyclic pathway.

A manner how DBNs can be employed for network inference and how they can be learned, their relationship with the hidden markov model

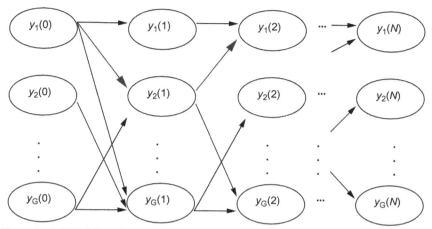

Figure 3 A GRN inferred using DBNs applied on an input time series gene expression data for *G* genes whose expression is measured in *N* time points.

(HMM), Boolean and stochastic Boolean networks, and DBNs with continuous variables is presented in Ref. [35]. Moreover, Boolean networks, linear and nonlinear equations models can be considered as a special case of DBNs.

To overcome the high complexity needed for GRNs inference by DBNs, a model with constraint of the potential regulators has been proposed [36]. This constraint considers those genes that have changes in gene expression level at the previous or at the same time points regarding their target genes. The proposed model uses the time lag of changes in expression levels of regulator and target genes, which increases the accuracy of the inferred networks. The time points of initial over- or under-regulation of the genes are determined. The genes with changes in previous and current time points are denoted as potential regulators to those genes with expression changes in the following time points. In such a way, a subset of potential regulators for every target gene is chosen.

Another approach named as Bayesian Orthogonal Least Squares (BOLS) for inference of GRNs is proposed in Ref. [37]. This approach combines the orthogonal least squares, second-order derivatives for network pruning, and BN. In the inferred networks, that are sparse, only limited number of genes regulates every gene and the number of false inferred regulatory relationships is small.

An effective algorithm for structure learning as an extension of K2 algorithm is proposed in Ref. [38]. This algorithm is utilized for learning of large-scale BNs by introducing sorting of the genes to improve the efficiency in the large-scale network inference. The assessment of the efficiency of the proposed algorithm is performed by performing Monte Carlo simulation and then comparing to the greedy hill-climbing algorithm.

4.4 Association Networks

Association networks are static networks that can describe the possible structure of the GRNs by an undirected graph. They can be applied on time series and steady-state gene expression data. If two nodes/genes are connected by an edge, then it is not possible to determine which gene is regulated and which one is regulator. To identify which genes are coexpressed and where should be an edge, similarity metrics such as Pearson coefficient or mutual information is applied and additionally a threshold is set. For higher set threshold values, the inferred GRNs are sparser.

Although the association networks do not determine the edges directions in the networks, they are suitable to be employed in inference of large-scale networks because of their low computational costs [2]. The directions of the regulatory interactions can be determined by computing the similarity between genes, their possible regulators, and with additional knowledge about interaction with TFs.

A proposed algorithm ARACNE is based on mutual information between gene expression data [39]. It defines the network edges as statistical dependences, whereby the directed regulatory relationships using data about TFs and their TFBSs can be determined. Using ARACNE, the number of falsely predicted gene interactions in the networks can be reduced significantly. The computational complexity of this algorithm is $O(N^3 + N^2 M^2)$, where N is the number of genes and M is the number of samples. The lower complexity makes this algorithm to be suitable for inference of large-scale GRNs [39].

Very popular models are GGMs that use partial correlation coefficients to determine the conditional dependencies between genes [40]. GGMs can distinguish directed or undirected interactions between genes, unlike the correlation networks where the edges correspond to correlation between genes.

Let X is a gene expression data matrix with n rows and p columns, where n is the number of experimental conditions and p is the number of genes. Supposing that data entries from matrix X follow the normal distribution $N_P(\mu, \Sigma)$, where $\mu = \left(\mu_1, \ldots, \mu_p\right)^T$ is the means vector and $\Sigma = (\sigma ij)_{1 \leq i, j \leq p}$ is a positive definite covariance matrix. The matrix Σ is decomposed of two parts: variance components σ_i^2 and Brevis–Pearson correlation matrix $P = \left(\rho_{ij}\right)$. A partial correlation matrix $Z = \left(\varsigma_{ij}\right)$ is composed of the correlation coefficients between any two genes i and j with regard to all other genes. The matrix Z is associated with the inverse matrix of the standard correlation coefficients matrix P. Their relationship is given by the following equations [41]:

$$\Omega = \left(\omega_{ij}\right) = P^{-1} \tag{6}$$

and

$$\varsigma_{ij} = -\frac{\omega_{ij}}{\sqrt{\omega_{ii}\omega_{jj}}} \tag{7}$$

In Eq. (6), instead of correlation matrix P, the covariance matrix Σ can be used. Partial correlation coefficients ς_{ij} are correlation coefficients of conditional bivariant normal distributions of the genes i and j. Two variables that follow normal distribution are conditionally independent if and only if their partial coefficients are equal to zero. The conditional independence of the random variables is determined by the zero entries in the inverse correlation matrix Ω.

To infer a GRN by using the GGMs from a data set, the correlation matrix P is estimated by unbiased sampling of the covariance matrix, given by:

$$\hat{\Sigma} = \left(\hat{\sigma}_{ij}\right) = \frac{1}{n-1}(X - \overline{X})^T(X - \overline{X}) \tag{8}$$

The estimation of partial correlation coefficients is calculated by Eqs. (6) and (7) from the sample correlation matrix. The entries from estimated correlation matrix $\hat{Z}$, which differentiate from zero, are determined by statistical tests. The network inference finishes with a visualization of correlation structure by a graph, whose edges correspond to nonzero partial correlation coefficients.

The main shortcoming of the described classical GGMs is that they can be applied when the number of experimental conditions n is greater than the number of genes p, because they cannot calculate the partial correlations. The commonly used statistical tests for GGMs selection are valid only for data with large number of samples [40]. If $p > n$ then covariance matrix is not positive definite, so its inverse matrix cannot be calculated. Also, the existence of an additional linear dependence between variables leads to multicollinearity.

Therefore, to obtain positive definite covariance matrix, covariance matrix estimation is performed by shrinkage estimators and thus, its inverse matrix could be found [42,43]. Then, the edges in the graph are determined by model selection of the network graphs.

4.5 Differential and Difference Equations Models

Concentration of RNAs, proteins, and other metabolites changes through time. Therefore, differential equations systems can be an appropriate model to describe gene regulatory relationships [44]. Ordinary differential equations (ODEs) systems use continuous gene expression data directly and can easily cover positive and negative feedback loops.

The main constraint of this model based on ODEs is the assumed constant or linear changes of the concentration of regulators, although their changes through time are actually nonlinear.

The dynamics of gene expression data changes is described by the following differential equation:

$$\frac{dx}{dt} = f(x, p, u, t) \tag{9}$$

where $x(t) = (x_1(t), x_2(t, \ldots, x_n(t)))$ is a vector of gene expression data for n genes at time t, f is the function describing the changes of variables x_i depending on the model parameters p and external perturbations u. GRNs inference aims to determine the function f and parameters p for given measured signals x and u at the time t[2].

Equation (9) can have more solutions, so structure and parameters identification of the model requires identification of the function f based on *a priori* knowledge or some approximations. The function f can be linear or nonlinear and when this function is nonlinear, to simplify, its linearity is supposed and Eq. (9) transforms into the following equation:

$$\frac{dx_i}{dt} = \sum_{j=1}^{N} w_{ij} x_j + b_i u, \quad i = 1, \ldots, N \tag{10}$$

where w_{ij} are entries of weight matrix W and parameters b_i determine the external disturbance u to gene expression. This model is also called a model of regulatory matrices composed of weight coefficients w_{ij} that present the regulatory dependences. If a weight coefficient is positive, then corresponding gene has activating role, while a weight coefficient is negative, then that gene has inhibitory role. If weight coefficients values are zeros, then genes do not interact mutually.

In linear models, network inference from small number of samples is easier to carry out. The identification of function f and the parameters in the nonlinear models is more difficult because the number of samples in gene expression data is smaller than the number of genes and finding numerical solutions is more complex.

Another way to describe the changes of gene expression is by using S-systems with activating and inhibitory components, given by following equation:

$$\frac{dX_i}{dt} = \alpha_i \prod_{j=1}^{N} X_j^{g_{ij}} - \beta_i \prod_{j=1}^{N} X_j^{h_{ij}} \qquad (11)$$

where α_i and β_i are positive constants and h_{ij} and g_{ij} are kinetic exponents [2]. In these models, there are many parameters whose identification requires carrying out numerous experiments, and therefore to find solutions, these differential equations are approximated.

An optimized model for GRNs inference that uses known *a priori* biological knowledge from available databases for genome, proteome, transcriptome, and scientific literature has been proposed in Ref. [45]. This model is based on differential equations whose particular solutions are obtained by singular values decomposition. The obtained solutions are optimized by using mathematical programming.

A special case of differential equations system is the model of pairwise linear differential equations, proposed in Ref. [46]. In this model, it is supposed that gene regulation can be represented by pairwise linear equations. This model uses only gene expression data and neglects regulation on posttranscriptional level.

Beside ODEs, difference equations can describe the dynamics of GRNs. Unlike the differential equations models that deal with continuous variables, the variables in the difference equations model are discrete. Discretization of the gene expression data leads to information loss [44]. However, difference equations are more suitable when time series gene expression data are available. The change of gene expression data is described by the following equation:

$$\frac{x_i(t + \Delta t) - x_i(t)}{\Delta t} = \sum_{j=1}^{N} w_{ij} x_j(t) + b_i u, \quad i = 1, \dots, N \qquad (12)$$

Difference equations model can be transformed into a system of linear algebraic equations that can be solved easily by linear algebra methods [2].

4.6 Other Models for Inference of GRNs

Besides the above-mentioned models, numerous models for GRNs reconstruction are proposed.

Collateral-Fuzzy Gene Regulatory Network Reconstruction (CF-GeNe), proposed by Sehgal *et al.*, applies collateral assessment of the missing values [47]. This model utilizes the fuzzy nature of gene coregulation determined by fuzzy *c*-means clustering algorithm. This clustering algorithm allows one gene to belong to several clusters, i.e., biological processes. CF-GeNe can handle noisy data and missing values and it determines the optimal number of clusters.

Fujita *et al.* had proposed a model of GRNs using sparse autoregressive vector in Ref. [48]. This model can infer gene regulatory relationships when the number of samples is lesser than the number of genes without using *a priori* knowledge and it can deal with the feedback loops.

The linear model in the finite state space proposed in Ref. [49] infers gene regulatory relationships including discrete and continuous aspects of the gene regulation. The model assumptions are that gene activity is determined by the state of the TFBSs, each binding sites can be located in one of the final number of states, genes may be repressed or they can have some activity and the state of the binding sides depends on the concentration of TFs.

Li *et al.* had proposed another model that uses the state space with hidden variables for the GRNs reconstruction [50]. This model is dynamic and it is consisted of observations and states. The observations $(O_1, O_2, \ldots, O_T)$ are generated from the vector of states $(S_1, S_2, \ldots, S_T)$ according to the formal model given by:

$$S_t = AS_{t-1} + W_t, \quad O_t = BS_t + V_t \tag{13}$$

where A denotes the transition state probability $P(S_t|S_{t-1})$ from the state at time $t-1$ to t, B denotes the probability $P(O_t|S_t)$ of observation to be determined by the state in the same time point, while W_t and V_t represent the perturbations of the states and the observations, respectively. This model can be considered as a subtype of DBNs. The hidden variables include the regulatory motifs such as feedback loops and autoregulation.

A qualitative model for GRNs reconstruction employing Petri nets is proposed in Ref. [51]. This model, which is based on Boolean networks, uses minimization logic to transform Boolean rules into Petri nets. It overcomes the super-exponential number of states in the Boolean networks that depends on the number of nodes.

For hierarchical reconstruction of GRNs, Lee and Yang have proposed a model, which uses the clustering of gene expression data [52]. This model can infer regulatory relationships in large-scale networks. This method uses the recurrent neural networks to infer GRNs and applies the learning algorithm to update the main network parameters in discrete time steps.

Another method called FBN, applies the clustering of gene expression data to obtain modules (clusters) and then, it infers the gene regulatory relationships between clusters [53]. This method uses fuzzy clustering to reduce the search space for BNs learning.

4.7 Recent Models for Inference of GRNs by Integration of *A Priori* Knowledge

The GRNs inference based on gene expression data is very complex and difficult task, particularly because the present technical biological noise in microarray data should not be ignored. Furthermore, the number of experiments or conditions is lesser than the number of genes whose expression profiles are measured. Such shortcomings of the microarray data lead to unsatisfactory precision and accuracy of inferred networks, i.e., erroneous edges in inferred networks. To increase the accuracy and precision, employing other types of biological data and *a priori* knowledge such as knowledge obtained from scientific literature, protein–DNA interactions data, and other available databases is needed [54,55]. The capabilities of these models to reveal complex systems come from the model extensions by including *a priori* knowledge and using complementary and diverse data types [56].

One such method is suggested by Li, which combines qualitative and quantitative biological data for prediction of GRNs [57]. This method uses parallel processing and multiprocessor system to speed up the structural learning of BNs.

Based on comparison of the inference capabilities in Refs. [58,59], Ristevski and Loskovska [60] have suggested a novel model for GRNs inference, which performs in two stages. The first stage of the proposed model uses GGMs, because they are a good starting point to reveal the "hub" genes. The GRNs structure G is represented by an adjacency matrix, whose entries G_{ij} can be either 1 or 0, which means presence or absence of a directed edge between ith and jth node of the network G, respectively. As a result of the first phase of the proposed model, a matrix of *a priori* knowledge *Gprior* is obtained, whose elements are computed by:

$$
Gprior_{ij} = \begin{cases} \dfrac{1}{2}\dfrac{|pcor_{ij}| - pcor_{\min}}{pcor_{\max} - pcor_{\min}} + \dfrac{1}{2} \\ 0, \text{ if } |pcor_{ij}| < pcor_{\min} \text{ or edge direction is from } j \text{ to } i \end{cases} \tag{14}
$$

where $pcor_{\max}$ and $pcor_{\min}$ are the maximum and minimum (set threshold) partial correlation coefficient, respectively [60]. This matrix of *a priori* knowledge *Gprior*, whose entries $Gprior_{ij} \in [0, 1]$, presents a basis for the second phase of the proposed model.

To integrate the *a priori* knowledge obtained in first phase, the second phase uses a function *Gprior'* as a measure of matching between the given network G and the obtained *a priori* knowledge *Gprior*[55]. The integration of *a priori* knowledge *Gprior* is according to prior distribution of the network structure G, which follows Gibbs distribution, given by the following equation [54,55]:

$$
P(G|\beta) = \frac{e^{-\beta Gprior'(G)}}{Z(\beta)} \tag{15}
$$

where the denominator is normalization constant calculated from all possible network structures Γ by the formula $Z(\beta) = \sum_{G \in \Gamma} e^{-\beta Gprior'(G)}$. In the second stage of the proposed model structure Bayesian learning using Markov chain Monte Carlo simulations is performed [60]. The flow chart of this model is illustrated in Fig. 4. This model has shown even better inference capabilities of networks inference, compared to Boolean networks, GGMs, and DBNs in the case when it was applied on experimental data sets as well as simulated datasets [59].

Beside gene expression data, the network inference using available heterogeneous -omics data, like transcriptomics, proteomics, interactomics, and metabolomics data, becoming more flexible. Integration of these data and using *a priori* knowledge can contribute to achieve more reliable comprehension of the regulatory relationships.

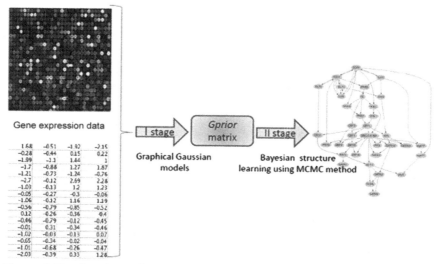

Figure 4 The flowchart of the two-stage inference model that integrates *a priori* knowledge [61].

5. COMPUTATIONAL APPROACHES FOR INFERENCE OF MicroRNA-MEDIATED REGULATORY NETWORKS

5.1 MicroRNA-Mediated Regulatory Networks

miRNAs repress translation of thousands of genes including TFs and hence significantly affect many types of cellular processes. Mostly, miRNAs and TFs regulate their mutual targets synchronously, composing complex networks named as *miRNA-mediated regulatory networks* [19]. The network is structured by the nodes and edges as connections between nodes. The nodes can represent TFs, miRNAs, target genes of miRNAs and TFs, and regulators of miRNAs, while the edges representing the regulatory relationships between the nodes. Figure 5 shows an miRNA-mediated regulatory networks, where full lines present transcriptional level regulation, whereas dashed edges present regulation on posttranscriptional level.

5.2 Types of Regulatory Relationships

There are several types of regulatory mechanisms [62]:
- TF regulates gene expression, denoted as *TF–gene* interaction. TFs can regulate gene expression by repressing or activating their target genes forming transcriptional regulatory networks.

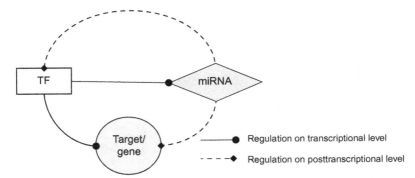

Figure 5 An miRNA-mediated regulatory network.

- TF regulates miRNA, denoted as *TF–miRNA* relationship. TFs are playing the key role in regulation of expression of miRNAs. Identifying the regulators of miRNAs is crucial to fully understand the miRNA-mediated regulatory networks.
- *MiRNA–TF* denotes that miRNA regulates TF. MiRNA–TF regulatory networks play an important role as functional entity in the cell regulatory processes in different cell types including cancer.
- MiRNA regulation on gene expression is denoted as *miRNA–gene*. Single miRNA targets hundreds of genes and even more, miRNAs often acting together by overlapping their targets. This makes miRNAs key elements in complex regulatory networks.
- *Gene–gene* interactions, which are covered in above-described GRNs.
- *TF–TF* or PPIs, forming PPI networks.

The most commonly used repositories, computational models, and tools for inferring/revealing of mutual regulatory interactions between TFs, miRNAs, and genes are listed in Table 1.

The most commonly used algorithms for the miRNAs target predictions are TargetScan 6.2 [63], Diana-microT [64], miRanda—microRNA Target Detection [65], miRTarbase [66], etc. These algorithms use different combination of features to identify whether particular sequence is a target of miRNAs or not. These algorithms exhaustively search for structural indication suggesting the presence of an interaction and they are often uncorrelated, which can lead to the nonoverlapping prediction results. Impossibility to integrate in a single model all possible interplaying options, which can influence the results of the miRNAs targeting and different type of sequence resources used as reference data set, is a shortcoming of the above-mentioned methods.

Table 1 Computational Models/Tools Used to Reveal Regulatory Relationships Between miRNAs, TFs, and Genes

Type of Interaction	Repositories/Databases or Computational Models/Tools
TF–gene	Match [88] CircuitsDB [89] Transcriptional Regulatory Element Database (TRED) [71] Human Transcriptional Regulation Interactions database (HTRIdb) [72] TRANScription FACtor database (TRANSFAC®) [20] mirGen 2.0 [90] ChIPBase [91]
TF–miRNA	Match [88] CircuitsDB [89] TransmiR [92] ChIPBase [91]
Gene–gene	Models listed in Section 4 of this chapter
miRNA–TF	TargetScan 6.2 [63] CircuitsDB [89]
miRNA–gene	Diana-microT [64] Tarbase 6.0 [73] miRecords [74] miRTarbase [66] TargetScan 6.2 [63] miRanda—microRNA Target Detection [65] CircuitsDB [89] doRiNa [93] miRNA—Target Gene Prediction at EMBL [94]
TF–TF/PPI	Biological General Repository for Interaction Datasets (BioGRID) [76] Human Protein Reference Database (HPRD) [77] IntAct [78] MIPS-Mammalian Protein–Protein Interaction Database (MIPS-MPPI) [79] KEGG [75]

Besides simple training-prediction model utilized in miRNAs targets prediction, diverse machine learning algorithms had also been employed such as support vector machines (SVMs) and random walk [19].

There are several computational methods to identify miRNA targets by using sequence analysis, which do not deal with the temporal dynamics of miRNA-regulated networks.

Schulz *et al.* had developed a tool named as MIRna Dynamic Regulatory Events Miner (mirDREM) [67]. Reconstructing of dynamic regulatory networks by mirDREM covers effects of TFs and miRNAs on their targets over time by integrating time series gene expression data with protein–DNA interaction data and the miRNAs expression level and their binding activities to predict their targets.

In Ref. [68], a feature dependency analysis across samples is performed in order to determine regulators (miRNAs and TFs) that significantly describe common and subtype-specific gene expression changes. To rank subtype-specific features, a score based on increasing in squared loss on samples, which belong to a subtype excluding the regulator from the learned model, is used.

Liao *et al.* had developed a data decomposition method—network component analysis (NCA) for reconstruction of regulatory signals and control strengths using partial and qualitative network connectivity information [69]. This method is applied on transcription regulatory network.

Ripoli *et al.* had proposed fuzzy logic approach to reveal miRNAs role to gene expression regulation [70].

Sun *et al.* developed an integrative framework for miRNA–TF regulatory networks construction for glioblastoma multiforme (GBM) [62]. The aim of this model is to identify GBM-specific miRNA–TF regulatory network and critical miRNA elements in a given pathway. Although GRNs modeling including TFs and miRNAs is very complex task, it will clarify both directly and indirectly regulatory mechanisms and mutual interactions between regulators and their targets. Computational models are very useful to uncover these complex regulatory relationships, particularly because the biological experiments' processes are very expensive and time demanding.

Lai *et al.* presented a systems' biology approach that combine data-driven modeling and model-driven experiments to examine the role of miRNA-mediated repression in GRNs [11]. Experimental approaches have constraints when handling complex biological systems regulations on transcriptional and posttranscriptional level by TFs and miRNAs. For mathematical modeling of GRNs, the authors integrated data from literature, biological databases, and experiments from different resources. Extracting experimental verified data for transcriptional level regulators is from literature or databases such as TRED [71], HTRIdb [72], TRANSFAC [20] or miRGen 2.0. Tarbase 6.0 [73], miRecords [74], and miRTarBase [66] provide information about miRNA–gene interactions, while KEGG [75], BioGRID [76], HPRD [77], IntAct [78], and MIPS-MPPI [79] are repositories for PPIs [11].

Similar to protein-coding genes, the miRNA transcription is closely controlled by upstream TFs. To discover the biological roles of the miRNAs, their targets' functions should be clarified. The miRNA expression and microarray data can be employed to examine specific TF–miRNA regulations. Self-regulation of miRNA genes is a mechanism that works as a buffering system for their expression modulation [80]. Feedback loops between specific miRNAs and the upstream TFs are another type of regulatory relationships in the miRNA-mediated regulatory networks [80]. These feedback circular connections are very important units in balancing TF and miRNA expression in the living organisms. Integration of more feedback circuits that exist between miRNAs and TFs increases the biological meaning, reliability, and complexity of the miRNA-mediated regulatory networks.

Le et al. suggested framework for complex regulatory network construction with three components: genes, miRNAs, and TFs [10]. Their model performed in three steps: data preparation, BN learning and integration, and network inference. The aim of the network inference is to find the global network for the subgraphs that show the interactions among miRNAs and TFs and network motifs composed of at least two regulators using network motifs finding algorithms.

Most of the existing computational models and tools find out statistically correlation and association between miRNAs and mRNAs. Correlation and association are not necessarily measures that provide an insight into causal gene regulation. Le et al. [81] refer the causal effects discovery as miRNA causal regulatory relationships. Their method uses miRNAs and mRNAs expression data and validates the causal effects of miRNAs on mRNAs assuming that miRNAs and mRNAs mutually interact. This method can be used to identify which gene set is casually regulated by particular miRNAs. Moreover, this method can theoretically infer the causal associations between every pair variables in the data set, for instance TFs, miRNAs, and mRNAs.

Pio et al. suggested semi-supervised learning approach for miRNA target prediction [82]. Their approach, beside the positive examples, utilizes unlabeled examples. The nontraditional classifier is learned using SVMs algorithm to learn to combine the results of several prediction algorithms. For validation of suggested model, a set of experimentally verified miRNA–miRNA interaction from miRTarBase and a set of miRNA target prediction are used.

Examination of protein changes following miRNA knockout (technique in which one of an miRNA is inoperative/"knocked out" of the organism) or knockdown (technique by which the miRNAs expression of an organism's genome is reduced) is a helpful basis to assign the specific interaction function [83]. The possibility of indirect effects can be difficult to eliminate, because each miRNA can have many targets.

Laboratory experiments for characterization of individual regulatory interactions can reveal much more information about these interactions. By using expression data, target predictions and biological knowledge, candidates for regulatory interactions can be obtained by pointing on the messages predicted to be most responsive to the miRNA, coexpressed with the miRNA in the related cells, in those regulatory networks' nodes that are subject of interest.

5.3 Robustness of miRNA-Mediated Regulatory Networks

A good procedure is to disturb only particular interaction and monitor the phenotypic effects. A beneficial technique is disrupting a single miRNA–target interaction by using antisense reagents that hybridize to the target site, thus to disallow miRNA pairing. The phenotypic effects of these preserved interactions are very challenging task, especially their detection in the wet lab, although the simultaneously perturbation of all miRNA interactions by their knocking out usually does not have considerable phenotypic effects [83]. One of the more reasons of toleration of such disturbances for miRNA targets, which are gene regulatory proteins, is the regulatory network buffering. Many regulatory interactions, including many miRNA–target interactions, belong to complex regulatory networks with bifurcating pathways and feedback control enabling accurate reaction regardless of an inoperative node in the network. With this ability to buffer the effects of missing a node, such networks must be disturbed somewhere else before the missing miRNA interaction has evident phenotypic effects [83]. Perturbation of the miRNA node is expected to make the network susceptive to discover the importance of the rest of regulatory nodes.

Recent studies have uncovered that target hub genes, which carry vast number of TFBSs, are possible subject to massive regulation by many miRNAs. It means that nodes with more connections will more probably obtain new connections during time. The top genes with big number of both miRNA binding sites and TFBS are boosted in the functions related to development and differentiation of cells. Many of these target hub genes are transcription regulators, proposing a crucial pathway for miRNAs to indirectly regulate genes by repressing TFs [19].

miRNAs could be also target of hub genes. There is a class of miRNAs regulated by a large number of TFs, while the others are regulated by only a few TFs. miRNA expression profiles in embryonic developmental stages and adult tissues or cancer samples had disclosed that the miRNAs from the first class have higher expression levels in embryonic developmental stages, while the second class miRNAs are more expressed in adult tissues or cancer samples.

Regulator hub genes are more likely to have interactions with miRNAs, because they regulate large number of targets. miRNAs together with master TFs prefer to coregulate their targets. Regulator hub genes are very important constituents in the GRNs, since perturbations on them can disturb functions of numerous target genes. As miRNAs buffer stochastic perturbations, their preference to regulator hub genes could provide robustness of the regulatory network [19].

6. MODEL VALIDATION

Validation of inferred miRNA-mediated and GRNs represents an assessment of the accuracy of the inferred networks, compared to the available knowledge in so-called "gold standard" networks. To validate regulatory relationships inferred by using computational models, reliable biological experimental data are needed. In order to ensure more accurate and reliable model prediction, validation of the model with the data that are not included in the parameter estimation is required.

As commonly used validation criteria, receiver operating characteristic (ROC) curve and area under the ROC curve (AUC) are used.

In a graph between two nodes, it might be or not an edge, or using the formalism of machine learning, each edge (instance) of the network belongs to either positive (p) or negative (n) class, and classifier results belong to either class p or class n [84].

For a given two-class classifier and test samples, four cases can occur:
- True positive (TP), if the instance is positive and it is classified as positive;
- False negative (FN), if the instance is positive and it is classified as negative;
- True negative (TN), if the instance is negative and it is classified as negative;
- False positive (FP), if the instance is negative and it is classified as positive.

Based on the defined TP, FN, TN, and FP, following variables are defined [85,86]:

tpr (true-positive rate) (recall):

$$tpr = \frac{TP}{P} = \frac{TP}{TP + FN} \tag{16}$$

fpr (false-positive rate):

$$fpr = \frac{FP}{N} = \frac{FP}{FP + TN} \tag{17}$$

precision:

$$precision = \frac{TP}{TP + FP} \tag{18}$$

accuracy:

$$accuracy = \frac{TP + TN}{P + N} = \frac{TP + TN}{TP + FN + FP + TN} \tag{19}$$

An ROC curve is a plot of a function where on the x-axis, the fpr—and on the y-axis—the tpr are applied, as shown in Fig. 6. In other words, an ROC curve represents the ratio between sensitivity and (1 - specificity) [87]. If the ROC curve is more above the line $y = x$, then classification is better.

To facilitate comparison of inference capabilities, the area under ROC curve (AUC) can also be used. The AUC is the area covered by the ROC curve with the x-axis, as shown in Fig. 6. The statistical meaning of the

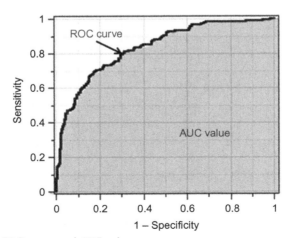

Figure 6 The ROC curve and AUC value.

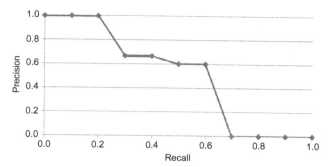

Figure 7 Precision–recall operating characteristics (P-ROC) curve.

AUC corresponds to the probability that the classifier will rank a randomly selected positive instance higher than a selected negative instance [84].

Alternatively, precision–recall operating characteristic (P-ROC, PR) curve can be used as validation criterion, where on the x-axis recall and on the y-axis precision are applied, as shown in Fig. 7.

7. CONCLUSION AND FURTHER WORKS

This overview of the most commonly used models for inference of miRNA-mediated and GRNs has shown that there is still a need for development of models that can integrate *a priori* knowledge in order to increase models inference capabilities. Such *a priori* knowledge significantly can improve the accuracy and biological reliability of the inferred regulatory networks. Inferred network edges, which are not present in the biological regulatory repositories and database, are indications for further experimental analysis to confirm or reject their presence as true regulatory relationships. Nevertheless, despite the advantages of described models, it can be concluded that there is no "silver bullet" inference model, which will have highly effective and accurate inference capabilities.

To assign the specific interaction function, a helpful base is protein changes examination of following miRNA knockout or knockdown. Laboratory experiments for characterization of individual regulatory interactions can reveal much more information about regulatory interactions.

By validation of the inferred networks, the main problem is the lack of reference "gold standard" networks. In addition, greater efforts should be made toward upgrading of existing regulatory databases with confirmed regulatory relationships between genes, miRNAs, TFs, and the other components involved in the cell regulatory processes.

Various -omics data uncover diverse perspectives of regulatory networks. Hence, integration of heterogeneous data and using biological *a priori* knowledge remains still challenging and partially unsolved issue in the inference of regulatory networks.

REFERENCES

[1] B. Ristevski, A survey of models for inference of gene regulatory networks, Nonlinear Anal. Modell. Control 18 (4) (2013) 444–465.

[2] M. Hecker, S. Lambeck, S. Toepfer, E. van Someren, R. Guthke, Gene regulatory network inference: data integration in dynamic models—a review, Biosystems 96 (2009) 86–103.

[3] P. Brazhnik, A. de la Fuente, P. Mendes, Gene networks: how to put the function in genomics, Trends Biotechnol. 20 (11) (2002) 467–472.

[4] Z. Shuang, L. Mo-Fang, Mechanisms of microRNA-mediated gene regulation, Sci. China C Life Sci. 52 (12) (2009) 1111–1116.

[5] Y. Nikolsky, J. Bryant (Eds.), Protein Networks and Pathway Analysis, Humana Press, Clifton, NJ, 2009, pp. 303–352.

[6] http://www.mirbase.org.

[7] Z. Wang, MicroRNA Interference Technologies, Springer-Verlag, New York, 2009.

[8] C. Li, Y. Feng, G. Coukos, L. Zhang, Therapeutic microRNA strategies in human cancer, AAPS J. 11 (4) (2009) 747–757.

[9] J.G. Joung, Z. Fei, Identification of microRNA regulatory modules in Arabidopsis via a probabilistic graphical model, Bioinformatics 25 (3) (2009) 383–393.

[10] T.D. Le, L. Liu, B. Liu, A. Tsykin, G.J. Goodall, K. Satou, J. Li, Inferring microRNA and transcription factor regulatory networks in heterogeneous data, BMC Bioinformatics 14 (2013) 92.

[11] X. Lai, A. Bhattacharya, U. Schmitz, M. Kunz, J. Vera, O. Wolkenhauer, A systems' biology approach to study microRNA-mediated gene regulatory networks, Biomed. Res. Int. 2013 (2013) Article ID 703849.

[12] A. Drakaki, D. Iliopoulos, MicroRNA gene networks in oncogenesis, Curr. Genomics 10 (2009) 35–41.

[13] S.K. Shenouda, S.K. Alahari, MicroRNA function in cancer: oncogene or a tumor suppressor? Cancer Metastasis Rev. 28 (3–4) (2009) 369–378.

[14] N.A. Kolchanov, T.I. Merkulova, E.V. Ignatieva, et al., Combined experimental and computational approaches to study the regulatory elements in eukaryotic genes, Brief. Bioinform. 8 (4) (2007) 266–274.

[15] P.J. Park, ChIP-seq: advantages and challenges of a maturing technology, Nat. Rev. Genet. 10 (10) (2009) 669–680.

[16] P. Collas (Ed.), Chromatin Immunoprecipitation Assays, Humana Press, Totowa, NJ, 2009, pp. 133–143.

[17] W. Zhao, E. Serpedin, E.R. Douherty, Recovering genetic regulatory networks from chromatin immunoprecipitation and steady-state microarray data, EURASIP J. Bioinform. Syst. Biol. 2008 (2008) 248747.

[18] H. Bolouri, Modeling genomic regulatory networks with big data, Trends Genet. 30 (5) (2014) 182–191.

[19] Y. Zhou, Interconnection of microRNA and transcription factor-mediated regulatory networks, in: Y. Gusev (Ed.), MicroRNA Profiling in Cancer—A Bioinformatics Perspective, Pan Stanford Publishing Pte. Ltd., Singapore, 2010

[20] E. Wingender, et al., The TRANSFAC system on gene expression regulation, Nucleic Acids Res. 29 (1) (2001) 281–283.

[21] A. Sandelin, W. Alkema, P. Engström, W.W. Wasserman, B. Lenhard, JASPAR: an open-access database for eukaryotic transcription factor binding profiles, Nucleic Acids Res. 32 (2004) D91–D94.

[22] M. Nicolau, M. Schoenauer, On the evolution of scale-free topologies with gene regulatory network model, Biosystems 98 (3) (2009) 137–148.

[23] S. Liang, S. Fuhrman, R. Somogyi, REVEAL, a general reverse engineering algorithm for inference of genetic network architectures, Pac. Symp. Biocomput. 3 (1998) 18–19.

[24] Y.K. Kwon, K.H. Cho, Analysis of feedback loops and robustness in network evolution based on Boolean models, BMC Bioinformatics 8 (2007) 430.

[25] I. Shmulevich, E.R. Dougherty, W. Zhang, From Boolean to probabilistic Boolean networks as models of genetic regulatory networks, Proc. IEEE 90 (11) (2002) 1778–1792.

[26] N. Friedman, M. Goldszmidt, Learning Bayesian networks with local structure, in: Proceedings of the 12th International Conference on Uncertainty in Artificial Intelligence, 1996, pp. 252–262.

[27] M. Grzegorczyk, D. Husmeier, Improving the structure MCMC sampler for Bayesian networks by introducing a new edge reversal move, Mach. Learn. 71 (2008) 265–305.

[28] N. Friedman, M. Linian, I. Nachman, D. Pe'er, Using Bayesian networks to analyze expression data, J. Comput. Biol. 7 (2000) 601–620.

[29] D. Husmeier, R. Dybowskiand, S. Roberts (Eds.), Probabilistic Modeling in Bioinformatics and Medical Informatics, Springer-Verlag, London, 2005.

[30] L. Kaderali, N. Radde, Inferring gene regulatory networks from expression data, Stud. Comput. Intell. 94 (2008) 33–74.

[31] R.E. Neapolitan, Learning Bayesian Networks, Prentice Hall, New York, 2003.

[32] A. Shermin, M.A. Orgun, Using dynamic Bayesian networks to infer gene regulatory networks from expression profiles, in: SAC '09, Proceedings of the 2009 ACM Symposium on Applied Computing, 2009, pp. 799–803.

[33] Y. Zhang, Z. Deng, H. Jiang, P. Jia, Inferring Gene Regulatory Networks from Multiple Data Sources via a Dynamic Bayesian Networks with Structural EM, Springer-Verlag, Berlin, Heidelberg, 2007, pp. 204–214.

[34] R. Daly, K.D. Edwards, J.S. O'Neill, S. Aitken, A.J. Millar, M. Girolami, Using higher-order dynamic Bayesian networks to model periodic data from the circadian clock of Arabidopsis thaliana, in: PRIB 2009, 2009, pp. 67–78.

[35] K. Murphy, S. Mian, Modelling gene expression data using dynamic Bayesian networks, in: Technical Report, Computer Science Division, University of California, Berkeley, CA, 1999.

[36] M. Zou, S.D. Conzen, A new dynamic Bayesian network (DBN) approach for identifying gene regulatory networks from time course microarray data, Bioinformatics 21 (1) (2005) 71–79.

[37] C.S. Kim, Bayesian Orthogonal Least Squares (BOLS) algorithm for reverse engineering of gene regulatory networks, BMC Bioinformatics 8 (2007) 251.

[38] K. Numata, S. Imoto, S. Miyano, A structure learning algorithm for inference of gene networks from microarray gene expression data using Bayesian networks, in: 7th IEEE International Conference on Bioinformatics and Bioengineering, BIBE 2007, 2007, pp. 1280–1284.

[39] A.A. Margolin, I. Nemenman, K. Basso, C. Wiggins, G. Stolovitzky, R.D. Favera, A. Califano, ARACNE: an algorithm for the reconstruction of gene regulatory networks in a mammalian cellular context, BMC Bioinformatics 7 (Suppl. 1) (2006) S7.

[40] J. Schäfer, K. Strimmer, Learning large-scale graphical Gaussian models from genomic data, CPP776, in: Science of Complex Networks: From Biology to the Internet and WWW; CNET 2004, 2004, pp. 263–276.

[41] J. Schäfer, K. Strimmer, A shrinkage approach to large-scale covariance matrix estimation and implications for functional genomics, Stat. Appl. Genet. Mol. Biol. 4 (1) (2005) Article 32.

[42] F. Jaffrezic, G.T. Klopp, Gene network reconstruction from microarray data, BMC Proc. 3 (Suppl. 4) (2009) S12.

[43] J. Schäfer, R. Opgen-Rhein, K. Strimmer, Reverse engineering genetic networks using the GeneNet package, R. News 6/5 (2006) 50–53.

[44] L.F.A. Wessels, E.P. van Someren, M.J.T. Reinders, A comparison of genetic network models, Pac. Symp. Biocomput. 6 (2001) 508–519.

[45] J. Li, X.S. Zhang, An optimization model for gene regulatory networks reconstruction with known biological information, in: 1st International Symposium on Optimization and Systems Biology (OSB'07), Beijing, China, 2007, pp. 35–44.

[46] J. Gebert, N. Radde, G.-W. Weber, Modeling gene regulatory networks with piecewise linear differential equations, Eur. J. Oper. Res. 181 (3) (2007) 1148–1165.

[47] M.S.B. Sehgal, I. Gondal, L.S. Dooley, CF-GeNe: fuzzy framework for robust gene regulatory network inference, J. Comput. 1 (7) (2006) 1–8.

[48] A. Fujita, J.R. Sato, H.M. Garay-Malpartida, R. Yamaguchi, S. Miyano, M.C. Sogayar, C.E. Ferreira, Modeling gene expression regulatory networks with the sparse vector autoregressive model, BMC Syst. Biol. 1 (2007) 39.

[49] A. Brazma, T. Schlitt, Reverse engineering of gene regulatory networks: a finite state linear model, Genome Biol. 4:P5 (2003) 1–31.

[50] Z. Li, S.M. Shaw, M.J. Yedwabnick, C. Chan, Using a state-space model with hidden variables to infer transcription factor activities, Bioinformatics 22 (6) (2006) 747–754.

[51] L.J. Steggles, R. Banks, A. Wipat, Modelling and analysing genetic networks: from Boolean networks to Petri nets: Technical Report, University of Newcastle upon Tyne, Computing Science, 2006, pp. 127–141.

[52] W.-P. Lee, K.-C. Yang, A clustering-based approach for inferring recurrent neural networks as gene regulatory networks, Neurocomputing 71 (2008) 600–610.

[53] F. Wang, D. Pan, J. Ding, A new approach combined fuzzy clustering and Bayesian networks for modeling gene regulatory networks, in: Proceedings of the 2008 International Conference on BioMedical Engineering and Informatics, 1, 2008, pp. 29–33.

[54] A.V. Werhli, D. Husmeier, Reconstructing gene regulatory networks with Bayesian networks by combining expression data with multiple sources of priori knowledge, Stat. Appl. Genet. Mol. Biol. 6 (2007) Article 15.

[55] S. Imoto, T. Higuchi, T. Goto, K. Tashiro, S. Kuhara, S. Miyano, Combining microarrays and biological knowledge for estimating gene networks via Bayesian networks, in: Proceedings of the Computational Systems Bioinformatics (CSB '03), 2003, pp. 104–113.

[56] T. Ideker, J. Dutkowski, L. Hood, Boosting signal-to-noise in complex biology: prior knowledge is power, Cell 144 (6) (2011) 860–863.

[57] S. Li, Integrate qualitative biological knowledge to build gene networks by parallel dynamic Bayesian network structure learning, in: Bioinformatics and Bioengineering, BIBE 2007, 2007, pp. 87–92.

[58] B. Ristevski, S. Loskovska, ROC curves comparison of inferred gene regulatory networks, in: 13th International Multiconference Information Society 2010, Intelligent Systems, Ljubljana, Slovenia, 2010, pp. 39–42.

[59] B. Ristevski, S. Loshkovska, A comparison of models for gene regulatory networks inference, in: 2nd International Conference, ICT Innovations 2010, Ohrid, Republic of Macedonia, 2010, pp. 59–68.

[60] B. Ristevski, S. Loskovska, A novel model for inference of gene regulatory networks, HealthMed J. 5 (6) (2011) 2024–2033.

[61] B. Ristevski, Inference of gene regulatory networks by integrating prior knowledge, in: R. Hofestädt, N. Kolchanov (Eds.), German/Russian Network of Computational Systems Biology: Report 2012, Berichte aus der Medizinischen Informatik und Bioinformatik, Shaker-Verlag, Aachen, 2012.

[62] J. Sun, X. Gong, B. Purow, Z. Zhao, Uncovering microRNA and transcription factor mediated regulatory networks in glioblastoma, PLoS Comput. Biol. 8 (7) (2012) e1002488.

[63] B.P. Lewis, C.B. Burge, D.P. Bartel, Conserved seed pairing, often flanked by adenosines, indicates that thousands of human genes are microRNA targets, Cell 120 (1) (2005) 15–20.

[64] M. Maragkakis, T. Vergoulis, et al., DIANA-microT web server upgrade supports fly and worm miRNA target prediction and bibliographic miRNA to disease association, Nucleic Acids Res. 39 (2011) W145–W148.

[65] D. Betel, M. Wilson, A. Gabow, D.S. Marks, C. Sander, The microRNA.org resource: targets and expression, Nucleic Acids Res. 36 (Database Issue) (2008) D149–D153.

[66] S.D. Hsu, Y.T. Tseng, S. Shrestha, et al., miRTarBase update 2014: an information resource for experimentally validated miRNA-target interactions, Nucleic Acids Res. 42 (Database Issue) (2014) D78–D85.

[67] M.H. Schulz, K.V. Pandit, C.L.L. Cardenas, N. Ambalavanan, N. Kaminskiand, Z.B. Joseph, Reconstructing dynamic microRNA-regulated interaction networks, Proc. Natl. Acad. Sci. U. S. A. 110 (2013) 15686–15691.

[68] M. Setty, et al., Inferring transcriptional and microRNA-mediated regulatory programs in glioblastoma, Mol. Syst. Biol. 8 (2012) Article 605.

[69] J.C. Liao, et al., Network component analysis: reconstruction of regulatory signals in biological systems, Proc. Natl. Acad. Sci. U.S.A. 100 (26) (2003) 15522–15527.

[70] A. Ripoli, et al., The fuzzy logic of microRNA regulation: a key to control cell complexity, Curr. Genomics 11 (5) (2010) 350–353.

[71] F. Zhao, Z. Xuan, L. Liu, M.Q. Zhang, TRED: a Transcriptional Regulatory Element Database and a platform for in silico gene regulation studies, Nucleic Acids Res. 33 (Database Issue) (2005) D103–D107.

[72] L.A. Bovolenta, M.L. Acencio, N. Lemke, HTRIdb: an open-access database for experimentally verified human transcriptional regulation interactions, BMC Genomics 13 (Database) (2012) 405.

[73] T.I. Vergoulis, P. Vlachos, et al., Tarbase 6.0: capturing the exponential growth of miRNA targets with experimental support, Nucleic Acids Res. 40 (D1) (2012) D222–D229.

[74] F. Xiao, Z. Zuo, G. Cai, S. Kang, X. Gao, T. Li, miRecords: an integrated resource for microRNA-target interactions, Nucleic Acids Res. 37 (Database Issue) (2009) D105–D110.

[75] M. Tanabe, M. Kanehisa, Using the KEGG database resource, Curr. Protoc. Bioinformatics 38(1) (2012) 12:1.12.1–1.12.43.

[76] C. Stark, B.J. Breitkreutz, T. Reguly, L. Boucher, A. Breitkreutz, M. Tyers, BioGRID: a general repository for interaction datasets, Nucleic Acids Res. 1 (34) (2006) 535–539.

[77] T.S.K. Prasad, et al., Human protein reference database—2009 update, Nucleic Acids Res. 37 (2009) D767–D772.

[78] S. Orchard, et al., The MIntAct project—IntAct as a common curation platform for 11 molecular interaction databases, Nucleic Acids Res. 42 (2014) D358–D363.

[79] P. Pagel, S. Kovac, M. Oesterheld, et al., The MIPS mammalian protein-protein interaction database, Bioinformatics 21 (6) (2005) 832–834.

[80] Y. Meng, C. Shao, M. Chen, Toward microRNA-mediated gene regulatory networks in plants, Brief. Bioinform. 12 (6) (2011) 645–659.

[81] T.D. Le, L. Liu, A. Tsykin, G.J. Goodall, B. Liu, B.-Y. Sun, J. Li, Inferring microRNA–mRNA causal regulatory relationships from expression data, Bioinformatics 29 (6) (2013) 765–771.

[82] G. Pio, D. Malerba, D. D'Elia, M. Ceci, Integrating microRNA target predictions for the discovery of gene regulatory networks: a semi-supervised ensemble learning approach, BMC Bioinformatics 15 (Suppl. 1) (2014) S4.

[83] D.P. Bartel, MicroRNA target recognition and regulatory functions, Cell 136 (2) (2009) 215–233.

[84] T. Fawcett, An introduction to ROC analysis, Pattern Recogn. Lett. 27 (2006) 861–874.

[85] P. Baldi, S. Brunak, Bioinformatics: The Machine Learning Approach, The MIT Press, London, 2001.

[86] J. Huang, C.X. Ling, Using AUC and accuracy in evaluating learning algorithms, IEEE Trans. Knowl. Data Eng. 17 (3) (2005) 299–310.

[87] L.M. de Campos, A scoring function for learning Bayesian networks based on mutual information and conditional independence tests, J. Mach. Learn. Res. 7 (2006) 2149–2187.

[88] A.E. Kel, E. Gossling, I. Reuter, E. Cheremushkin, O.V. Kel-Margoulis, et al., MATCH: a tool for searching transcription factor binding sites in DNA sequences, Nucleic Acids Res. 31 (2003) 3576–3579.

[89] O. Friard, A. Re, D. Taverna, M. De Bortoli, D. Corá, CircuitsDB: a database of mixed microRNA/transcription factor feed-forward regulatory circuits in human and mouse, BMC Bioinformatics 11 (2010) 435.

[90] P. Alexiou, T. Vergoulis, et al., miRGen 2.0: a database of microRNA genomic information and regulation, Nucleic Acids Res. 38 (Database Issue) (2010) D137–D141.

[91] J.H. Yang, J.H. Li, S. Jiang, H. Zhou, L.H. Qu, ChIPBase: a database for decoding the transcriptional regulation of long non-coding RNA and microRNA genes from ChIP-Seq data, Nucleic Acids Res. 41 (2013) D177–D187.

[92] J. Wang, M. Lu, C. Qiu, Q. Cui, TransmiR: a transcription factor-microRNA regulation database, Nucleic Acids Res. 38 (Suppl. 1) (2010) D119–D122.

[93] G. Anders, S.D. Mackowiak, M. Jens, et al., doRiNA: a database of RNA interactions in post-transcriptional regulation, Nucleic Acids Res. 40 (Database Issue) (2012) D180–D186.

[94] J. Brennecke, A. Stark, R.B. Russell, S.M. Cohen, Principles of microRNA-target recognition, PLoS Biol. 3 (3) (2005) e85.

ABOUT THE AUTHOR

Blagoj Ristevski is currently an assistant professor at the St. Kliment Ohridski University in Bitola, Republic of Macedonia. He is a head of the Department of Information Systems at Faculty of Information and Communication Technologies—Bitola. From 2002 to 2007, he worked as a teaching and research assistant at Faculty of Technical Sciences in Bitola, afterward until 2014 he worked as an assistant professor at Faculty of Administration and Information Systems Management—Bitola, Republic of Macedonia.

He received his Ph.D. degree in Computer Science and Engineering from the University Ss. Cyril and Methodius in Skopje, Faculty of Electrical

Engineering and Information Technology, Macedonia with the doctoral thesis "Modelling, Analysis and Validation of Gene Regulatory Networks" in 2011. He received Magister degree in Computer Science and Engineering and Graduate Engineer degree in Electrical Engineering from the same Faculty in 2007 and 2001, respectively.

He is an author and a coauthor of many research papers published in international journals and conference proceedings. Since 2009, he has done several research stays at research centers at University of Göttingen and University of Bielefeld, Germany; University of Groningen, The Netherlands; and University of Sofia, Bulgaria. His current research interests are Bioinformatics, Gene Regulatory Networks, Reverse Engineering, Database Management Systems, Algorithms, and Data Mining and Cryptography.

CHAPTER FOUR

Proving Programs Terminate Using Well-Founded Orderings, Ramsey's Theorem, and Matrices

William Gasarch
Department of Computer Science, University of Maryland, College Park, Maryland, USA

Contents

Advances in Computers, Volume 97
ISSN 0065-2458
http://dx.doi.org/10.1016/bs.adcom.2014.12.002

Abstract

Many programs allow the user to input data several times during its execution. If the program runs forever, the user may input data infinitely often. A program terminates no matter what the user does. We define a program to terminate if no matter what the user does the program will halt.

We discuss various ways to prove that a program terminates. The proofs use well-founded orders, Ramsey Theorem, and matrices. These techniques are used by real program checkers.

1. INTRODUCTION

We describe several ways to prove that programs terminate. By this, we mean terminate on *any* sequence of inputs. The methods employed are well-founded orders, Ramsey's theorem, and matrices. This chapter is self contained; it does not require knowledge of any of these topics or of programming languages. The methods we describe are used by real program checkers.

Our account is based on the articles of Cook and coauthors [1–7] and Lee and coauthors [8, 9]. Termination checkers that use the methods discussed in this chapter include:

1. Loopfrog (http://www.verify.inf.unisi.ch/loopfrog/termination).
2. Terminator (http://www7.in.tum.de/~rybal/papers/).
3. ACL2 (Applicative common lisp 2) (http://acl2s.ccs.neu.edu/acl2s/doc/).
4. APoVE (Automatic program verification environment) (http://aprove. informatik.rwth-aachen.de/).
5. Julia (http://julia.scienze.univr.it/).

Convention 1. The statement *The Program Terminates* means that it terminates no matter what the user does. The user will be supplying inputs as the program runs; hence, we are saying that the user cannot come up with some (perhaps malicious) inputs that make the program run forever. A more realistic scenario is if the programs input is a sequence of requests for devices.

In Section 2, we establish a standard notation. In Sections 3 and 4, we prove particular programs terminate using well-founded orderings. In

Section 5, we present a general theorem that encapsulates the technique of using well-founded orderings. In Section 6, we prove a program terminates by using Ramsey theory. In Section 7, we prove a general theorem that encapsulates the technique using Ramsey theory. In Sections 8 and 9, we use Ramsey theory and matrices to prove particular programs terminate, and also state a general theorem that encapsulates the technique. In Sections 10 and 11, we use Ramsey theory and invariants to prove particular programs terminate.

All of the results are about showing particular types of programs can be proven to terminate. In Section 12, we state (without proof) many theorems about particular types of programs for which one can decide if the program terminates.

In Section 13, we discuss informally how much Ramsey theory we need. In particular, in most cases, the transitive Ramsey theorem (which is a weaker version of Ramsey theory) suffices.

In the Appendix, we give some strange examples of programs and the proofs that they terminate, and then give a tutorial on Ramsey's theorem and the transitive Ramsey theorem.

2. NOTATION AND DEFINITIONS

Notation 1.
1. N is the set $\{0,1,2,3,\ldots,\}$.
2. Z is the set of integers $\{\ldots,-2,-1,0,1,2,\ldots\}$.
3. R is the set of reals.

Notation 2.
1. In a program, the command
   $x = \mathbf{Input}(Z)$
   means that x gets an integer provided by the user.
2. More generally, if A is any set, then
   $x = \mathbf{Input}(A)$
   means that x gets a value from A provided by the user.
3. If we represent the set A by listing it out, we will write (for example)
   $x = \mathbf{Input}(y, y + 2, y + 4, y + 6,\ldots)$
   rather than the proper but cumbersome
   $x = \mathbf{Input}(\{y, y + 2, y + 4, y + 6,\ldots\})$

In a program, the command

$(x,y,z) = ($**Input**$(\mathsf{Z}), $**Input**$(\mathsf{N}), $**Input**$(\mathsf{N}))$

means that x gets an integer provided by the user, y gets a natural provided by the user, and z gets a natural provided by the user. One can generalize this to longer vectors of variables.

In a program, the command

$(x,y,z) = (y - z, x + y + z, $**Input**$(\mathsf{Z}))$ means that *simultaneously* x gets $y - z$, y gets $x + y + z$, and z gets an integer provided by the user. One can generalize this to longer vectors of variables and any computable functions of them.

All of the programs we discuss do the following: initially the variables get values supplied by the user, then there is a **While** loop. Within the **While** loop, the user can specify which one of a set of statements get executed through the use of a variable called *control*. We focus on these programs for two reasons: (1) programs of this type are a building block for more complicated programs and (2) programs of this type will illustrate our points well. One drawback is that the programs we present will not do anything of interest.

Example 1.

1. Program 1 does not terminate since the user can set $(x,y,z) = (1,1,1)$ and then keep setting control=3.

2. Let $n, m \in \mathsf{N}$. Let g_i as $1 \le i \le m$ be computable functions from Z^{n+1} to Z^n. These functions are used in Program 2 which is very general. All of the programs in this chapter will essentially be of this type.

$(x,y,z) = ($**Input**$(\mathsf{N}), $**Input**$(\mathsf{N}), $**Input**$(\mathsf{N}))$
While $x > 0$ and $y > 0$ and $z > 0$
    control $= $**Input**$(1,2,3)$
    if control $== 1$
        $(x,y,z) = (x^2 + 10, y - x, z - 10)$
    else
    if control $== 2$
        $(x,y,z) = (y^2 + 17, y - z^2, x - y)$
    else
    if control $== 3$
        $(x,y,z) = (y + 17, xyz, x + y + z)$

Listing 1: Program 1

Comment: X is $(x[1],\ldots,x[n])$
Comment: The g_i are computable functions from Z^{n+1} to Z^n
$X = (\textbf{Input}(Z),\textbf{Input}(Z),\ldots,\textbf{Input}(Z))$
While $x[1] > 0$ and $x[2] > 0$ and $\cdots$ and $x[n] > 0$
  control $= \textbf{Input}(1,2,3,\ldots,m)$
  if control $== 1$
    $X = g_1(X, \textbf{Input}(Z))$
  else
  if control $== 2$
    $X = g_2(X, \textbf{Input}(Z))$
  else

    .

    .

    .

  else
  if control $== m$
    $X = g_m(X,\textbf{Input}(Z))$

Listing 2: Program 2

We define this type of program formally. We call it a *program* though it is actually a program of this restricted type. We also give intuitive comments in parenthesis.

Definition 1.

1. A *program* is a tuple (S, I, R) where the following hold.
   - S is a decidable set of states. (If $(x_1,\ldots, x_n)$ are the variables in a program and they are of types $T_1,\ldots,T_n$, then $S = T_1 \times \cdots \times T_n$.)
   - I is a decidable subset of S. (I is the set of states that the program could be in initially.)
   - $R \subseteq S \times S$ is a decidable set of ordered pairs. ($R(s, t)$ iff s satisfies the condition of the **While** loop and there is some choice of instruction that takes s to t. Note that if s does not satisfy the condition of the **While** loop, then there is no t such that $R(s, t)$. This models the **While** loop termination condition.)

2. A *computation* is a (finite or infinite) sequence of states $s_1, s_2,\ldots$ such that
   - $s_1 \in I$.
   - For all i such that s_i and s_{i+1} exist, $R(s_i, s_{i+1})$.
   - If the sequence is finite and ends in s, then there is no pair in R whose first coordinate is s. Such an s is called *terminal*.

3. A program *terminates* if every computation of it is finite.

4. A *computational segment* is a sequence of states $s_1, s_2, \ldots, s_n$ such that, for all $1 \leq i \leq n - 1$, $R(s_i, s_{i+1})$. Note that we do not insist that $s_1 \in I$ nor do we insist that s_n is a terminal state.

Consider Program 3.

$$(x,y) = (\textbf{Input}(\mathbb{Z}), \textbf{Input}(\mathbb{Z}))$$
While $x > 0$
            control = **Input**(1,2)
            if control $=$ 1
                    $(x,y) = (x + 10, y - 1)$
            else
            if control $=$ 2
                    $(x,y) = (y + 17, x - 2)$

Listing 3: Program 3

Program 3 can be defined as follows:

- $S = I = \mathbb{Z} \times \mathbb{Z}$.
- $R = \{((x,y), (x + 10, y - 1)) : x, y \geq 1\} \bigcup \{((x,y), (y + 17, x - 2)) : x, y \geq 1\}$.

3. A PROOF USING THE ORDER $(\mathbb{N}, \leq)$

We show that every computation of Program 4 terminates. To prove this, we will find a quantity that, during every iteration of the **While** Loop, decreases. None of x, y, z qualify. However, the quantity $x + y + z$ does. We use this in our proof.

$$(x,y,z) = (\textbf{Input}(\mathbb{Z}), \textbf{Input}(\mathbb{Z}), \textbf{Input}(\mathbb{Z}))$$
While $x > 0$ and $y > 0$ and $z > 0$
            control = **Input**(1,2,3)
            if control $=$ 1 then
                    $(x,y,z) = (x + 1, y - 1, z - 1)$
            else
            if control $=$ 2 then
                    $(x,y,z) = (x - 1, y + 1, z - 1)$
            else
            if control $=$ 3 then
                    $(x,y,z) = (x - 1, y - 1, z + 1)$

Listing 4: Program 4

Theorem 1. *Every computation of Program 4 is finite.*
Proof. *Let*

$$f(x,y,z) = \begin{cases} 0 \text{ if any of } x,y,z \text{ are} \leq 0 \\ x+y+z \text{ otherwise} \end{cases} \tag{1}$$

Assume, by way of contradiction, that there is a nonterminating computation.

$$(x_1,y_1,z_1),(x_2,y_2,z_2),\ldots,$$

Before every iteration of the **While** loop, $f(x,y,z) > 0$. After every iteration of the **While** loop, $f(x,y,z)$ has decreased. Hence,

$$f(x_1,y_1,z_1) > f(x_2,y_2,z_2) > \ldots,$$

This is impossible since the range of f is **N**.   ∎

The keys to the proof of Theorem 1 are (1) $x + y + z$ decreases with every iteration and (2) there is no infinite decreasing sequence of naturals. We will later state a general theorem that can be used on any program that satisfies generalizations of those properties.

4. A PROOF USING THE ORDERING ($N \times N \times N \times N$, $<_{\text{lex}}$)

To prove that every computation of Program 5 is finite, we need to find a quantity that, during every iteration of the **While** Loop, decreases. None of x,y,z qualify. No arithmetic combination of w,x,y,z qualifies.

Definition 2. Let P be an order and $k \geq 1$. The *lexicographic order* on P^k is the order

$$(a_1,\ldots,a_k) <_{\text{lex}} (b_1,\ldots,b_k)$$

if for the least i such that $a_i \neq b_i$, $a_i < b_i$.

```
(w,x,y,z) = (Input(Z),Input(Z),Input(Z),Input(Z))
While w > 0 and x > 0 and y > 0 and z > 0
        control = Input(1,2,3)
        if control == 1 then
                x = Input(x + 1,x + 2,...)
                w = w − 1
```

Listing 5: Program 5

(Continued)

```
else
if control == 2 then
        y = Input(y + 1, y + 2, . . .,)
        x = x - 1
else
if control == 3 then
        z = Input(z + 1, z + 2, . . .)
        y = y - 1
```

Listing 5: Program 5—Cont'd

Example 2. In the order $(\mathsf{N}^4, <_{\text{lex}})$

$$(1, 10, 10000000000, 99999999999999) <_{\text{lex}} (1, 11, 0, 0).$$

We leave the following lemma to the reader.

Lemma 1. *If P is an well-founded order and $k \geq 1$, then $(P, <_{\text{lex}})$ is a well-founded order.*

Theorem 2. *Every computation of Program 5 is finite.*

Proof. Assume, by way of contradiction, that there is a nonterminating computation.

$$(w_1, x_1, y_1, z_1), (w_2, x_2, y_2, z_2), \ldots,$$

Let

$$f(w, x, y, z) = \begin{cases} (0, 0, 0, 0) & \text{if any of } w, x, y, z \text{ are } \leq 0 \\ (w, x, y, z) & \text{otherwise} \end{cases} \tag{2}$$

We will be concerned with the order $(\mathsf{N}^4, <_{\text{lex}})$.

Claim 1. In every iteration of the **While** loop, $f(w, x, y, z)$ decreases. ∎

Proof of Claim 1. Consider an iteration of the **While** loop. There are three cases.

1. control=1: w decreases by 1, x increases by an unknown amount, y stays the same, z stays the same. Since the order is lexicographic and w is the first coordinate, the tuple decreases no matter how much x increases.
2. control=2: w stays the same, x decreases by 1, y increases by an unknown amount, z stays the same. Since the order is lexicographic, w is the first coordinate and stays the same, and x is the second coordinate and decreases, the tuple decreases no matter how much y increases.

3. control=3: w stays the same, x stays the same, y decreases by 1, z increases by an unknown amount. This case is similar to the two other cases.   ∎

Before every iteration of the **While** loop, $f(w,x,y,z) > 0$. After every iteration of the **While** loop, $f(w,x,y,z)$ has decreased. Hence,

$$f(w_1,x_1,y_1,z_1) > f(w_1,x_2,y_2,z_2) > \ldots,$$

This is impossible since the range of f if P, and by Lemma 4.3, P has no infinite descending sequences.   ∎

5. A GENERAL THEOREM ABOUT PROVING PROGRAMS TERMINATE USING WELL-FOUNDED ORDERINGS

The proofs of Theorems 1 and 2 look very much alike. There is a general theorem, due to Floyd [10], that captures both of these proofs and many more.

Definition 3. An order T is *well founded* if every nonempty subset has a minimal element. Note that if T is well founded, then there are no infinite descending sequences of elements of T.

Theorem 3. *Let $PROG = (S,I,R)$ be a program. Assume that there is a well-founded order $(P, <_P)$ and a map $f : S \to P$ such that if $R(s,t)$ then $f(t) <_P f(s)$. Then any computation of $PROG$ is finite.*

Proof. Assume the premise holds. We denote $<_P$ by $<$. Assume, by way of contradiction, that the program does not terminate. Then there exists an infinite sequence of states

$$s_1, s_2, s_3, \ldots,$$

such that, for all i, $R(s_i, s_{i+1})$. By the premise on f, we have

$$f(s_1) > f(s_2) > f(s_3) > \cdots$$

This contradicts $<$ being a well-founded order.   ∎

Note 1. It turns out that this theorem is iff. That is, if every computation of $PROG$ is finite, then there is a (perhaps contrived) well order that satisfies the premise.

6. A PROOF USING RAMSEY'S THEOREM

In the proof of Theorem 2, we showed that during every single step of Program 5 the quantity (w,x,y,z) decreased with respect to the order $<_{lex}$. The proof of termination was easy in that we only had to deal with one step but hard in that we had to deal with the lexicographic order on $\mathsf{N} \times \mathsf{N} \times \mathsf{N} \times \mathsf{N}$ rather than just the order N.

In this section, we will prove that Program 5 terminates in a different way. We will not need an order on 4-tuples. We will only deal with $w,x,$ y,z individually. However, we will need to prove that, for *each* finite computational segment, at least one of w,x,y,z decreases.

We will use the infinite Ramsey's theorem. In the Appendix, we will give some history and the proof of Ramsey's theorem. For now we state it and use it.

Notation 3.
1. If $n \geq 1$, then K_n is the complete graph with vertex set $V = \{1,\ldots,n\}$.
2. K_{N} is the complete graph with vertex set N.

Definition 4.
Let $c,n \geq 1$. Let G be K_n or K_{N}. Let COL be a c-coloring of the edges of G. A set of vertices V is *homogeneous with respect to COL* if all the edges between vertices in V are the same color. We will drop the *with respect to COL* if the coloring is understood.

Infinite Ramsey's theorem:

Theorem 4. *Let $c \geq 1$. For every c-coloring of the edges of K_{N}, there exists an infinite homogeneous set.*

Theorem 5. *Every computation of Program 5 is finite.*

Proof. We show Program 5 terminates. Assume, by way of contradiction, that there is an infinite computation. Let this computation be

$$(w_1, x_1, y_1, z_1), (w_2, x_2, y_2, z_2), \ldots.$$

We show that for each finite computational segment one of w,x,y will decrease. Let $i < j$. We look at the finite computational segment

$$(w_i, x_i, y_i, z_i), (w_{i+1}, x_{i+1}, y_{i+1}, z_{i+1}), \ldots, (w_j, x_j, y_j, z_j).$$

There are several cases.

1. If control=1 ever occurs in the segment, then $w_i > w_j$. No other case makes w increase, so we are done. In all later cases, we can assume that control is never 1 in the segment.

2. If control=2 ever occurs in the segment, then $x_i > x_j$. Since control=1 never occurs and control=3 does not make x increase, x decreases and we are done. In all later cases, we can assume that control is never 1 or 2 in the segment.

3. If control=3 is the only case that occurs in the segment, then $y_i > y_j$.

Since in for each finite computational segment one of w,x,y decreases, we have that, for all $i < j$, either $w_i > w_j$ or $x_i > x_j$ or $y_i > y_j$. We use this to create a coloring of the edges of K_N. Our colors are W, X, Y. In the coloring below, each case assumes that the cases above it did not occur.

$$COL(i,j) = \begin{cases} W \text{ if } w_i > w_j; \\ X \text{ if } x_i > x_j; \\ Y \text{ if } y_i > y_j. \end{cases} \qquad (3)$$

By Ramsey's theorem, there is an infinite set

$$i_1 < i_2 < i_3 < \cdots$$

such that

$$COL(i_1, i_2) = COL(i_2, i_3) = \cdots.$$

(We actually know more. We know that *all* pairs (i_j, i_k) have the same color. We do not need this fact here; however, see the second note after Theorem 8.)

Assume the color is W (the cases for X, Y are similar). Then

$$w_{i_1} > w_{i_2} > w_{i_3} > \cdots.$$

Hence, eventually w must be less than 0. When this happens the program terminates. This contradicts the program not terminating. ■

7. A GENERAL THEOREM ABOUT PROVING PROGRAMS TERMINATE USING RAMSEY THEOREM

The keys to the proof of Theorem 5 are (1) in every finite computational segment one of w,x,y decreases, and (2) by Ramsey's theorem any nonterminating computation leads to an infinite decreasing sequence in a well-founded set. These ideas are from Theorem 1 of [5], though similar ideas were in [9].

Theorem 1 of [5] is a very general statement about program termination. We present three theorems in increasing order of generality. The last one is Theorem 1 of [5].

Theorem 6. *Let* $PROG = (S,I,R)$ *be a program of the form of Program 2. Note that the variables are* $x[1],\ldots,x[n]$. *Assume that for each computational segment* $t_1,\ldots,t_L$ *there exists a* $1 \leq k \leq m$ *such that* $x[k]$ *in* t_1 *is strictly less than* $x[k]$ *in* t_L. *Then any computation of PROG is finite.*

Proof. We show Program (S,I,R) terminates. Assume, by way of contradiction, that there is an infinite computation. Let this computation be

$$s_1, s_2, s_3, \ldots$$

where each s_i is an n-tuple of values for $(x[1],\ldots,x[n])$.

By the premise, for every $i < j$, in the finite computational segment

$$s_i, s_{i+1}, \ldots, s_j$$

there is a k such that $x[k]$ in s_i is less than $x[k]$ in s_j.

We use this to create a coloring of the edges of K_N. Our colors are $\{1,\ldots,m\}$. $COL(i,j)$ is the least index k such that $x[k]$ in s_i is greater than $x[k]$ in s_j.

By Ramsey's theorem, there is an infinite set

$$i_1 < i_2 < i_3 < \cdots$$

and a color L such that

$$L = COL(i_1, i_2) = COL(i_2, i_3) = \cdots.$$

Hence, the value of $x[L]$ in s_1 is larger than it is in s_2 is larger than it is in s_3, etc. This means that there is a time when the value of $x[L]$ is ≤ 0. Hence, the program terminates. This is a contradiction. ∎

To prove that a program terminates, we might use some function of the variables rather than the variables themselves. The next theorem, which is a generalization of Theorem 6, captures this.

Theorem 7. *Let* $PROG = (S,I,R)$ *be a program of the form of Program 2. Note that the variables are* $x[1],\ldots,x[n]$. *We denote the vector of variables by* $\vec{x}$. *Assume there exists functions* $f_1(\vec{x}), \ldots, f_M(\vec{x})$ *with range* $\mathbb{N}$ *such that the following holds:*

For each computational segment $t_1, \ldots, t_L$, there exists a $1 \leq k \leq M$ such that $f_k(\vec{x})$ in t_1 is strictly less than $f_k(\vec{x})$ in t_L. Then any computation of PROG is finite.

Proof Sketch. This proof is virtually identical to the proof of Theorem 6. The only difference comes toward the end, so we do the last few lines.

$COL(i,j)$ is the least index k such that $f(\vec{x})$ in s_i is greater than $f(\vec{x})$ in s_j. By Ramsey's theorem, there is an infinite set

$$i_1 < i_2 < i_3 < \cdots$$

and a color L such that

$$L = COL(i_1, i_2) = COL(i_2, i_3) = \cdots.$$

Hence, the value of $f_L(\vec{x})$ in s_1 is larger than it is in s_2 is larger than it is in s_3, etc. This means that there is a time when the value of $f_L(\vec{x})$ is ≤ -1. This is a contradiction since f has range **N**.

In the statement of Theorem 7, the functions f mapped to the natural numbers. What was it about the natural numbers that we used? At first glance it seems like we only use that $-1 \notin$ **N**. However, we really used that **N** is well founded. This leads to a more general theorem.

Theorem 8. *Let $PROG = (S, I, R)$ be a program of the form of Program 2. Note that the variables are $x[1], \ldots, x[n]$. We denote the vector of variables by $\vec{x}$. Assume there exists functions $f_1(\vec{x}), \ldots, f_M(\vec{x})$ such that f_i has range P_i where P_i is a well-founded set. For each computational segment $t_1, \ldots, t_n$, there exists a $1 \leq k \leq M$ such that $f_k(\vec{x})$ in t_1 is strictly less than (using the order P_k) $f_k(\vec{x})$ in t_n. Then any computation of PROG is finite.*

Proof Sketch. This proof is virtually identical to the proof of Theorem 6. The only difference comes toward the end, so we do the last few lines.

$COL(i,j)$ is the least index k such that $f(\vec{x})$ in s_i is greater than (using the order P_k) $f(\vec{x})$ in s_j.

By Ramsey's theorem, there is an infinite set

$$i_1 < i_2 < i_3 < \cdots$$

and a color L such that

$$L = COL(i_1, i_2) = COL(i_2, i_3) = \cdots.$$

Hence, the value of $f_L(\vec{x})$ in s_1 is larger (using the order P_k) than it is in s_2 is larger than (using the order P_k) it is in s_3, etc. Hence, we have an infinite decreasing sequence in P_k. This is a contradiction since P_k is a well-founded ordering.

Note 2. It turns out that this theorem is iff. That is, if every computation of *PROG* is finite, then there are (perhaps contrived) functions f_i and well-founded orderings P_i as stated in Theorem 8. This is the actual statement of Theorem 1 of [5].

Note 3. The proofs of Theorems 5, 6, and 8 do not need the full strength of Ramsey's theorem. Consider Theorem 6. For any i, j, k if $COL(i, j) = a$ (so a is the least number such that $x[a]$ in s_i is greater than $x[a]$ in s_j), $COL(j, k) = a$ (so a is the least number such that $x[a]$ in s_j is greater than $x[a]$ in s_k), one can show $COL(i, k) = a$. Such colorings are called *transitive*. Hence, we only need Ramsey's theorem for transitive colorings. We discuss this further in Section 13.

8. A PROOF USING MATRICES AND RAMSEY'S THEOREM

Part of the proof of Theorem 5 involved showing that, for any finite computational segment of Program 5, one of w, x, y, z decreases. Can such proofs be automated?

Ben-Amram [15] developed a way to partially automate such proofs. He uses matrices and Ramsey's theorem. An earlier version by Lee *et al.* [9] used size-change graphs instead of matrices. We discuss the difference later.

We use Ben-Amram's matrix techniques to give a proof that Program 5 terminates. We will then discuss their general technique.

Program 5 has variables w, x, y, z. To use Theorem 6 on it, we need to know that in every finite computational segment one of these variables decreases. We would rather reason about what happens during one step. Let us capture what we do know about one step.

If control=1, then

$$
\begin{aligned}
w &= w - 1 \\
x &= \mathbf{Input}(x + 1, x + 2, \ldots) \\
y &= y \\
z &= z
\end{aligned}
$$

We represent this by a matrix. The rows and columns are both indexed by the variables, so it will be a four by four matrix. In the (say) (w, y) entry, we put the difference between the new y and the old w. If we do not know the difference, we put ∞ (this will happen most of the time). It is easy to see that the matrix is:

$$C_1 = \begin{pmatrix} -1 & \infty & \infty & \infty \\ \infty & \infty & \infty & \infty \\ \infty & \infty & 0 & \infty \\ \infty & \infty & \infty & 0 \end{pmatrix}$$

The matrix for control=2 is

$$C_2 = \begin{pmatrix} 0 & \infty & \infty & \infty \\ \infty & -1 & \infty & \infty \\ \infty & \infty & \infty & \infty \\ \infty & \infty & \infty & 0 \end{pmatrix}$$

The matrix for control=3 is

$$C_3 = \begin{pmatrix} 0 & \infty & \infty & \infty \\ \infty & 0 & \infty & \infty \\ \infty & \infty & -1 & \infty \\ \infty & \infty & \infty & \infty \end{pmatrix}$$

Clearly if the program executes any one of these commands, then some variable decreases. In terms of the matrices, this means that some entry on the diagonal is negative.

We need that any finite sequence of instructions leads to some variable decrease. We want to express any finite sequence of instructions as a matrix. How?

Definition 5. If A and B are $n \times n$ matrices, then we define (just for this chapter) the product AB in the following (nonstandard) way:

$$AB[i,j] = \min_{1 \leq k \leq n} \{a_{ik} + b_{kj}\}.$$

By convention, for any $x \in \mathbb{N} \cup \{\infty\}$, $\infty + x = x + \infty = \infty$.

We leave the proof of the following easy lemma to the reader.

Lemma 2. Let $\vec{x}$ be variables and $g_1(\vec{x})$, $g_2(\vec{x})$ be computable functions. Let $PROG_1$ be the short program $\vec{x} = g_1(\vec{x})$. Let $PROG_2$ be the short program $\vec{x} = g_2(\vec{x})$. (We think of $PROG_1$ and $PROG_2$ as being what happens in the various control cases.) Let C_1 be the matrix that represents what is known whenever $PROG_1$ is executed. Let C_2 be the matrix that represents what is known whenever $PROG_2$ is executed. Then the matrix product $C_1 C_2$ as defined above represents what is known when $PROG_1$ and then $PROG_2$ are executed.

Hence, every finite sequence of instructions corresponds to some finite product of C_1's, C_2's, and C_3's. In the case at hand, we need to only show that every such product has a negative number on some diagonal. We state this in general.

Theorem 9. *Let* $PROG = (S,I,R)$ *be a program in the form of Program 2. Let* $C_1, C_2, \ldots, C_m$ *be the matrices associated to control=1, $\ldots$, control=m cases. If every product of the C_i's yields a matrix with a negative integer on the diagonal, then the program terminates.*

Proof. Consider computational segment $s_1, \ldots, s_n$. Let the corresponding matrices be $C_{i_1}, \ldots, C_{i_n}$. By the premise, the product of these matrices has a negative integer on the diagonal. Hence, some variable decreases. By Theorem 6, the program terminates. ∎

Note 4. Lee *et al.* used size–change graphs rather than matrices. Their results can be interpreted as matrices where, instead of having the difference, you have whether or not the (say) old y is bigger than the old x, or smaller, or unknown. [9]

In the case at hand, it may seem difficult to show that *every* product C_1's, C_2's, and C_3's has a negative number on the diagonal. However, we can show this:

Theorem 10. *Every computation of Program 5 is finite.*

Proof. Let C_1, C_2, C_3 be the matrices that represent the cases of Control=1,2,3 in Program 5. (These matrices are above.) We show that the premise of Theorem 9 holds. To do this, we prove items 0–7 below. Item 0 is easily proven directly. Items 1,2,3,4,5,6,7 are easily proven by induction on the number of matrices being multiplied.

0. $C_1 C_2 = C_2 C_1,\ C_1 C_3 = C_3 C_1,\ C_2 C_3 = C_3 C_2.$
1. For all $a \geq 1$,

$$C_1^a = \begin{pmatrix} -a & \infty & \infty & \infty \\ \infty & \infty & \infty & \infty \\ \infty & \infty & 0 & \infty \\ \infty & \infty & \infty & 0 \end{pmatrix}$$

2. For all $b \geq 1$,

$$C_2^b = \begin{pmatrix} 0 & \infty & \infty & \infty \\ \infty & -b & \infty & \infty \\ \infty & \infty & \infty & \infty \\ \infty & \infty & \infty & 0 \end{pmatrix}$$

3. For all $c \geq 1$,

$$C_3^c = \begin{pmatrix} 0 & \infty & \infty & \infty \\ \infty & 0 & \infty & \infty \\ \infty & \infty & -c & \infty \\ \infty & \infty & \infty & \infty \end{pmatrix}$$

4. For all $a,b \geq 1$,

$$C_1^a C_2^b = \begin{pmatrix} -a & \infty & \infty & \infty \\ \infty & -b & \infty & \infty \\ \infty & \infty & 0 & \infty \\ \infty & \infty & \infty & 0 \end{pmatrix}$$

5. For all $a,c \geq 1$,

$$C_1^a C_3^c = \begin{pmatrix} -a & \infty & \infty & \infty \\ \infty & 0 & \infty & \infty \\ \infty & \infty & -c & \infty \\ \infty & \infty & \infty & \infty \end{pmatrix}$$

6. For all $b,c \geq 1$,

$$C_2^b C_3^c = \begin{pmatrix} 0 & \infty & \infty & \infty \\ \infty & -b & \infty & \infty \\ \infty & \infty & \infty & \infty \\ \infty & \infty & \infty & \infty \end{pmatrix}$$

7. For $a,b,c \geq 1$,

$$C_1^a C_2^b C_3^c = \begin{pmatrix} -a & \infty & \infty & \infty \\ \infty & \infty & \infty & \infty \\ \infty & \infty & \infty & \infty \\ \infty & \infty & \infty & 0 \end{pmatrix}$$

Since the multiplication of these matrices is commutative, we need only concern ourselves with $C_1^a C_2^b C_3^c$ for $a,b,c \in \mathbb{N}$. In all of the cases below, $a,b,c \geq 1$.

1. C_1^a: w decreases.
2. C_2^b: x decreases.
3. C_3^c: y decreases.
4. $C_1^a C_2^b$: Both w and x decrease.
5. $C_1^a C_3^c$: Both w and y decrease.
6. $C_2^b C_3^c$: x decreases.
7. $C_1^a C_2^b C_3^c$: w decreases. ∎

The keys to the proof of Theorem 10 (1) represent how the old and new variables relate after one iteration with a matrix, (2) use these matrices and a type of matrix multiplication to determine that for every finite computational segment some variable decreases, and (3) use Theorem 6 to conclude the program terminates.

Theorem 9 leads to the following algorithm to test if a program terminates. There is one step (alas, the important one) which we do not say how to do. If done in the obvious way, it may not halt.

1. Input Program P.
2. Form matrices for all the cases of control. Let them be $C_1, \ldots, C_m$.
3. Find a finite set of types of matrices $\mathcal{M}$ such that any product of the C_i's (allowing repeats) is in $\mathcal{M}$. (If this step is implemented by looking at all possible products until a pattern emerges, then this step might not terminate.)
4. If all of the elements of $\mathcal{M}$ have some negative diagonal element, then output *YES the program terminates!*
5. If not, then output *I DO NOT KNOW if the program terminates!*

If all products of matrices fit a certain pattern, as they did in the proof of Theorem 10, then this idea for an algorithm will terminate. Even in that case, it may output *I DO NOT KNOW if the program terminates!* However, this algorithm can be used to prove that some programs terminate, just not all. It cannot be used to prove that a program will not terminate.

The premise of Theorem 9 is designed so that we can apply Theorem 6. Hence, we are only looking at the variables of the program and the natural numbers. We generalize Theorem 9 so it feeds into Theorem 7. We omit the proof which is similar to that of Theorem 9.

Let $PROG = (S, I, R)$ be a program in the form of Program 2. Note that the variables are $x[1], \ldots, x[n]$. We denote the vector of variables by $\vec{x}$. Let functions $f_1(\vec{x}), \ldots, f_M(\vec{x})$ have range N. We can now form $k \times k$ matrices $C_1, \ldots, C_m$ such that matrix $C_L[i, j]$ is the difference between the new $f_j(\vec{x})$ and the old $f_i(\vec{x})$.

Theorem 11. *Let $PROG = (S, I, R)$ be a program in the form of Program 2. Note that the variables are $x[1], \ldots, x[n]$. We denote the vector of variables by $\vec{x}$. Let functions $f_1(\vec{x}), \ldots, f_M(\vec{x})$ have range N. Assume that $C_1, \ldots, C_m$ are the matrices associated to them as noted above. If every product of the matrices has a negative number on the diagonal, then the program terminates.*

Is there a further generalization of Theorem 9 that feeds into Theorem 8. Recall in the premise of Theorem 8 the functions f have range in some well-founded order. The matrices we work with deal with differences. Since the different f's in Theorem 8 have ranges in different well-founded orders, we cannot take their difference. What if we require that the f's all have the same well-founded order as their range? This still does not work since some well-founded order (e.g., $(N \times N, <_{lex})$) do not have a notion of difference. The approach of Lee *et al.* that used size-change graphs instead of matrices (see note after Theorem 9) might work here.

$$(x,y) = (\textbf{Input}(Z),\textbf{Input}(Z))$$
While $x > 0$ and $y > 0$
$\qquad$ control $= \textbf{Input}(1,2)$
$\qquad$ if control $== 1$ then
$\qquad\qquad (x,y) = (x - 1,x)$
$\qquad$ else
$\qquad$ if control $== 2$ then
$\qquad\qquad (x,y) = (y - 2,x + 1)$

Listing 6: Program 6

9. ANOTHER PROOF USING MATRICES AND RAMSEY'S THEOREM

We prove Program 6 terminates using matrices. The case control$=1$ is represented by the matrix

$$C_1 = \begin{pmatrix} -1 & 0 \\ \infty & \infty \end{pmatrix}.$$

The case control$=2$ is represented by the matrix

$$C_2 = \begin{pmatrix} \infty & -2 \\ 1 & \infty \end{pmatrix}.$$

This will not work! Note that C_2 has no negative numbers on its diagonal. Hence, we cannot use these matrices in our proof! What will we do? Instead of using x,y, we will use x,y, and $x + y$. We comment on whether or not you can somehow use C_1 and C_2 after the proof.

Theorem 12. *Every computation of Program 6 is finite.*

Proof. We will use Theorem 11 with functions x, y, and $x + y$. Note that $x + y$ is not one of the original variables which is why we need Theorem 11 rather than Theorem 9.

The control=1 case of Program 6 corresponds to

$$D_1 = \begin{pmatrix} -1 & 0 & 1 \\ \infty & \infty & \infty \\ \infty & \infty & \infty \end{pmatrix}$$

The control=2 case of Program 6 corresponds to

$$D_2 = \begin{pmatrix} \infty & 1 & \infty \\ -2 & \infty & \infty \\ \infty & \infty & -1 \end{pmatrix}$$

We show that the premises of Theorem 11 hold. The following are true and easily proven by induction on the number of matrices being multiplied.

1. For all $a \geq 1$,

$$D_1^a = \begin{pmatrix} -a & -a+1 & -a+2 \\ \infty & \infty & \infty \\ \infty & \infty & \infty \end{pmatrix}$$

2. For all $b \geq 1$, b odd, $b = 2d - 1$,

$$D_2^b = \begin{pmatrix} -d & \infty & \infty \\ \infty & -d & \infty \\ \infty & \infty & -2d \end{pmatrix}$$

3. For all $b \geq 2$, b even, $b = 2e$,

$$D_2^b = \begin{pmatrix} \infty & -e+1 & \infty \\ -e-2 & \infty & \infty \\ \infty & \infty & -2e-1 \end{pmatrix}$$

4. For all $a, b \geq 1$, b odd, $b = 2d - 1$,

$$D_1^a D_2^b = \begin{pmatrix} -a-d & -a-d+1 & -a-2d+2 \\ \infty & \infty & \infty \\ \infty & \infty & \infty \end{pmatrix}$$

5. For all $a,b \geq 1$, b even, $b = 2e$,

$$D_1^a D_2^b = \begin{pmatrix} -a-e-1 & -a-e+1 & -a-2e+1 \\ \infty & \infty & \infty \\ \infty & \infty & \infty \end{pmatrix}$$

6. For all $a,b \geq 1$, a is odd,

$$D_2^a D_1^b = \begin{pmatrix} \infty & \infty & \infty \\ -(\lfloor a/2 \rfloor + b + 2) & -(\lfloor a/2 \rfloor + b + 1) & -(\lfloor a/2 \rfloor + b) \\ \infty & \infty & \infty \end{pmatrix}$$

7. If $a,b \geq 1$, a is even,

$$D_2^a D_1^b = \begin{pmatrix} -(a/2) + b & -(a/2) + b - 1 & -\lfloor a/2 \rfloor + b - 2 \\ \infty & \infty & \infty \\ \infty & \infty & \infty \end{pmatrix}$$

We use this information to formulate a lemma.

Convention. If we put < 0 (≤ 0) in an entry of a matrix, it means that the entry is some integer less than 0 (less than or equal to 0). We might not know what it is.

Claim. For all $n \geq 2$, any product of n matrices all of which are D_1's and D_2's must be of one of the following types:

1.

$$\begin{pmatrix} <0 & \leq 0 & \leq 0 \\ \infty & \infty & \infty \\ \infty & \infty & \infty \end{pmatrix}$$

2.

$$\begin{pmatrix} \infty & \infty & \infty \\ <0 & <0 & <0 \\ \infty & \infty & \infty \end{pmatrix}$$

3.

$$\begin{pmatrix} <0 & \infty & \infty \\ \infty & <0 & \infty \\ \infty & \infty & <0 \end{pmatrix}$$

4.

$$\begin{pmatrix} \infty & <0 & \infty \\ <0 & \infty & \infty \\ \infty & \infty & <0 \end{pmatrix}$$

This can be proved easily by induction on n. ∎

One can show that every computation of Program 6 terminates using the original matrices, 2×2 matrices C_1, C_2. Ben-Amram has done this and has allowed us to place his proof in the Appendix of this chapter.

10. A PROOF USING TRANSITION INVARIANTS AND RAMSEY'S THEOREM

We present an example from Ref. [5] of a program (Program 6) where the proof of termination using Ramsey's theorem is obtained by using transition invariants (to be defined). Podelski and Rybalchenko found this proof by hand and later their termination checker found it automatically. A proof of termination using a well-founded order seems difficult to find. Ben-Amram and Lee [16, 8] have shown that a termination proof that explicitly exhibits a well-founded order can be automatically derived when the matrices only use entries $0, -1$, and ∞. Alas, Program 6 is not of this type; however, using some manipulation Ben-Amram (unpublished) has used this result to show that Program 6 terminates. (The proof is in the Appendix.) Hence, there is a proof that Program 6 terminates that uses a well-founded order; however, it was difficult to obtain.

Theorem 13. *Every computation of Program 6 is finite.*

Proof. We assume that the computational segment enters the **While** loop, else the program has already terminated.

We could try to show that, in each finite computational segment, either x or y decreases. This statement is true but seems hard to prove directly. Instead we show that either x or y or $x + y$ decreases. This turns out to be easier. Intuitively we are loading our induction hypothesis. We now proceed formally.

We show that the premises of Theorem 7 hold with $f_1(x,y) = x$, $f_2(x,y) = y$, and $f_3(x,y) = x + y$. It may seem as if knowing that $x + y$ decreases you know that either x or y decreases. However, in our proof, we will *not* know which of x, y decreases. Hence, we must use x, y, and $x + y$.

Claim 2. For each finite computational segment, one of $x, y, x+y$ decreases.

Proof of Claim 2. We want to prove that, for all $n \geq 2$, for each computational segment of length n

$$(x_1, y_1), (x_2, y_2), \ldots, (x_n, y_n),$$

either $x_1 > x_n$ or $y_1 > y_n$ or $x_1 + y_1 > x_n + y_n$. However, we will prove something stronger. We will prove that, for all $n \geq 2$, for each computational segment of length n

$$(x_1, y_1), (x_2, y_2), \ldots, (x_n, y_n),$$

one of the following occurs.
(1) $x_1 > 0$ and $y_1 > 0$ and $x_n < x_1$ and $y_n \leq x_1$ (so x decreases),
(2) $x_1 > 0$ and $y_1 > 0$ and $x_n < y_1 - 1$ and $y_n \leq x_1 + 1$ (so $x + y$ decreases),
(3) $x_1 > 0$ and $y_1 > 0$ and $x_n < y_1 - 1$ and $y_n < y_1$ (so y decreases),
(4) $x_1 > 0$ and $y_1 > 0$ and $x_n < x_1$ and $y_n < y_1$ (so x and y both decrease, though we just need one of them).

(We will later refer to the OR of these four statements as *the invariant*.)
We prove this by induction on n.
Base Case: $n = 2$ so we only look at one instruction.
If $(x_2, y_2) = (x_1 - 1, x_1)$ is executed, then (1) holds.
If $(x_2, y_2) = (y_1 - 2, x_1 + 1)$ is executed, then (2) holds.
Induction Step: We prove Claim 1 for $n + 1$ assuming it for n. There are four cases, each with two subcases.
1. $x_n < x_1$ and $y_n \leq x_1$.
    (a) If $(x_{n+1}, y_{n+1}) = (x_n - 1, x_n)$ is executed, then
       • $x_{n+1} = x_n - 1 < x_1 - 1 < x_1$
       • $y_{n+1} = x_n < x_1$
    Hence, (1) holds.
    (b) If $(x_{n+1}, y_{n+1}) = (y_n - 2, x_n + 1)$ is executed, then
       • $x_{n+1} = y_n - 2 \leq x_1 - 2 < x_1$
       • $y_{n+1} = x_n + 1 \leq x_1$
    Hence, (1) holds.
2. $x_n < y_1 - 1$ and $y_n \leq x_1 + 1$
    (a) If $(x_{n+1}, y_{n+1}) = (x_n - 1, x_n)$ is executed, then
       • $x_{n+1} = x_n - 1 < y_1 - 2 < y_1 - 1$
       • $y_{n+1} = x_n < y_1 - 1 < y_1$
    Hence, (3) holds.

(b) If $(x_{n+1}, y_{n+1}) = (y_n - 2, x_n + 1)$ is executed, then

- $x_{n+1} = y_n - 2 \leq x_1 - 1 < x_1$
- $y_{n+1} = x_n < y_1$

Hence, (4) holds.

3. $x_n < y_1 - 1$ and $y_n < y_1$

   (a) If $(x_{n+1}, y_{n+1}) = (x_n - 1, x_n)$ is executed, then

- $x_{n+1} = x_n - 1 < y_1 - 2 < y_1 - 1$
- $y_{n+1} = x_n < y_1 - 1 < y_1$.

Hence, (3) holds.

   (b) If $(x_{n+1}, y_{n+1}) = (y_n - 2, x_n + 1)$ is executed, then

- $x_{n+1} = y_n - 2 < y_1 - 2 < y_1 - 1$
- $y_{n+1} = x_n < y_1 - 1 < y_1$

Hence, (3) holds.

4. $x_n < x_1$ and $y_n < y_1$

   (a) If $(x_{n+1}, y_{n+1}) = (x_n - 1, x_n)$ is executed, then

- $x_{n+1} = x_n - 1 < x_1 - 1 < x_1$
- $y_{n+1} = x_n < x_1$

Hence, (1) holds.

   (b) If $(x_{n+1}, y_{n+1}) = (y_n - 2, x_n + 1)$ is executed, then

- $x_{n+1} = y_n - 2 < y_1 - 2 < y_1 - 1$.
- $y_{n+1} = x_n < x_1 < x_1 + 1$.

Hence, (2) holds.

We now have that, for each finite computational segment either x, y, or $x + y$ decreases.

The following claim is obvious.

Claim 3. If any of $x, y, x + y$ is 0, then the program terminates.

By Claims 1 and 3, the premise of Theorem 7 is satisfied. Hence, Program 6 terminates. ∎

Consider the following four orderings on $\mathsf{N} \times \mathsf{N}$ and the OR of them.

- T_1 is the ordering $(x', y') <_1 (x, y)$ iff $x > 0$ and $y > 0$ and $x' < x$ and $y' \leq x$.
- T_2 is the ordering $(x', y') <_2 (x, y)$ iff $x > 0$ and $y > 0$ and $x' < y - 1$ and $y' \leq x + 1$.
- T_3 is the ordering $(x', y') <_3 (x, y)$ iff $x > 0$ and $y > 0$ and $x' < y - 1$ and $y' < y$.
- T_4 is the ordering $(x', y') <_4 (x, y)$ iff $x > 0$ and $y > 0$ and $x' < x$ and $y' < y$.
- $T = T_1 \cup T_2 \cup T_3 \cup T_4$. We denote this order by $<_T$.

Note that (1) each T_i is well founded and (2) for each computational segment

$$(x_1, y_1), (x_2, y_2), \ldots, (x_n, y_n)$$

we have $(x_1, y_1) <_T (x_n, y_n)$

It is easy to see that these properties of T are all we needed in the proof. This is Theorem 1 of [5] which we state and prove.

Definition 6. Let $PROG = (S, I, R)$ be a program.

1. An ordering T, which we also denote $<_T$, on $S \times S$ is *transition invariant* if for each computational segment $s_1, \ldots, s_n$ we have $s_n <_T s_1$.
2. An ordering T is *disjunctive well founded* if there exists well-founded orderings $T_1, \ldots, T_k$ such that $T = T_1 \cup \cdots \cup T_k$. Note that the T_i need not be total orderings, they need only be well founded. This will come up in the proof of Theorem 15.

Theorem 14. *[5] Let $PROG = (S, I, R)$ be a program. If there exists a disjunctive well-founded transition invariant, then every run of $PROG$ terminates.*

Proof. Let $T = T_1 \cup \cdots \cup T_k$ be the disjunctive well-founded transition invariant for $PROG$. Let $<_c$ be the ordering for T_c.

Assume, by way of contradiction, that there is an infinite sequence $s_1, s_2, s_3, \ldots$, such that each $(s_i, s_{i+1}) \in R$. Define a coloring COL by, for $i < j$,

$$COL(i, j) = \text{the least } L \text{ such that } s_j <_L s_i.$$

By Ramsey's theorem, there is an infinite set

$$i_1 < i_2 < i_3 < \cdots$$

such that

$$COL(i_1, i_2) = COL(i_2, i_3) = \cdots.$$

Let that color be L. For notational readability, we denote $<_L$ by $<$ and $>_L$ by $>$. We have

$$s_{i_1} > s_{i_2} > \cdots >$$

This contradicts $<$ being well founded.   ■

Note 5. It turns out that this theorem is iff. That is, if every computation of $PROG$ is finite, then there is a (perhaps contrived) transition invariant.

Finding an appropriate T is the key to the proofs of termination for the termination checkers Loopfrog and Terminator.

The proof of Theorem 14 seems to need the full strength of Ramsey's theorem (unlike the proofs of Theorems 6, 7, and 8, see the note following its proof). In the Appendix, we give an example, due to Ben-Amram, of a program with a disjunctive well-founded transition invariant where the coloring is not transitive.

If in the premise of Theorem 14 all of the T_i's are total (that is, every pair of elements is comparable), then the transitive Ramsey theorem suffices for the proof.

11. ANOTHER PROOF USING TRANSITION INVARIANTS AND RAMSEY'S THEOREM

Showing Program 7 terminates seems easy: eventually y is negative and after that point x will steadily decrease until $x < 0$. But this proof might be hard for a termination checker to find since x might increases for a very long time. Instead we need to find the right disjunctive well-founded transition invariant.

$(x,y) = (\textbf{Input}(\mathbb{Z}), \textbf{Input}(\mathbb{Z}))$
While $x > 0$
$$(x,y) = (x + y, y - 1)$$

Listing 7: Program 7

Theorem 15. *Every run of Program 7 terminates.*

Proof. We define orderings T_1 and T_2 which we also denote $<_1$ and $<_2$.
- $(x',y') <_1 (x,y)$ iff $0 < x' < x$.
- $(x',y') <_2 (x,y)$ iff $0 \le y' < y$.
Let
$$T = T_1 \cup T_2.$$

Clearly T_1 and T_2 are well founded (though see note after the proof). Hence, T is disjunctive well founded. We show that T is a transition invariant.

We want to prove that, for all $n \ge 2$, for each computational segment of length n

$$(x_1, y_1), (x_2, y_2), \ldots, (x_n, y_n)$$

either $(x_n, y_n) <_1 (x_1, y_1)$ or $(x_n, y_n) <_2 (x_1, y_1)$.

We illustrate this with an example. Say $(x_1,y_1) = (5,4)$. Then the computation will initially look like this:

$$(5,4),(9,3),(12,2),(14,1),(15,0)$$

This looks odd since x is increasing and we want it to be 0. But note that

$$(5,4)>_2(9,3)>_2(12,2)>_2(14,1)>_2(15,0)$$

so the pairs are decreasing in the $<_2$ ordering.
After that the computation looks like this:

$$(15,-1),(14,-2),(12,-3),(9,-4),(5,-5),(0,-6)$$

At this point the computation terminates. We note that

$$(15,-1)>_1(14,-2)>_1(12,-3)>_1(9,-4)>_1(5,-5)>_1(0,-6)$$

Hence, in this part of the computation, the pairs decrease in the $<_1$ ordering. Hence, the every step of the computation decreases in the T ordering.
By splitting the computational segment

$$(x_1,y_1),(x_2,y_2),\ldots,(x_n,y_n)$$

into two parts depending on if y is ≥ 0 or $y < 0$ we can show that either $(x_1,y_1) >_1 (x_n,y_n)$ or $(x_1,y_1) >_2(x_n,y_n)$, so $(x_1,y_1) >_T(x_n,y_n)$. Hence, we can apply Theorem 8 to conclude that the program terminates.   ∎

T_1 and T_2 are *partial orders* not *total orders*. In fact, for both T_1 and T_2 there are an infinite number of minimal elements. In particular,
- the minimal elements for T_1 are $\{(x,y) : x \leq 0\}$ and
- the minimal elements for T_2 are $\{(x,y) : y < 0\}$.

Recall that the definition of a transition invariant, Definition 6, allows partial orders. We see here that this is useful.

12. SOLVING SUBCASES OF THE TERMINATION PROBLEM

The problem of determining if a program is terminating is unsolvable. This problem is *not* the traditional Halting problem since we allow the program to have a potentially infinite number of user-supplied inputs.

Definition 7.

1. Let $M_1^{(\cdots)}, M_2^{(\cdots)}, \ldots$ be a standard list of oracle Turing machines. These Turing machines take input in two ways: (1) the standard way, on a tape, and (2) we interpret the oracle as the user-supplied inputs.

2. If $A \subseteq N$ and $s \in N$ then $M_{i,s}^A \downarrow$ means that if you run M_i^A (no input on the tape) it will halt within s steps.

3. Let $M_1^{(\cdots)}, M_2^{(\cdots)}, \ldots$ be a standard list of oracle Turing machines.

$$TERM = \{i : (\forall A)(\exists s)[M_{i,s}^A \downarrow]\}.$$

Definition 8.

1. If A and B are subsets of N, then $A \leq_m B$ means that there is a computable function f such that $x \in A$ iff $f(x) \in B$. (The m is a historical anachronism—it means that f may be many-to-one. There was also a definition $\leq_1$ where we insist f be one-to-one. We do not care anymore, and I personally wonder why anyone ever did.)

2. $X \in \Pi_1^1$ if there exists an oracle Turing machine $M^{(\cdots)}$ such that

$$X = \{x : (\forall A)(\exists x_1)(\forall x_2)\cdots(Q_n x_n)[M^A(x, x_1, \ldots, x_n) = 1]\}.$$

(Q_n is a quantifier.)

3. A set X is Π_1^1-complete if $X \in \Pi_1^1$ and, for all $Y \in \Pi_1^1$, $Y \leq_m X$.

The following were proven by Kleene [17, 18] (see also [19]).

Theorem 16.

1. $X \in \Pi_1^1$ *if there exists an oracle Turing machine* $M^{(\cdots)}$ *such that*

$$X = \{x : (\forall A)(\exists y)[M^A(x, y) = 1]\}.$$

2. *TERM is* Π_1^1*-complete.*

3. *If X is* Π_1^1*-complete, then, for all Y in the arithmetic hierarchy, $Y \leq_m X$.*

4. *For all Y in the arithmetic hierarchy, $Y \leq_m TERM$. This follows from (2) and (3). (See Definition 13 for the definition of the arithmetic Hierarchy.)*

Hence, *TERM* is much harder than the halting problem. Therefore, it will be very interesting to see if some subcases of it are decidable.

Definition 9. Let $n \in N$. Let *FUN(n)* be a set of computable functions from Z^{n+1} to Z^n. Let $m \in N$. An $(F(n), m)$ *program* is a program of the form of Program 2 where the functions g_i used in Program 7 are all in *FUN(n)*.

Open Question. For which *FUN(n),m* is the Termination problem restricted to $(FUN(n), m)$ programs decidable?

We list all results we know. Some are not quite in our framework. Some of the results use the **While** loop condition $Mx \geq b$ where M is a matrix and b is a vector. Such programs can easily be transformed into programs of our form.

1. Tiwari [20] has shown that the following problem is decidable: Given matrices A, B and vector c, all over the rationals, is Program 8 in $TERM$. Note that the user is inputting a real.

   $x = \mathbf{Input}(\mathbb{R})$
   while $(Bx > b)$
   $\qquad x = Ax + c$

   Listing 8: Program 8

2. Braverman [21] has shown that the following problem is decidable: Given matrices A, B_1, B_2 and vectors b_1, b_2, c, all over the rationals, is Program 9 in $TERM$. Note that the user is inputting a real.

   $x = \mathbf{Input}(\mathbb{R})$
   while $(B_1 x > b_1)$ and $(B_2 x \geq b_2)$
   $\qquad x = Ax + c$

   Listing 9: Program 9

3. Ben-Amram *et al.* [22] have shown that the following problem is undecidable: Given matrices A_0, A_1, B and vector v all over the integers, and $i \in \mathbb{N}$ does Program 10 terminate.

   $x = \mathbf{Input}(\mathbb{Z})$
   while $(Bx \geq b)$
   $\qquad$ if $x[i] \geq 0$
   $\qquad\qquad$ then $x = A_0 x$
   $\qquad$ else
   $\qquad\qquad x = A_1 x$

   Listing 10: Program 10

4. Ben-Amram [15] has shown a pair of contrasting results:
   - The termination problem is undecidable for $(FUN(n), m)$ programs where $m = 1$ and $FUN(n)$ is the set of all functions of the form

     $$f(x[1], \ldots, x[n]) = \min\{x[i_1] + c_1, x[i_2] + c_2, \ldots, x[i_k] + c_k\}$$

     where $1 \leq i_1 < \cdots < i_k$ and $c_1, \ldots, ck \in \mathbb{Z}$.
   - The Termination problem is decidable for $(FUN(n), m)$-programs when $m \geq 1$ and $FUN(n)$ is the set of all functions of the form

     $$f(x[1], \ldots, x[n]) = x[i] + c$$

   where $1 \leq i \leq n$ and $c \in \mathbb{Z}$. Note that Program 6 falls into this category.

5. Ouakine and coauthors [23–27] have proven that, for many types of programs that involve matrices, it is decidable if the program terminates.

13. HOW MUCH RAMSEY THEORY DO WE NEED?

Podelski and Rybalchenko [7] noted that the proofs of Theorems 5, 6, 7, and 8 do not need the strength of the full Ramsey's theorem. In the proofs of these theorems, the coloring is transitive.

Definition 10. A coloring of the edges of K_n or K_N is *transitive* if for every $i < j < k$; if $COL(i,j) = COL(j,k)$, then both are equal to $COL(i,k)$.

Definition 11. Let $c, n \geq 1$. Let G be K_n or K_N. Let COL be a c-coloring of the edges of G. A set of vertices V is a *monochromatic increasing path with respect to COL* if $V = \{v_1 < v_2 < \cdots \}$ and

$$COL(v_1, v_2) = COL(v_2, v_3) = \cdots.$$

(If $G = K_n$, then the $\cdots$ stop at some $k \leq n$.) We will drop the *with respect to COL* if the coloring is understood. We will abbreviate *monochromatic increasing path* by *MIP* from now on.

Here is the theorem we really need. We will refer to it as *the transitive Ramsey's theorem*.

Theorem 17. *Let $c \geq 1$. For every transitive c-coloring of K_N, there exists an infinite MIP.*

The transitive Ramsey theorem is weaker than Ramsey's theorem. We show this in three different ways: (1) Reverse Mathematics, (2) Computable Mathematics, and (3) Finitary Version.

Definition 12.
1. For all $c \geq 1$, let $RT(c)$ be Ramsey's theorem for c colors.
2. Let RT be $(\forall c)[RT(c)]$.
3. For all $c \geq 1$, let $TRT(c)$ be the transitive Ramsey's theorem for c colors.
4. Let TRT be $(\forall c)[TRT(c)]$. (This is the theorem that we really need.)

13.1 Reverse Mathematics

Reverse mathematics [28] looks at exactly what strength of axioms is needed to prove results in mathematics. A weak axiom system called RCA_0 (Recursive Comprehension Axiom) is at the base. Intuitively a statement proven in RCA_0 is proven constructively.

Notation 4.

Let A and B be statements.

- $A \rightarrow B$ means that one can prove B from A in RCA_0.
- $A \equiv B$ means that $A \rightarrow B$ and $B \rightarrow A$.
- $A \nrightarrow B$ means that, only using the axioms in RCA_0, one cannot prove B from A. It may still be the case that A implies B but proving this will require a stronger base axiom system.

The following are known. Items 1 and 2 indicate that the proof-theoretic complexity of RT is greater than that of TRT.

1. $RT \rightarrow TRT$. The usual reasoning for this can easily be carried out in RCA_0.
2. Hirschfeldt and Shore [29] have shown that $TRT \nrightarrow RT$.
3. For all c, $RT(2) \equiv RT(c)$. The usual reasoning for this can easily be carried out in RCA_0. Note how this contrasts to the next item.
4. Cholak *et al.* [30] showed that $RT(2) \nrightarrow (\forall c)[RT(c)]$.

The proof of Theorem 5 showed that, over RCA_0,

$$TRT(3) \rightarrow \text{Program 5 terminates.}$$

Does the following hold over RCA_0?

$$\text{Program 5 terminates} \rightarrow TRT(3).$$

We do not know.

In the spirit of the reverse mathematics program, we ask the following: For each c, is there a program P_c such that the following holds over RCA_0?

$$P \text{ terminates} \Longleftrightarrow TRT(c).$$

The following is open: for which $i, j \geq 2$ does $TRT(i) \rightarrow TRT(j)$?

13.2 Computable Mathematics

Computable mathematics [31] looks at theorems in mathematics that are proven noneffectively and questions if there is an effective (that is computable) proof. The answer is usually no. Then the question arises as to how noneffective the proof is. Ramsey's theorem and the transitive Ramsey's theorem have been studied and compared in this light [29, 32–35].

Definition 13. Let $M_1^{(\cdots)}, M_2^{(\cdots)}, \ldots$ be a standard list of oracle Turing machines.

1. If A is a set, then $A' = \{e : M_e^A(e)\downarrow\}$. This is also called *the Halting problem relative to A*. Note that $\emptyset' = HALT$.
2. A set A is called *low* if $A'\le_T HALT$. Note that decidable sets are low. It is known that there are undecidable sets that are low; however, they have some of the properties of decidable sets.
3. We define the levels of the arithmetic hierarchy.
   - A set is in Σ_0 and Π_0 if it is decidable.
   - Assume $n \ge 1$. A set A is in Σ_n if there exists a set $B \subseteq \mathbb{N} \times \mathbb{N}$ that is in Π_{n-1} such that

   $$A = \{x : (\exists y)[(x, y) \in B]\}.$$

   - Assume $n \ge 1$. A set A is in Π_n if $\overline{A}$ is in Σ_n.
   - A set is in the *arithmetic hierarchy* if it is in Σ_n or Π_n for some n.

The following are known. Items 1 and 3 indicate that the Turing degree of the infinite homogenous set induced by a coloring is greater than the Turing degree of the infinite homogenous set induced by a transitive coloring.

1. Jockusch [34] has shown that there exists a computable 2-coloring of the edges of $K_\mathbb{N}$ such that, for all infinite homogeneous sets H, H is not computable in the halting set.
2. Jockusch [34] has shown that for every computable 2-coloring of the edges of $K_\mathbb{N}$, there exists an infinite homogeneous sets $H \in \Pi_2$.
3. For all c, for every computable transitive c-coloring of the edges of $K_\mathbb{N}$, there exists an infinite MIP P that is computable in the halting set. This is folklore.
4. There exists a computable transitive 2-coloring of the edges of $K_\mathbb{N}$ with no computable infinite MIP. This is folklore.
5. Hirschfeldt and Shore [29] have shown that there exists a computable transitive 2-coloring of the edges of $K_\mathbb{N}$ with no infinite low MIP.

13.3 Finitary Version

There are finite versions of both Ramsey's theorem and the transitive Ramsey's theorem. The finitary version of the transitive Ramsey's theorem yields better upper bounds.

Notation 5. Let $c, k \ge 1$.
1. $R(k, c)$ is the least n such that, for any c-coloring of the edges of K_n, there exists a homogeneous set of size k.

2. $TRT(k, c)$ is the least n such that, for any transitive c-coloring of the edges of K_n, there exists a MIP of length k.

It is not obvious that $R(k, c)$ and $TRT(k, c)$ exist; however, they do.

The following is well known [12–14] and will be proved in the $c = 2$ case in the Appendix.

Theorem 18. *For all* k, $c \geq 1$, $c^{k/2} \leq R(k, c) \leq c^{ck-c+1}$.

Improving the upper and lower bounds on the $R(k, c)$ (often called *the Ramsey numbers*) is a long-standing open problem. The best known asymptotic results for the $c = 2$ case are by Conlon [36]. For some exact values, see Radziszowski's dynamic survey [37].

The following theorem is easy to prove; however, neither the statement nor the proof seems to be in the literature. We will prove it in the Appendix.

Theorem 19. *For all* k, $c \geq 1$, $TRT(k, c) = (k-1)^c + 1$.

14. OPEN PROBLEMS

1. For which $(FUN(n), m)$ is the Termination problem restricted to $(FUN(n), m)$ programs decidable?

2. Find a natural example showing that Theorem 14 requires the full Ramsey theorem.

3. Prove or disprove that Theorem 14 is equivalent to Ramsey's theorem.

4. Classify more types of Termination problems into the classes Decidable and Undecidable. It would be of interest to get a more refined classification. Some of the undecidable problems may be equivalent to HALT while others may be complete in some level of the arithmetic hierarchy or Π_1^1-complete

5. Prove or disprove the following conjecture: for every c there is a program P_c such that, over RCA_0, $TRT(c) \Longleftrightarrow$ every run of Program P_c terminates.

15. SUMMARY

In this survey, we discussed various ways to prove that a program always terminates. The techniques used were well-founded orderings, Ramsey theory, and matrices. These techniques work on some programs but not all programs. We then discussed classes of programs where decidability of termination has been proven.

The applications of Ramsey theory only used the transitive Ramsey theorem. We discussed the distinction between the two.

Lastly, we listed several open problems.

ACKNOWLEDGMENTS

I would like to thank Daniel Apon, Amir Ben-Amram, Peter Cholak, Byron Cook, Denis Hirschfeldt, Jon Katz, John Ouaknine, Andreas Podelski, Brian Postow, Andrey Rybalchenko, and Richard Shore for helpful discussions. We would also like to again thank Amir Ben-Amram for patiently explaining to me many subtle points that arose in this chapter. We would also like to thank Daniel Apon for a great proofreading job.

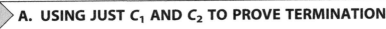

A. USING JUST C_1 AND C_2 TO PROVE TERMINATION

Definition A.1. If C is a set of square matrices of the same dimension, then $\text{clos}(C)$ is the set of all finite products of elements of C. For example, if $C = \{C_1, C_2\}$, then $C_1^2 C_2 C_1^3 C_2^{17} \in \text{clos}(C_1, C_2)$.

This section is due to Ben-Amram and is based on a paper of his [15]. He gives an example of a proof of termination of Program 6 where he uses the matrices C_1, C_2 that come out of Program 6 directly (in contrast to our proof in Theorem 12 which used 3×3 matrices by introducing $x + y$). Of more interest: there *is* an element of $\text{clos}(C_1, C_2)$ that has no negative numbers on the diagonal, namely C_2 itself. Hence, we cannot use Theorem 9 to prove termination.

Theorem A.1. *Every computation of Program 6 is finite.*

Proof. The case control$=1$ is represented by the matrix

$$C_1 = \begin{pmatrix} -1 & 0 \\ \infty & \infty \end{pmatrix}.$$

The case control$=2$ is represented by the matrix

$$C_2 = \begin{pmatrix} \infty & -2 \\ +1 & \infty \end{pmatrix}.$$

We find a representation of a *superset* of $\text{clos}(C_1, C_2)$. Let

$$\mathcal{E} = \bigcup_Y \mathcal{E}_Y \text{ where } Y \in \{C_1, C_2, C_1C_2, C_2C_1\}$$

and

$$\mathcal{E}_Y = \{YZ^a, \; a \geq 1\}.$$

Thus, $\mathcal{E}$ is an infinite set of matrices formed by uniting four classes, each of a simple structure (periodic sets, in an appropriate sense of the word). We show that $clos(C_1, C_2) \subseteq \mathcal{E}$. We prove this by induction on the number of matrices that are multiplied to form the element of $clos(C_1, C_2)$.

The base case is trivial since clearly $C_1, C_2 \in \mathcal{E}$.

We show the induction step by multiplying each of the four "patterns" in $\mathcal{E}$ *on the left* by each of the matrices C_1, C_2. We use the following identities: $C_1^2 = ZC_1 = C_1 Z = C_1 C_2$, $C_2^2 = Z$, $ZC_2 = C_2 Z$.

1. $C_1(C_1 Z^a) = C_1^2 Z^a = C_1 Z Z^a = C_1 Z^{a+1}$
2. $C_2(C_1 Z^a) = (C_2 C_1) Z^a$
3. $C_1(C_2 Z^a) = (C_1 C_2) Z^a$
4. $C_2(C_2 Z^a) = C_2^2 Z^a = Z Z^a = Z^{a+1}$
5. $C_1(C_1 C_2 Z^a) = C_1^2 C_2 Z^a = C_1 Z C_2 Z^a = C_1 C_2 Z Z^a = (C_1 C_2) Z^{a+1}$
6. $C_2(C_1 C_2 Z^a) = C_2(C_1 Z Z^a = (C_2 C_1) Z^{a+1}$
7. $C_1(C_2 C_1 Z^a) = (C_1 C_2) C_1 Z^a = C_1(Z C_1) Z^a = C_1^2 Z^{a+1} = C_1 Z^{a+2}$
8. $C_2(C_2 C_1 Z^a) = Z C_1 Z^a = C_1 Z^{a+1}$

We have shown that $clos(C_1, C_2) \subseteq \mathcal{E}$. Next, we verify that for every class $\mathcal{E}_Y$, either every matrix in $\mathcal{E}_Y$ or every product of a certain finite number of matrices in $\mathcal{E}_Y$, has a negative integer on the diagonal. This suffices for a proof of termination by Theorem 14, since every class induces a well-founded order (if an order is not well founded, every finite power of it is not well founded either). The second case occurs here only once (for the second class) and the negative number occurs already for a product of two such matrices.

1. $M = C_1 Z^a$, for some $a \Rightarrow M = \begin{pmatrix} -1-a & -a \\ \infty & \infty \end{pmatrix}$
2. $M_1 = C_2 Z^a$, $M_2 = C_2 Z^b \Rightarrow M_1 M_2 = C_2^2 Z^{a+b} = Z^{a+b+1}$
3. $M = C_1 C_2 Z^a \Rightarrow M = C_1 Z Z^a = C_1 Z^{a+1}$
4. $M \in C_2 C_1 Z^a \Rightarrow M = \begin{pmatrix} \infty & \infty \\ -3 & -2 \end{pmatrix} Z^a = \begin{pmatrix} \infty & \infty \\ -3 & -2-a \end{pmatrix}$. ∎

B. A VERIFICATION THAT NEEDS THE FULL RAMSEY THEORY

The proof of Theorem 14 seems to need the full strength of Ramsey's theorem (unlike the proof of Theorem 8, see the note following its proof). We give an example, due to Ben-Amram, of a program with a disjunctive well-founded transition invariant where the coloring is not transitive. Consider Program not-transitive

$x = \textbf{Input}(\mathbb{Z})$
While $x > 0$
$$x = x \div 2$$

Listing A.1: Program not-transitive

It clearly terminates and you can use the transition invariant $\{(x,x') : x > x'\}$ to prove it. This leads to a transitive coloring. But what if instead your transition-invariant-generator came up with the following rather odd relations instead:

1. $T_1 = \{(x,x') : x > 3x'\}$
2. $T_2 = \{(x,x') : x > x' + 1\}$

Note that $T_1 \cup T_2$ is a disjunctive well-founded transition invariant. We show that the coloring associated to $T_1 \cup T_2$ is not transitive.

- $COL(4,2) = 2$. That is, $(4,2) \in T_2 - T_1$.
- $COL(2,1) = 2$. That is, $(2,1) \in T_2 - T_1$.
- $COL(4,1) = 1$. That is, $(4,1) \in T_1$.

Hence, COL is not a transitive coloring.

C. RAMSEY'S THEOREM

Ramsey theory is a deep branch of combinatorics. For two books on the subject, see Refs. [11, 14].

We will present the finite and infinite Ramsey theorem, and also the finite and infinite transitive Ramsey theorem. The only theorem used in this chapter is the infinite transitive Ramsey theorem; however, we give you more so you will have some context.

It is somewhat remarkable that this branch of pure math has an application in programming languages. See www.cs.umd.edu/~gasarch/ramsey/ramsey.html or Ref. [38] for other applications of Ramsey theory. These applications are largely to other theorems in mathematics or theoretical computer science. Hence, one could argue that the application to proving programs terminate is the first *real* application.

C.1. If There Are Six People at a Party...

The following is well-known recreational math problem:

Question. Show that if there are six people at a party, either three of them mutually know each other or three of them mutually do not know each other. We call such a set of people *homogenous* since they all bear the same relationship to each other. We will call set of three either homogenous-K (all three pairs know each other) or homogenous-DK (none of the pair knows each other).

Solution. Let the people be A,B,C,D,E,F. Look at how F relates to the rest: there must be either ≥ 3 that he knows or ≥ 3 that he does not know. We will assume that there are ≥ 2 that he knows (the other case is similar).

We can assume that F knows A,B, and C. If any of A,B,C know each other, then we have a homogenous-K set: F and the pair of A,B,C who know each other. If none of A,B,C know each other, then we have a homogenous-DK set: namely A,B,C. (End of Proof)

What if you only had five people at the party? Are you still guaranteed a homogenous set? No: Take A,B,C,D,E where the following pairs know each other: (A,B), (B,C), (C,D), (D,E), (E,A), and the remaining pairs do not know each other. We leave it to the reader that in this scenario there is no homogenous set.

What if you want to have a homogenous set of size four? It turns out that if there are 18 people at a party, there must be a homogenous set of size four; however, if there are 17 people at a party, there is a scenario where there is no homogenous set of size four.

What if you want to have a homogenous set of size five? It turns out that if there are 49 people at a party, there must be a homogenous set of size five; however, if there are 43 people at a party, there is a scenario where there is no homogenous set of size five. It is an open problem to determine the exact number. See http://www.cs.umd.edu/~gasarch/BLOGPAPERS/ramseykings.pdf for an interesting take on the problem.

What if you want to have a homogenous set of size m? It turns out that if there is a large number $R(m)$ such that if there are $R(m)$ people at a party, there must be a homogenous set. We will prove this.

What if you want to have an infinite (countable) homogenous set? It turns out that there is an infinite number of people at a party,[1] then there is an infinite homogenous set. We will prove this.

We will now state this more mathematically and prove the last assertions, though in the reverse order.

---

[1] Perhaps they all fit because person i is of height $2^{-i} \times 6$ ft and of width 2^{-i} ft.

C.2. Notation

Note A.1. In the graph theory literature, there are (at least) two kinds of coloring. We present them in this note so that if you happen to read the literature and they are using coloring in a different way then in these notes, you will not panic.

- Vertex Coloring. Usually one says that the vertices of a graph are c-colorable if there is a way to assign each vertex a color, using no more than c colors, such that no two adjacent vertices (vertices connected by an edge) are the same color. Theorems are often of the form "if a graph G has property BLAH BLAH then G is c-colorable" where they mean vertex c-colorable. We **will not** be considering these kinds of colorings.
- Edge Colorings. Usually this is used in the context of Ramsey theory and Ramsey-type theorems. Theorems begin with "for all c-coloring of K_n," there exists BLAH such that BLAH. We **will** be considering these kinds of colorings.

Let us go back to our party! We can think of the 6 people as vertices of K_6. We can color edge $\{i,j\}$ RED if i and j know each other, and BLUE if they do not.

Definition A.2. Let $n \geq 2$. Then K_n has a homogenous K_m if there is a set V' of m vertices (in V) such that
- there is an edge between every pair of vertices in V': $\{\{i,j\} \mid i,j \in V'\} \subseteq E$
- all the edges between vertices in V' are the same color: there is some $l \in [c]$ such that $COL(\{i,j\}) = l$ for all $i,j \in V'$.

Notation A.1. K_N is the graph (V,E) where

$$V = N$$
$$E = \{\{x,y\} \mid x,y \in N\}$$

We now restate our 6-people-at-a-party theorem:

Theorem A.2. *Every 2-coloring of the edges of K_6 has a homogenous set of size 3.*

The *finite Ramsey's theorem*, usually called *Ramsey's theorem*, is as follows:

Theorem A.3. *For all c, for all m, there exists an n such that every c-coloring of the edges of K_n has a homogenous set of size m.*

The *infinite Ramsey's theorem* is as follows:

Theorem A.4. *For all c, every c-coloring of the edges of K_N has an infinite homogenous set.*

We need a way to state these theorems more succinctly. We introduce some notation.

Notation A.2.

1. If A is a set, then $\binom{A}{2}$ is the set of all unordered pairs of distinct elements of A. Note that the phrase *for all c-colorings of K_n* can now be states as *for all* $COL : \binom{[n]}{2} \to [c]$.

2. $R_c(m)$ is the least n such that for any c-coloring of $\binom{[n]}{2}$, there is a homogenous set of size m. $R(m)$ is $R_2(m)$. We have not shown that $R_c(m)$ exists; however, we will state theorems like $\ldots R_c(m) \leq \ldots$ which will mean that $R_c(m)$ exists and we have a bound for it.

3. $R_c(\infty) = \infty$ means that for any c-coloring of $\binom{N}{2}$ there is an infinite homogenous set.

In the sections below, we state the infinite and finite Ramsey's theorem using this notation.

C.3. Proof of the Infinite Ramsey Theorem

We will prove the infinite Ramsey theorem. We prove this one first for three reasons

1. The infinite one is the only one that we use in this chapter.

2. The infinite one is *easier* to prove than the finite one. The combinatorist Joel Spencer has said *infinite combinatorics is easier than finite combinatorics since all of those messy constants go away.*

3. We can derive the finite Ramsey theorem (usually just called *Ramsey's theorem*) from the infinite one. We will present this proof as well two more as standard proofs.

Theorem A.5. $R(\infty) = \infty$.

Proof. Let COL be a 2-coloring of K_N. We define an infinite sequence of vertices,

$$x_1, x_2, \ldots,$$

and an infinite sequence of sets of vertices,

$$V_0, V_1, V_2, \ldots,$$

that are based on COL.

Here is the intuition: Vertex $x_1 = 1$ has an infinite number of edges coming out of it. Some are RED, and some are BLUE. Hence, there are an infinite number of RED edges coming out of x_1, or there are an infinite number of BLUE edges coming out of x_1 (or both). Let c_1 be a color such that x_1 has an infinite number of edges coming out of it that are colored c_1. Let V_1 be the set of vertices v such that $COL(\{v,x_1\}) = c_1$. Then keep iterating this process.

We now describe it formally.

$$V_0 = \mathbf{N}$$
$$x_1 = 1$$
$$c_1 = \begin{cases} \text{RED} & \text{if } |\{v \in V_0 | COL(\{v,x_1\}) = \text{RED}\}| \text{ is infinite} \\ \text{BLUE} & \text{otherwise} \end{cases}$$
$$V_1 = \{v \in V_0 | COL(\{v,x_1\}) = c_1\} \, (\text{note that } |V_1| \text{ is infinite})$$

Let $i \geq 2$, and assume that V_{i-1} is defined. We define x_i, c_i, and V_i:

$$x_i = \text{the least number in } V_{i-1}$$

$$c_i = \begin{cases} \text{RED} & \text{if } |\{v \in V_{i-1} | COL(\{v,x_i\}) = \text{RED}\}| \text{ is infinite} \\ \text{BLUE} & \text{otherwise} \end{cases}$$
$$V_i = \{v \in V_{i-1} | COL(\{v,x_i\}) = c_i\} \, (\text{note that } |V_i| \text{ is infinite})$$

How long can this sequence go on for? Well, x_i can be defined if V_{i-1} is nonempty. We can show by induction that, for every i, V_i is infinite. Hence, the sequence

$$x_1, x_2, \ldots,$$

is infinite.

Consider the infinite sequence

$$c_1, c_2, \ldots$$

Each of the colors in this sequence is either RED or BLUE. Hence, there must be an infinite sequence $i_1, i_2, \ldots$ such that $i_1 < i_2 < \cdots$ and

$$c_{i_1} = c_{i_2} = \cdots$$

Denote this color by c, and consider the vertices

$$x_{i_1}, x_{i_2}, \cdots$$

It is easy to see they form an infinite homogenous set. ∎

We leave it as an easy exercise to prove c-color case:

Theorem A.6. $R_c(\infty) = \infty$.

C.4. Proof of the Finite Ramsey Theorem from the Infinite Ramsey Theorem

Theorem A.7. *For every $m \geq 2$, $R(m)$ exists.*

Proof. Suppose, by way of contradiction, that there is some $m \geq 2$ such that $R(m)$ does not exist. Then, for every $n \geq m$, there is some way to color K_n so that there is no monochromatic K_m. Hence, there exist the following:

1. COL_1, a 2-coloring of K_m that has no monochromatic K_m
2. COL_2, a 2-coloring of K_{m+1} that has no monochromatic K_m
3. COL_3, a 2-coloring of K_{m+2} that has no monochromatic K_m

$\vdots$

j. COL_j, a 2-coloring of K_{m+j-1} that has no monochromatic K_m

$\vdots$

We will use these 2-colorings to form a 2-coloring COL of K_N that has no monochromatic K_m.

Let $e_1, e_2, e_3, \ldots$ be a list of all unordered pairs of elements of N such that every unordered pair appears exactly once. We will color e_1, then e_2, etc.

How should we color e_1? We will color it the way an infinite number of the COL_i's color it. Call that color c_1. Then how to color e_2? Well, first consider ONLY the colorings that colored e_1 with color c_1. Color e_2 the way an infinite number of those colorings color it. And so forth.

We now proceed formally:

$$J_0 = N$$
$$COL(e_1) = \begin{cases} RED & \text{if} |\{j \in J_0 | COL_j(e_1) = RED\}| \text{ is infinite} \\ BLUE & \text{otherwise} \end{cases}$$
$$J_1 = \{j \in J_0 | COL(e_1) = COL_j(e_1)\}$$

Let $i \geq 2$, and assume that $e_1, \ldots, e_{i-1}$ have been colored. Assume, furthermore, that J_{i-1} is infinite and, for every $j \in J_{i-1}$,

$$COL(e_1) = COL_j(e_1)$$
$$COL(e_2) = COL_j(e_2)$$
$$\vdots$$
$$COL(e_{i-1}) = COL_j(e_{i-1})$$

We now color e_i:

$$COL(e_i) = \begin{cases} \text{RED} & \text{if } |\{j \in J_{i-1} | COL_j(e_i) = \text{RED}\}| \text{ is infinite} \\ \text{BLUE} & \text{otherwise} \end{cases}$$
$$J_i = \{j \in J_{i-1} | COL(e_i) = COL_j(e_i)\}$$

One can show by induction that, for every i, J_i is infinite. Hence, this process never stops.

Claim. If K_N is 2-colored with COL, then there is no monochromatic K_m. ∎

Proof. Suppose, by way of contradiction, that there is a monochromatic K_m. Let the edges between vertices in that monochromatic K_m be

$$e_{i_1}, \ldots, e_{i_M},$$

where $i_1 < i_2 < \cdots < i_M$ and $M = \binom{m}{2}$. For every $j \in J_{i_M}$, COL_j and COL agree on the colors of those edges. Choose $j \in J_{i_M}$ so that all the vertices of the monochromatic K_m are elements of the vertex set of K_{m+j-1}. Then COL_j is a 2-coloring of the edges of K_{m+j-1} that has a monochromatic K_m, in contradiction to the definition of COL_j. ∎

Hence, we have produced a 2-coloring of K_N that has no monochromatic K_m. This contradicts Theorem A.5. Therefore, our initial supposition—that $R(m)$ does not exist—is false. ∎

We leave it as an easy exercise to prove c-color case:

Theorem A.8. *For all c, for all m, $R_c(m)$ exists.*

C.5. A Direct Proof of the Finite Ramsey's Theorem

The proof of Ramsey's theorem given for Theorem A.7 did not give a bound on $R(m)$. The following proof gives a bound. It is similar in spirit to the proof of Theorem A.5.

Theorem A.9. *For every $m \geq 2$, $R(m) \leq 2^{2m-2}$.*

Proof. Let COL be a 2-coloring of $K_{2^{2m-2}}$. We define a sequence of vertices,

$$x_1, x_2, \ldots, x_{2m-1},$$

and a sequence of sets of vertices,

$$V_0, V_1, V_2, \ldots, V_{2m-1},$$

that are based on COL.

Here is the intuition: Vertex $x_1 = 1$ has $2^{2m-2} - 1$ edges coming out of it. Some are RED, and some are BLUE. Hence, there are at least 2^{2m-3} RED edges coming out of x_1, or there are at least 2^{2m-3} BLUE edges coming out of x_1.

Let c_1 be a color such that x_1 has at least 2^{2m-3} edges coming out of it that are colored c_1. Let V_1 be the set of vertices v such that $COL(\{v,x_1\}) = c_1$. Then keep iterating this process.

We now describe it formally.

$$V_0 = [2^{2m-2}]$$
$$x_1 = 1$$

$$c_1 = \begin{cases} \text{RED} & \text{if } |\{v \in V_0 | COL(\{v,x_1\}) = \text{RED}\}| \geq 2^{2m-3} \\ \text{BLUE} & \text{otherwise} \end{cases}$$
$$V_1 = \{v \in V_0 | COL(\{v,x_1\}) = c_1\} \text{(note that } |V_1| \geq 2^{2m-3})$$

Let $i \geq 2$, and assume that V_{i-1} is defined. We define x_i, c_i, and V_i:

$$x_i = \text{the least number in } V_{i-1}$$

$$c_i = \begin{cases} \text{RED} & \text{if } |\{v \in V_{i-1} | COL(\{v,x_i\}) = \text{RED}\}| \geq 2^{(2m-2)-i} \\ \text{BLUE} & \text{otherwise} \end{cases}$$
$$V_i = \{v \in V_{i-1} | COL(\{v,x_i\}) = c_i\} \text{(note that } |V_i| \geq 2^{(2m-2)-i})$$

How long can this sequence go on for? Well, x_i can be defined if V_{i-1} is nonempty. Note that

$$|V_{2m-2}| \geq 2^{(2m-2)-(2m-2)} = 2^0 = 1$$

Thus if $i - 1 = 2m - 2$ (equivalently, $i = 2m - 1$), then $V_{i-1} = V_{2m-2} \neq \emptyset$, but there is no guarantee that $V_i (= V_{2m-1})$ is nonempty. Hence, we can define

$$x_1, \ldots, x_{2m-1}$$

Consider the colors

$$c_1, c_2, \ldots, c_{2m-2}$$

Each of these is either RED or BLUE. Hence, there must be at least $m - 1$ of them that are the same color. Let $i_1, \ldots, i_{m-1}$ be such that $i_1 < \cdots < i_{m-1}$ and

$$c_{i_1} = c_{i_2} = \cdots = c_{i_{m-1}}$$

Denote this color by c, and consider the m vertices

$$x_{i_1}, x_{i_2}, \cdots, x_{i_{m-1}}, x_{i_{m-1}} + 1$$

To see why we have listed m vertices but only $m - 1$ colors, picture the following scenario: You are building a fence row, and you want (say) 7 sections of fence. To do that, you need 8 fence posts to hold it up. Now think of the fence posts as vertices, and the sections of fence as edges between successive vertices, and recall that every edge has a color associated with it.

Claim. The m vertices listed above form a monochromatic K_m. ∎

Proof. First, consider vertex x_{i_1}. The vertices

$$x_{i_2}, \ldots, x_{i_{m-1}}, x_{i_{m-1}} + 1$$

are elements of V_{i_1} and hence the edges

$$\{x_{i_1}, x_{i_2}\}, \ldots, \{x_{i_1}, x_{i_{m-1}}\}, \{x_{i_1}, x_{i_{m-1}} + 1\}$$

are colored with c_{i_1} $(= c)$.

Then consider each of the remaining vertices in turn, starting with vertex x_{i_2}. For example, the vertices

$$x_{i_3}, \ldots, x_{i_{m-1}}, x_{i_{m-1}} + 1$$

are elements of V_{i_2} and hence the edges

$$\{x_{i_2}, x_{i_3}\}, \ldots, \{x_{i_2}, x_{i_{m-1}}\}, \{x_{i_2}, x_{i_{m-1}} + 1\}$$

are colored with c_{i_2} $(= c)$. ∎

Note that this is really the same proof as Theorem A.5 except that we had to keep track of the constants. This is an excellent example of Joel Spencer's quote given above.

We leave it as an easy exercise to prove c-color case:

Theorem A.10. For every c, $R_c(m) \le c^{m-c+1}$.

C.6. Another Direct Proof of the Finite Ramsey's Theorem

We give an alternative proof of the finite Ramsey's theorem that is similar in spirit to the original 6-people-at-a-party problem and yields slightly better bounds.

Given m, we really want n such that every 2-coloring of K_n has a RED K_m or a BLUE K_m. However, it will be useful to let the parameter for BLUE differ from the parameter for RED.

Notation A.3. Let $a,b \geq 2$. Let $R(a,b)$ denote the least number, if it exists, such that every 2-coloring of $K_{R(a,b)}$ has a RED K_a or a BLUE K_b. Note that $R(m) = R(m,m)$.

We state some easy facts.
1. For all a,b, $R(a,b) = R(b,a)$.
2. For $b \geq 2$, $R(2,b) = b$: First, we show that $R(2,b) \leq b$. Given any 2-coloring of K_b, we want a RED K_2 or a BLUE K_b. Note that a RED K_2 is just a RED edge. Hence, EITHER there exists one RED edge (so you get a RED K_2) OR all the edges are BLUE (so you get a BLUE K_b). Now we prove that $R(2,b) = b$. If $b = 2$, this is obvious. If $b > 2$, then the all-BLUE coloring of K_{b-1} has neither a RED K_2 nor a BLUE K_b; hence, $R(2,b) \geq b$. Combining the two inequalities ($R(2,b) \leq b$ and $R(2,b) \geq b$), we find that $R(2,b) = b$.
3. $R(3,3) \leq 6$. (This is the 6-people-at-a-party theorem.)

We want to show that, for every $n \geq 2$, $R(n,n)$ exists. In this proof, we show something more: that for all $a,b \geq 2$, $R(a,b)$ exists. We do not really care about the case where $a \neq b$, but that case will help us get our result. This is a situation where proving more than you need is easier.

Lemma A.1. For all $x,y \geq 1$, $\binom{x}{y-1} + \binom{x-1}{y-1} = \binom{x}{y}$.

Proof. One could prove this with algebra; however, we will prove it combinatorially. How many ways are there to choose y people out of x? The answer is of course $\binom{x}{y}$. We solve it a different way: consider one of the people, named Alice. If we do not choose Alice, then there are $\binom{x}{y-1}$ ways to choose y people. If we choose Alice, then there are $\binom{x-1}{y-1}$ ways to choose y people. Hence, there are $\binom{x}{y-1} + \binom{x-1}{y-1}$ was to choose y people. Hence, $\binom{x}{y-1} + \binom{x-1}{y-1} = \binom{x}{y}$. ∎

Theorem A.11.
1. For all $a,b \geq 3$: If $R(a-1,b)$ and $R(a,b-1)$ exist, then $R(a,b)$ exists and

$$R(a,b) \leq R(a-1,b) + R(a,b-1)$$

2. For all $a,b \geq 2$, $R(a,b)$ exists and $R(a,b) \leq \binom{a+b-2}{a-1}$.

3. For all $m \geq 2$, $R(m) \leq \binom{2^{2m}}{\sqrt{m}}$.

Proof.

1: Assume $R(a-1,b)$ and $R(a,b-1)$ exist. Let

$$n = R(a-1,b) + R(a,b-1)$$

Let COL be a 2-coloring of K_n, and let x be a vertex. Note that there are

$$R(a-1,b) + R(a,b-1) - 1$$

edges coming out of x (edges $\{x,y\}$ for vertices y).

Let NUM-RED-EDGES be the number of red edges coming out of x, and let NUM-BLUE-EDGES be the number of blue edges coming out of x. Note that

$$\text{NUM-RED-EDGES} + \text{NUM-BLUE-EDGES}$$
$$= R(a-1,b) + R(a,b-1) - 1$$

Hence, either

$$\text{NUM-RED-EDGES} \geq R(a-1,b)$$

or

$$\text{NUM-BLUE-EDGES} \geq R(a,b-1)$$

There are two cases:

Case A.1. NUM-RED-EDGES $\geq R(a-1,b)$. Let

$$U = \{y \mid COL(\{x,y\}) = \text{RED}\}$$

U is of size NUM-RED-EDGES $\geq R(a-1,b)$. Consider the restriction of the coloring COL to the edges between vertices in U. Since

$$|U| \geq R(a-1,b),$$

this coloring has a RED K_{a-1} or a BLUE K_b. Within Case 1, there are two cases:

(a) There is a RED K_{a-1}. Recall that all of the edges in

$$\{\{x,u\} \mid u \in U\}$$

are RED and hence all the edges between elements of the set $U \cup \{x\}$ are RED, so they form a RED K_a and WE ARE DONE.

(b) There is a BLUE K_b. Then we are DONE. ∎

Case A.2. NUM-BLUE-EDGES $\geq R(a, b - 1)$. Similar to Case 1.

2: To show that $R(a,b)$ exists and $R(a,b) \leq \binom{a+b-2}{a-1}$, we use induction on $n = a + b$. Since $a,b \geq 2$, the smallest value of $a + b$ is 4. Thus, $n \geq 4$.

Base Case: $n = 4$. Since $a + b = 4$ and $a,b \geq 2$, we must have $a = b = 2$. From Part 1, we know that $R(2,2)$ exists and $R(2,2) = 2$. Note that

$$R(2,2) = 2 \leq \binom{2+2-2}{2-1} = \binom{2}{1} = 2.$$

Induction Hypothesis: For all $a,b \geq 2$ such that $a + b = n$, $R(a,b)$ exists and $R(a,b) \leq \binom{a+b-2}{a-1}$.

Inductive Step: Let a,b be such that $a,b \geq 2$ and $a + b = n + 1$.

By Part 1, the induction hypothesis, and Lemma A.1, we have

$$R(a,b) \leq R(a,b-1) + R(a-1,b) \leq \binom{a+b-3}{a-1} + \binom{a+b-3}{a-2}$$
$$= \binom{a+b-2}{a-1}.$$

3: By Part 2, $R(m,m) \leq \binom{2m-2}{m-1}$. By Stirling's formula, this can be bounded above by $O(\frac{2^{2m}}{\sqrt{m}})$. ∎

We leave it as an easy exercise to prove c-color case:

Theorem A.12. *For every c, $R_c(a_1, \ldots, a_c) \leq \left(\frac{(\sum_{i=1}^{c})-c}{a_1!a_2!\cdots a_c!} \right).$*

C.7. Our Last Word on Ramsey Numbers

The best known asymptotic results for the $c = 2$ case are by Conlon [36] who has shown

$$R(m) \leq \frac{2^{2m}}{m^c \log_s / \log\log_s}.$$

For some exact values of the Ramsey numbers, see Radziszowski's dynamic survey [37].

What about lower bounds? Erdös found the first nontrivial bound and in the process invented the probabilistic method.

Theorem A.13. $R(m) \geq \Omega(m2^{m/2})$.

Proof. Let $n = cm2^{m/2}$ where we determine c later.

We need to find a 2-coloring of $\binom{[n]}{2}$ that has no homogenous set of size n. Or do we? We only have to show that such a coloring *exists*.

We do the following probabilistic experiment: for each edge randomly pick RED or BLUE to color it (the probability of each is $1/2$). We show that the probability the graph has a homogenous set of size m is less than one. Hence, there exists a coloring with no homogenous set of size m.

The number of colorings is $2^{\binom{n}{2}}$. The number of colorings that have a homogenous set of size m is bounded above by

$$\binom{n}{m} \times 2 \times 2^{\binom{n}{2} - \binom{m}{2}}.$$

Hence, the probability that the coloring has a homogenous set of size m is bounded above by

$$\frac{\binom{n}{m} \times 2 \times 2^{\binom{n}{2} - \binom{m}{2}}}{2^{\binom{n}{2}}} = \frac{\binom{n}{m} \times 2}{2^{-\binom{m}{2}}}.$$

Stirling's formula and algebra show that there is a choice for m where this is less than one. ∎

Note A.2. If the above proof is done carefully, then c can be taken to be $\frac{1}{e\sqrt{2}}$. The probabilistic method is when you show something exists by showing that the probability that it does not exist is less than one. It has many applications. See the book by Alon and Spencer [39].

D. THE TRANSITIVE RAMSEY THEOREM

D.1. A Common Math Competition Problem
The following problem will likely appear in some math competition in 2014:

Problem. Find x such that the following hold:

1. All sequences of 2014 distinct real numbers have a monotone subsequence of length x.
2. There exists a sequence of 2014 distinct real numbers that have a monotone subsequence of length $x + 1$.

Solution. $x = 45$.

(1) Let $x_1, x_2, \ldots, x_{2014}$ be a sequence of 2014 distinct reals. Assume, by way of contradiction, that there is no monotone subsequence of length 45. We define a map from [2014] to [44] × [44] as follows: Map x to the ordered pair (a,b) such that (1) the longest increasing subsequence that ends at x has a length a and (2) the longest decreasing subsequence that ends at x has a length h.

The map is 1–1: Assume, by way of contradiction, that if $i < j$, both map to (a,b). Assume that $x_i < x_j$ (the case of $x_i > x_j$ is similar). The longest increasing subsequence that ends at x_i has a length a. Since $x_i < x_j$, the longest increasing subsequence that ends at x_j has a length at least $a + 1$. Hence, j does not map to (a,b). *Contradiction.* Hence, the map is 1–1. The domain has a size 2014. The range has a size 44 × 44 = 1936. Hence, there is a 1–1 map between a set of size 2014 and a set of size < 2014, which is a contradiction.

(2) We construct a sequence of length 2025 (longer than we need) that has no monotone subsequence of length 46.

Let $y_1 < y_2 < \cdots < y_{45}$ be numbers such that $y_i + 46 < y_{i+1}$. Consider the sequence

$$y_1, y_1 - 1, y_1 - 2, \ldots, y_1 - 44,$$
$$y_2, y_2 - 1, y_2 - 2, \ldots, y_2 - 44,$$
$$\vdots$$
$$y_{45}, y_{44} - 1, y_{44} - 3, \ldots, y_{44} - 44.$$

This sequence has 45 × 45 = 2025 elements. We call each line a block. Within a block, the only monotone subsequences are decreasing and are of length ≤ 45. A monotone subsequence that uses different blocks must use one from each block and be increasing. Such a sequence must be of length ≤ 45.

This problem and solution are a subcase of a theorem by Erdős and Szekeres [40]. They showed the following:

- For all k, for all sequences of distinct reals of length $(k-1)^2 + 1$, there is either an increasing monotone subsequence of length k or a decreasing monotone subsequence of length k.

- For all k, there exists a sequence of distinct reals of length $(k-1)^2$ with either an increasing monotone subsequence of length k or a decreasing monotone subsequence of length k.

D.2. View in Terms of Colorings

Note that we can view a sequence $x_1,\ldots,x_n$ as a 2-coloring of $\binom{[n]}{2}$ via

$$COL(i<j) = \begin{cases} \text{RED} & \text{if } x_i < x_j \\ \text{BLUE} & \text{if } x_i > x_j \end{cases} \tag{A.1}$$

Using Ramsey theory, we would obtain the weak result that there is monotone subsequence of length roughly $\log_2 n$. A modification of the solution above yields a monotone subsequence of length roughly $\sqrt{n}$. The key is that this is not just any coloring—it is a transitive coloring. With that in mind, we can generalize the theorem of Erdős and Szekeres.

Definition A.3. A *transitive c-coloring of* $\binom{[n]}{2}$ is a mapping where if $COL(i,j) = COL(j,k)$, then that color is also $COL(i,k)$.

D.3. The Transitive Ramsey Theorem

Definition A.4. Let $c \geq 1$ and $n \in \mathbb{N} \cup \{\mathbb{N}\}$. Let COL be a c-coloring of $\binom{[n]}{2}$. A set of vertices V is a *monochromatic increasing path with respect to* COL if $V = \{v_1 < v_2 < \cdots \}$ and

$$COL(v_1,v_2) = COL(v_2,v_3) = \cdots .$$

(If $G = K_n$, then the $\cdots$ stop at some $k \leq n$.) We will drop the *with respect to* COL if the coloring is understood. We will abbreviate *monochromatic increasing path* by *MIP* from now on.

Definition A.5. $TRT_c(m)$ is the least n such that any transitive c-coloring of $\binom{[n]}{2}$ has a homogenous set. Note that by Ramsey's theorem (Theorem A.10), $TRT_c(m) \leq c^{cm-c+1}$. (Using Theorem A.12, there is a slightly lower, but still exponential, upper bound.) We will provide an alternative proof with a much smaller upper bound. $TRT_c(\infty)$ can be defined in the obvious way. By Ramsey's theorem, it exists and is ∞. We will supply an alternative proof that uses less machinery.

Theorem A.14. $TRT_c(m) \leq (m-1)^c + 1$.

Proof.

(1) Let $n = (m-1)^c + 1$. Assume, by way of contradiction, that there is transitive c-coloring of $\binom{[n]}{2}$ that has no MIP of length m.

We define a map from $\{1,\ldots,n\}$ to $\{1,\ldots,m-1\}^c$ as follows: Map x to the vector $(a_1,\ldots,a_c)$ such that the longest mono path of color i that ends at x has a length a_i. Since there are no MIPs of length m, the image is a subset of $\{1,\ldots,m-1\}^c$.

It is easy to show that this map is 1–1. Since $n > (m-1)^c$, this is a contradiction.

(2) $TRT_c(m) \geq (m-1)^c + 1$.

Fix $m \geq 1$. We show by induction on c, that, for all $c \geq 1$, there exists a transitive c-coloring of $\binom{[n]}{2}$ that has no MIP of length m.

Base Case: $c = 1$. We color the edges of K_{m-1} all RED. Clearly there is no MIP of length m.

Induction Step: Assume there is a transitive $(c-1)$-coloring COL of the edges of $K_{(m-1)^{c-1}}$ that has no homogeneous set of size m. Assume that RED is not used. Replace every vertex with a copy of K_{m-1}. Color edges between vertices in different groups as they were colored by COL. Color edges within a group RED. It is easy to see that this produces a transitive c-coloring of the edges and that there are no MIP of length m. ∎

Theorem A.15. $TRT_c(\infty) = \infty$

Proof. This is similar to the proof of Part 1 of Theorem A.14. ∎

REFERENCES

[1] B. Cook, A. Podelski, A. Rybalchenko, Abstraction refinement for termination, in: Static Analysis Symposium (SAS), Lecture Notes in Computer Science, vol. 3672, Springer, New York, 2005, pp. 87–101. http://www7.in.tum.de/~rybal/papers/.

[2] B. Cook, A. Podelski, A. Rybalchenko, Termination proofs for systems code, in: Proceedings of the 2006 ACM SIGPLAN Conference on Programming Language Design and Implementation, ACM, New York, 2006, pp. 415–426. http://www7.in.tum.de/~rybal/papers/.

[3] B. Cook, A. Podelski, A. Rybalchenko, Proving programs perminate, Commun. ACM 54 (5) (2011) 88–97. http://www7.in.tum.de/~rybal/papers/.

[4] A. Podelski, A. Rybalchenko, A complete method for the synthesis of linear ranking functions, in: Verification, Model Checking, and Abstract Interpretation, Lecture Notes in Computer science, vol. 2937, Springer, New York, 2004, pp. 239–251. http://www7.in.tum.de/~rybal/papers/.

[5] A. Podelski, A. Rybalchenko, Transition invariants, in: Proceedings of the Nineteenth Annual IEEE Symposium on Logic in Computer Science, Turku, FinlandIEEE, New York, 2004, pp. 32–41. http://www7.in.tum.de/~rybal/papers/.

[6] A. Podelski, A. Rybalchenko, Transition predicate abstraction and fair termination, in: Proceedings of the 32nd Symposium on Principles of Programming LanguagesACM, New York, 2005, pp. 132–144. http://www7.in.tum.de/~rybal/papers/.

[7] A. Podelski, A. Rybalchenko, Transition invariants and transition predicate abstraction for program termination, in: P.A. Abdulla, K.R.M. Leino (Eds.), TACAS, Lecture Notes in Computer Science, vol. 6605, Springer, New York, 2011, pp. 3–10. http://www7.in.tum.de/~rybal/papers/ or http://dx.doi.org/10.1007/978-3-642-19835-9_2.

[8] C.S. Lee, Ranking functions for size-change termination, ACM Trans. Program. Lang. Syst 31 (3) (2009) 81–92. http://doi.acm.org/10.1145/1498926.1498928.

[9] C.S. Lee, N.D. Jones, A.M. Ben-Amram, The size-change principle for program termination, in: Proceedings of the 28th Symposium on Principles of Programming Languages, ACM, New York, 2001, pp. 81–92. http://dl.acm.org/citation.cfm?doid=360204.360210.

[10] R. Floyd, Assigning meaning to programs, in: Proceedings of Symposium in Applied Mathematics, vol. 19, AMS, Providence, 1967, pp. 19–31. http://www.cs.virginia.edu/~weimer/2007-615/reading/FloydMeaning.pdf.

[11] F. Ramsey, On a problem of formal logic, Proc. Lond. Math. Soc. 30 (1) (1930) 264–286.

[12] W. Gasarch, Ramsey's theorem on graphs, 2005. http://www.cs.umd.edu/~gasarch/mathnotes/ramsey.pdf.

[13] R. Graham, B. Rothschild, J. Spencer, Ramsey Theory, Wiley, New York, 1990.

[14] B. Landman, A. Robertson, Ramsey Theory on the Integers, AMS, Providence, 2004.

[15] A.M. Ben-Amram, Size-change termination with difference constraints, ACM Trans. Program. Lang. Syst. 30 (3) (2008) 1–31. http://doi.acm.org/10.1145/1353445.1353450.

[16] A.M. Ben-Amram, Size-change termination, monotonicity constraints and ranking functions, Logic. Methods Comput. Sci 6 (3) (2010) 1–32. http://www2.mta.ac.il/~amirben/papers.html.

[17] S.C. Kleene, Hierarchies of number theoretic predicates, Bull. Am. Math. Soc 61 (3) (1955) 193–213. http://www.ams.org/journals/bull/1955-61-03/home.html.

[18] S.C. Kleene, Introduction to Metamathematics, D, Van Nostrand, Princeton, 1952.

[19] H. Rogers Jr., Theory of Recursive Functions and Effective Computability, McGraw Hill, New York, 1967.

[20] A. Tiwari, Termination of linear programs, in: R. Alur, D. Peled (Eds.), Proceedings of the 16th Annual International Conference on Computer Aided Verification, Boston, MA, Lecture Notes in Computer Science, vol. 3115, Springer, New York, 2004, pp. 70–82. http://www.csl.sri.com/users/tiwari/html/cav04.html.

[21] M. Braverman, Termination of integer linear programs, in: T. Ball, R. Jones (Eds.), Proceedings of the 18th Annual International Conference on Computer Aided Verification, Seattle, WA, Lecture Notes in Computer Science, vol. 4144, Springer, New York, 2006, pp. 372–385. http://www.cs.toronto.edu/~mbraverm/Pub-all.html.

[22] A.M. Ben-Amram, S. Genaim, A.N. Masud, On the termination of integer loops, ACM Trans. Program. Lang. Syst. 34 (4) (2012) 1–23.

[23] J. Ouaknine, J.S. Pinto, J. Worrell, On termination of integer linear loops, in: SODA '15: Proceedings of the Twenty-Sixth Annual ACM-SIAM Symposium on Discrete algorithms, Society for Industrial and Applied Mathematics, Philadelphia, PA, 2015, pp. 100–110.

[24] V. Chonev, J. Ouaknine, J. Worrell, The polyhedron-hitting problem, in: SODA '15: Proceedings of the Twenty-Sixth Annual ACM-SIAM Symposium on Discrete algorithms, Society for Industrial and Applied Mathematics, Philadelphia, PA, 2015, pp. 111–121.

[25] J. Ouaknine, J. Pinto, J. Worrell, Positivity problems for low-order linear recurrence sequences, in: SODA '14: Proceedings of the Twenty-Fifth Annual ACM-SIAM Symposium on Discrete Algorithms, Society for Industrial and Applied Mathematics, Philadelphia, PA, 2014, pp. 90–99.

[26] J. Ouaknine, J. Worrell, On the positivity problem for simple linear recurrence sequences, in: ICALP '14: Proceedings of the Forty-First International Colloquium on Automata, Languages, and Programming, Springer, Philadelphia, PA, 2014, pp. 80–88.

[27] V. Chonev, J. Ouaknine, J. Worrell, The orbit problem in higher dimensions, in: STOC '13: Proceedings of the Forty-Fifth Annual ACM Symposium on Theory of Computing, Society for Industrial and Applied Mathematics, Philadelphia, PA, 2014, pp. 80–88.

[28] S.G. Simpson, Subsystems of second order arithmetic, in: Perspectives in Mathematical Logic Series, Springer-Verlag, New York, 2009.

[29] D. Hirschfeldt, R. Shore, Combinatorial principles weaker than Ramsey's theorem for pairs, J. Symb. Log. 72 (1) (2007) 171–206. http://www.math.cornell.edu/~shore/papers.html.

[30] P. Cholak, C. Jockusch, T. Slaman, On the strength of Ramsey's theorem for pairs, J. Symb. Log. 66 (1) (2001) 1–55. http:www.nd.edu/~cholak/papers/.

[31] Y.L. Ershov, S.S. Goncharov, A. Nerode, J.B. Remmel (Eds.), Handbook of Recursive Mathematics, Elsevier, North-Holland, Inc., New York, 1998.

[32] W. Gasarch, A survey of recursive combinatorics, in: Y.L. Ershov, S.S. Goncharov, A. Nerode, J.B. Remmel (Eds.), Handbook of Recursive Algebra. Elsevier, North-Holland, Inc., New York, 1997, pp. 1041–1171. http://www.cs.umd.edu/~gasarch/papers/papers.html

[33] T. Hummel, Effective versions of Ramsey's theorem: avoiding the cone above, J. Symb. Log. 59 (4) (1994) 682–687. http://www.jstor.org/action/showPublication?journalCode=jsymboliclogic.

[34] C. Jockusch, Ramsey's theorem and recursion theory, J. Symb. Log. 37 (2) (1972) 268–280. http://www.jstor.org/pss/2272972.

[35] D. Seetapun, T.A. Slaman, On the strength of Ramsey's theorem, Notre Dame J. Formal Log. 36 (4) (1995) 570–581. http://projecteuclid.org/DPubS?service=UI&version=1.0&verb=Display&handle=euclid.ndjfl/1040136917.

[36] D. Conlon, A new upper bound for diagonal Ramsey numbers, Ann. Math. 170 (2) (2009) 941–960. http://www.dpmms.cam.ac.uk/~dc340.

[37] S. Radziszowski, Small Ramsey numbers, Electron. J. Comb. (2011). www.combinatorics.org. A dynamic survey so year is last update.

[38] V. Rosta, Ramsey theory applications, Electron. J. Comb. 13 (2014) 1–43. This is a dynamic survey.

[39] N. Alon, J. Spencer, The Probabilistic Method, Wiley, New York, 1992.

[40] P. Erdős, G. Szekeres, A combinatorial problem in geometry, Compos. Math. 2 (4) (1935) 463–470. http://www.renyi.hu/~p_erodso/1935-01.pdf.

ABOUT THE AUTHOR

William Gasarch is a full professor at the University of Maryland, College Park. He received his PhD in Computer Science from Harvard in 1985, with the thesis "Recursion Theoretic Techniques in Complexity Theory and Combinatorics." Since then, he has worked in complexity theory, combinatorics, learning theory, and communication complexity. He has a particular interest in Ramsey theory.

He has mentored over 30 high school students and over 20 undergraduates on projects. Several of the high school students have won competitions with their research.

He is the author or coauthor of more than 50 research papers. He has written a book, with Georgia Martin, on "Bounded Queries in Recursion Theory." He currently coblogs (with Lance Fortnow) complexity blog which is a well-read blog on complexity theory.

> CHAPTER FIVE

Advances in Testing JavaScript-Based Web Applications

Ali Mesbah[*,1]

*Department of Electrical and Computer Engineering, University of British Columbia, British Columbia, Canada
[1]Corresponding author: e-mail address: amesbah@ece.ubc.ca

Contents

Abstract

JavaScript is a flexible and expressive prototype-based scripting language that is used by developers to create interactive web applications. The language is interpreted, dynamic, weakly typed, and has first-class functions. It also interacts extensively with other web languages such as CSS and HTML at runtime. All these characteristics make JavaScript code particularly error-prone and challenging to analyze and test. In this chapter, we

Advances in Computers, Volume 97
ISSN 0065-2458
http://dx.doi.org/10.1016/bs.adcom.2014.12.003

explore recent advances made in analysis and testing techniques geared toward JavaScript-based web applications. In particular, we look at recent empirical studies, testing techniques, test oracle automation approaches, test adequacy assessment methods, fault localization and repair, and Integrated Development Environment support to help programmers write better JavaScript code.

1. INTRODUCTION

JavaScript has become the dominant language for implementing modern web applications. Today, as many as 97 of the top 100 most visited websites [1] have client-side JavaScript [2], often consisting of thousands of lines of code per application. JavaScript is an expressive language, used increasingly for (1) offloading core functionality to the client side and (2) implementing real-time applications on the server-side through environments such as Node.js [3].

JavaScript-based applications are particularly challenging to deal with for developers.

First, JavaScript is an interpreted language, meaning that there is typically no compiler that would help developers to detect erroneous or unoptimized code during development.

Second, it has a dynamic, weakly typed, and asynchronous nature. For instance, constructs such as eval allow text to turn into executable code at runtime, forming a serious hindrance for providing static guarantees about the behavior of the code [4] as well as performing proper instrumentation of the code for dynamic analysis. The weakly type nature of the language makes it particularly challenging to apply many established analysis techniques that work on statically typed languages such as Java. The language also enables asynchronous callbacks through mechanism such as setTimeout and the XMLHttpRequest (XHR) for server communication, which are error-prone [5] and difficult to follow [6].

JavaScript also has intricate features such as prototypes [7], first-class functions, and closures [8]. Prototype-based programming is a class-free style of object-oriented programming, in which objects can inherit properties from other objects directly. In JavaScript, prototypes can be redefined at runtime and immediately affect all the referring objects. The language has a very flexible model of objects and functions. Object properties and their values can be created, changed, or deleted at runtime and accessed via first-class functions. Due to such flexibility, the set of all available properties of an object is not easily retrievable statically. This poses a major challenge for scalable and precise static analysis for JavaScript [9, 10]. Empirical studies [11], however, have found that most dynamic features in JavaScript are frequently used by developers and cannot be disregarded in code analysis techniques.

Third, JavaScript extensively interacts with the Document Object Model (DOM) [12] to update the web page seamlessly at runtime. The DOM is a platform- and language-neutral standard object model for representing HTML and XML documents. It provides an Application Programming Interface (API) for dynamically accessing, traversing, and updating the content, structure, and style of such documents. Changes made dynamically, through JavaScript, to DOM elements are directly manifested in the browser's display. This allows a single page to be updated incrementally, which is substantially different from the traditional URL-based page transitions through hyperlinks, where the entire DOM was repopulated with a new HTML page from the server for every state change. This dynamic interplay between two separate entities, namely JavaScript and the DOM, is particularly error-prone in web applications [13].

Finally, JavaScript is an event-driven language allowing developers to register various event listeners on DOM nodes. While most events are triggered by user actions, timing events and asynchronous callbacks can be fired with no direct input from the user. To make things even more complex, a single event can propagate on the DOM tree and trigger multiple listeners according to the event capturing and bubbling properties of the event model [14]. Understanding these event-driven interactions in JavaScript is known to be challenging for developers [6].

All of these features make JavaScript-based web applications particularly error-prone [5, 13, 15], difficult to understand [6, 16], and challenging to analyze [9, 10, 17] and test [18-20].

While static analysis of client and server code of web applications can provide valuable insight into their dependability, the highly dynamic nature of today's client-side code makes dynamic analysis indispensable.

In this chapter, we provide an overview of the recent advancements made in analysis and testing techniques for modern JavaScript-based web applications. This chapter is further organized as follows: In Section 2, we discuss recent empirical studies conducted to understand the nature and challenges of analyzing JavaScript applications. In Section 3, we provide an overview of testing techniques that are specifically targeted toward JavaScript-based web applications such as state-based, invariant-based, feedback-directed, and symbolic analysis and concolic testing techniques.

In Section 4, we discuss web application test oracles, with particular attention to different ways of automating them. In Section 5, we present an overview of different methods used for assessing the adequacy of web application test cases, such as DOM coverage and JavaScript mutation testing. In Section 6, we explore how a test assertion failure can be linked to the faulty program code, and how a JavaScript fault can be localized and repaired automatically. And finally, in Section 7, we briefly mention some of the advancements made in integrated development environment (IDE) support to make it easier for developers to write and maintain JavaScript code.

2. EMPIRICAL STUDIES

In order to understand how JavaScript is used in today's web applications and what consequences it has for developers, various empirical studies have been conducted by analyzing web applications in the wild.

2.1 Insecure JavaScript Inclusions

Yue and Wang [21] analyze insecure practices of using JavaScript on the Web. They analyzed 6800 websites and found that 66% of the studied websites contain insecure practices related to including JavaScript files from external domains. In addition, they witnessed that around 44% of the sites use `eval` to generate and execute JavaScript code on the client side. Their study concludes that developers need to adopt and apply safer alternatives that exist today to reduce potential security risks. In a related study, Nikiforakis *et al.* [22] report on a large-scale analysis of 3 million pages of the top 10,000 Alexa sites in search of the trust relationships of these sites with their JavaScript library inclusions. They show that event top sites trust remote JavaScript providers that could be compromised and serve malicious code.

2.2 Dynamic JavaScript Features

To gain an understanding of which dynamic features of the JavaScript language developers depend on in practice, Richards *et al.* conducted an empirical study on 100 websites and 3 benchmarks [11]. Their results reveal that many of the dynamic features of the language are indeed used in practice. For instance, many libraries change the built-in prototypes in order to add behavior to different types. They also found that object properties are changed (added/deleted) at runtime, the use of `eval` to generate and execute code is frequent, and functions take a different number of parameters at runtime than statically declared. In a follow-up study [4], they focused on the runtime behavior of the `eval` function. Their analysis shows that between 50% and 80% of the 10,000 studied websites used `eval`. Authors conclude that JavaScript is a difficult terrain for static analysis since the dynamic features are prevalent and cannot simply be ignored to make approximate simplifications.

2.3 Dynamic DOM Induced by JavaScript

Through the execution of JavaScript code in browsers, the DOM tree representing a webpage at runtime can be incrementally updated without requiring a URL change.

Figures 1–3 present a simple example of how JavaScript code can dynamically modify the DOM. Figure 1 depicts a JavaScript code snippet using the popular jQuery library.[1] Figure 2 illustrates the initial state of the DOM before any modification has occurred. Once the page is loaded (line 1 in Fig. 1), the JavaScript code attaches an `onclick` event listener to the `DIV` DOM element with class attribute ``update`` (line 2). When a user clicks on this `DIV` element, the anonymous function associated with the event listener is executed (lines 2–8). The function then sends an asynchronous call to the server (line 4), passing a parameter read from the `DIV` element (i.e., ``sports``) (line 3). On the callback, the response content from the server is injected into the DOM element with ID ``sportsContainer`` (line 6). The resulting updated DOM state is shown in Fig. 3. This dynamic DOM manipulation has a significant impact on traditional web analysis techniques that treat web applications as a sequence of linked static HTML pages. In order to gain an understanding of the prevalence and extent of dynamic DOM manipulated through JavaScript in practice, Behfarshad and Mesbah

```
1  $(document).ready(function() {
2      $('div.update').click(function() {
3          var updateID = $(this).attr('rel');
4          $.get('/news/', { ref:updateID },
5          function(data) {
6              $(updateID+'Container').append(data);
7          });
8      })
9  });
```

Figure 1 JavaScript code for updating the DOM after a click event.

---

[1] http://jquery.com.

```
<body>
  <h1>Sports News</h1>
  <p>
    <span id="sportsContainer"/>
  </p>
  <div class="update" rel="sports">Update!</div>
</body>
```

Figure 2 The initial DOM state.

```
<body>
  <h1>Sports News</h1>
  <p>
    <span id="sportsContainer">
      <h3>US GP: Vettel fastest in Austin second practice</h3>
      <p>Vettel produced an ominous performance</p>
    </span>
  </p>
  <div class="update" rel="sports">Update!</div>
</body>
```

Figure 3 The updated DOM state after clicking on "Update!."

[23] conducted an empirical study on 500 websites. Their study reveals that dynamic DOM is prevalent in online web applications today. From the 500 websites they analyzed, 95% contained client-side dynamic DOM content, and on average, 62% of the analyzed web states of those websites were dynamic DOM. The study shows that today's web applications rely heavily on client-side code execution, and HTML is not just created on the server, but manipulated extensively within the browser through JavaScript code.

In a related but different study, Nederlof *et al.* [24] conducted a study to understand the software engineering implications of this change. They looked at deviations from many known best practices in such areas of performance, accessibility, and correct structuring of HTML documents. They assessed to what extent such deviations are manifested through client-side JavaScript manipulation only. To this end, they conducted a large-scale experiment, involving automated JavaScript-enabled crawling of over 4000 websites, resulting in over 100,000,000 pages, and around 1,000,000 unique client-side user interface states analyzed. Traditionally, each URL of a website pointed to a single HTML document on the server, providing a one-on-one mapping between the two. Figure 4 depicts the relation in current web applications. There are no entries underneath the diagonal since each URL points to at least one HTML/DOM state. The results show that per URL, there are 16 dynamic DOM states, on average. This means that if a traditional static HTML analysis tool would request

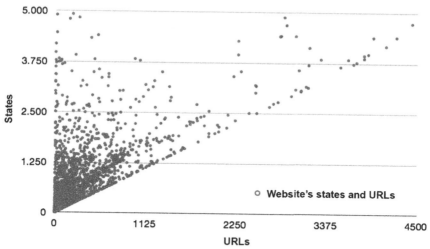

Figure 4 Number of HTML/DOM states per URL [24].

a certain URL once, without any context, it would miss more than half of the states. The study also found that 90% of the analyzed websites perform DOM manipulations after they are loaded into the browser. The findings also show that the majority of sites contain a substantial number of problems, making sites unnecessarily slow, inaccessible for the visually impaired, and with layout that is unpredictable due to errors in the dynamically modified DOM states. For instance, more than half of the sites contain errors such as ambiguous IDs and invalid HTML structure. These violations manifest themselves not just in HTML directly coming from the server but require code in the browser to execute before they become visible and detectable. Consequently, tools based on static analysis, or dynamic analysis using traditional hyperlink-based crawlers, will fail to analyze a large fraction of a modern web application.

2.4 JavaScript Bugs

A few studies have examined reported failures of web applications on the client side to characterize their nature and root causes.

Ocariza et al. [25] conducted an empirical characterization of the error messages printed to the browser console by JavaScript code execution of 50 websites, selected from the Alexa top 100 most visited sites. Their study reveals that runtime JavaScript errors (1) are galore in deployed websites: an average of four JavaScript runtime error messages appear even in popular production web applications; (2) fall into a small number of categories:

Permission Denied (52%), Undefined Symbol (28%), Null Exception (9%), and Syntax Errors (4%); and (3) are mostly (70%) nondeterministic, meaning that they vary from one execution to another, and that the speed of testing plays an important role in exposing such errors.

In a more recent study, Ocariza et al. [25] perform an empirical study of over 300 bug reports from various web applications and JavaScript libraries to help us understand the nature of the errors that cause these faults, and the failures to which these faults lead. The results of the study reveal that (1) around 65% of reported JavaScript faults are DOM-related—a fault is DOM-related if the parameter of a DOM access method (such as `getElementById(param)`) or the assignment value for a DOM access property is erroneous, thereby causing an incorrect retrieval or an incorrect update of a DOM element; (2) most (around 80%) high severity faults are DOM-related; (3) the vast majority (around 86%) of JavaScript faults are caused by errors manually introduced by JavaScript code programmers, as opposed to code automatically generated by the server; (4) error patterns exist in JavaScript bug reports (such as omitting `null`/`undefined` checks); and (5) DOM-related faults take longer to triage and fix than non-DOM-related JavaScript faults. Based on these findings, the authors suggest that testing efforts should target detecting DOM-related faults, as most high-impact faults belong to this category. One possible way to do this is to guide the test generation toward tests that cover DOM interaction points in the JavaScript code. This emphasis is particularly useful since DOM-related faults often have no accompanying error messages and thus can be more difficult to find.

3. TESTING TECHNIQUES

In the last decade, there are many advancements made in testing techniques and tools geared to JavaScript-based web applications.

3.1 Industrial Tools

Currently, many industrial tools exist that assist developers in parsing (e.g., Esprima,[2] Rhino[3]), optimizing (e.g., Google Closure Compiler[4]), and statically analyzing JavaScript code for common syntactical errors (e.g., JSHint[5]).

---

[2] http://esprima.org.
[3] https://developer.mozilla.org/en-US/docs/Mozilla/Projects/Rhino.
[4] https://developers.google.com/closure/compiler/.
[5] http://www.jshint.com.

Many testing frameworks have been developed to help developers to write test cases for JavaScript code. For instance, QUnit[6] is a popular JavaScript unit testing framework. Jasmine[7] is a behavior-driven development framework for testing JavaScript code. Mocha[8] is a JavaScript test framework that runs both on Node.js and the browser and has support for testing asynchronous methods. jsTestDriver[9] is a framework that automates running a JavaScript test suite in different browsers.

A challenge in testing web applications arises when the JavaScript code interacts with the DOM. In this case, an environment is needed that can support the creation and manipulation of the DOM and event listeners. This is what current browser automation frameworks aim for. For instance, frameworks such as Selenium,[10] PhantomJS,[11] and SlimerJS[12] provide APIs for driving a browser instance, firing events, and accessing DOM elements at runtime. These browser automation APIs can be utilized for writing DOM-based test cases that check the behavior of the web application (and indirectly its JavaScript code) from an end-user perspective.

Although such frameworks make it easier for the developer to write test cases, they still require a substantial level of manual effort.

3.2 State-Based Testing

Marchetto *et al.* [26] discuss a case study in which they assess the effectiveness of applying traditional web testing techniques [27–30] to modern web applications that have a rich client. Their analysis suggests that such traditional techniques have serious limitations in testing modern JavaScript-based web applications. In their work, Marchetto *et al.* [31] propose an approach for state-based testing of Ajax (Asynchronous JavaScript and XML) web applications based. They first generate traces of the application by manually interacting with the application. The traces are then used to construct a finite state model. Sequences of semantically interacting events in the model are transformed to test cases once the model is refined by the tester.

In order to automatically infer a model of the client side of JavaScript web applications, Mesbah *et al.* [32] proposed Crawljax,[13] a technique

---

[6] http://qunitjs.com.
[7] http://pivotal.github.io/jasmine/.
[8] http://visionmedia.github.io/mocha/.
[9] https://code.google.com/p/js-test-driver/.
[10] http://www.seleniumhq.org.
[11] http://phantomjs.org.
[12] http://www.slimerjs.org.
[13] http://crawljax.com.

and tool capable of detecting and executing User Interface (UI) event listeners that lead to various dynamic DOM states of a web application, recursively. While exploring, Crawljax infers a *state-flow graph* capturing the states of the user interface, and the possible event-based transitions between them, by analyzing the DOM before and after firing an event. Figure 5 presents a processing overview of Crawljax.

Definition 1 A **state-flow graph** for a web application **A** is a 3-tuple $\langle \mathbf{r}, \mathbf{V}, \mathbf{E} \rangle$ where:

1. **r** is the root node (called Index) representing the initial state after **A** has been fully loaded into the browser.
2. **V** is a set of vertices representing the UI states. Each $\mathbf{v} \in \mathbf{V}$ represents a unique run-time DOM state in **A**.
3. **E** is a set of edges between vertices. Each $(\mathbf{v}_1, \mathbf{v}_2) \in \mathbf{E}$ represents a clickable **c** connecting two states if and only if state $\mathbf{v}_2$ is reached by executing **c** in state $\mathbf{v}_1$.

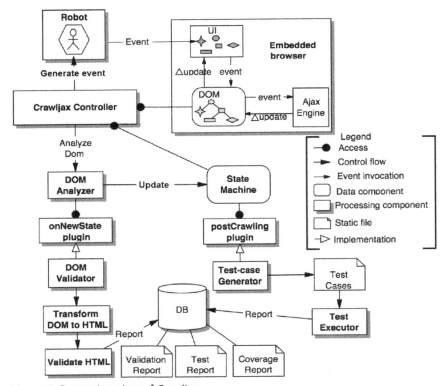

Figure 5 Processing view of Crawljax.

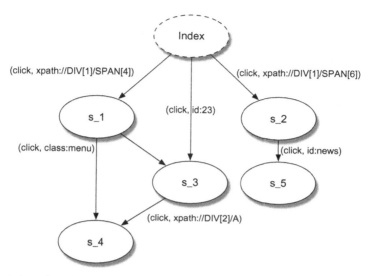

Figure 6 An inferred state-flow graph.

Figure 6 depicts a state-flow graph generated by Crawljax for a simple website. As it can be seen, the nodes are DOM states and edges are event types along with the DOM elements on which the events were fired. The DOM elements are identified using a combination of XPath expressions and other element attributes. The proposed exploration approach includes the following main steps:

Identifying clickables Since JavaScript code can be used to make any DOM element clickable, identification of clickable elements needs to be done dynamically. A list of *candidate clickable* is determined statically (e.g., all "div" or "a" tags), after which they are exercised dynamically. If a click event leads to a modified DOM tree, the element is considered clickable.

Comparing states While in principle a new DOM tree is considered a new state, the amount of change is important, since some small changes may be less relevant. Crawljax supports several ways of comparing DOM states, for different purposes. The simplest one is stripping the DOM states from all textual content and comparing the structure of the DOM trees as strings. Another more accurate but costly approach is string-based Levenshtein distance [33], where changes are considered relevant if the distance is beyond a given threshold.

Recurse When a new DOM state is identified, exploration needs to recurse to process the elements on the next state. To determine clickables

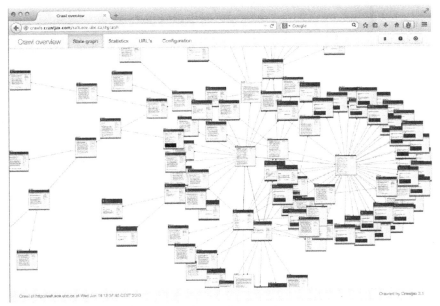

Figure 7 Visualization of a generated state-flow graph.

already processed on the new page, a *diff* algorithm is applied to guide the crawling process to the newly added elements.

Backtracking To navigate back to a state that has unexercised clickables, Crawljax records the path taken to that particular state and replays that path in order to backtrack. This is needed because in most JavaScript applications, dynamic DOM states are not registered with browsers history engine and as a result we cannot rely on the browser's Back-button to navigate to a previous state.

Providing input data Data entry points can be filled with random input values generated by Crawljax, or alternatively with custom input values for specific input fields, provided by the user.

The graph that is generated by Crawljax can be used for various purposes. For instance, it can be visualized (see Fig. 7) to help developers understand the navigational structure of their web application. In addition, the crawling process provided by Crawljax, which gives us access to dynamic DOM states of JavaScript applications, can be used for testing purposes.

3.3 Invariant-Based Testing

Mesbah *et al.* [19] build on the crawling capabilities of Crawljax and propose invariant-based testing of web applications. With access to different dynamic web states, the user interface can be checked against different constraints, expressed as *invariants*, which can act as oracles to automatically conduct sanity checks in any DOM state. They distinguish between *generic* and *application-specific* invariants on the DOM tree, between DOM-tree states, and on the run-time JavaScript variables. Each invariant is based on a fault model, representing specific faults that are likely to occur and which can be captured through the given invariant in JavaScript-based web applications. Examples of generic invariants include the requirement that any DOM should be composed of valid HTML, that there are no broken links, and that all element ID attributes are unique.

The state-flow graph automatically inferred through crawling can also be used for test generation. For example, it can be used to generate different event paths and cover the application's state space in different ways. Figure 8 shows an instance of a test case generated from the graph. These types of test cases can be used in regression testing of web applications in which the DOM states of a new version of the application are checked against a previous version's [34].

JSContest [35], proposed by Heidegger and Thiemann, provides a contract language for JavaScript, which allows to attach software contracts to definitions through in-comment annotations. Contracts can be as simple as type signatures and as complex as the programmer desires. These contracts are to be added to the JavaScript code by programmers as annotations. JSConTest then creates a test suite from the manually annotated program. It implements run-time contract monitoring and performs random testing with input data derived from these contracts.

```
 1   @Test
 2   public void test1() {
 3     browser.open(url);
 
 5     /*Element-info: SPAN News */
 6     Clickable c1 = new Eventable(new Identification(
 7       "xpath", "//DIV1/SPAN4"), "click");
 
 9     assertPresent(c1);
10     browser.enterRelatedInputValues(c1);
11     assertTrue(browser.fireEvent(c1));
12     assertEquals(oracle.getState("S_1").getDom(), browser.getDom());
 
14     /*Element-info: DIV World News */
15     Clickable c2 = new Eventable(new Identification(
16       "xpath", "//DIV2/DIV2"), "click");
 
18     assertPresent(c2);
19     assertTrue(browser.fireEvent(c2));
20     assertEquals(oracle.getState("S_3").getDom(), browser.getDom());
21     ...
22   }
```

Figure 8 A generated JUnit test case.

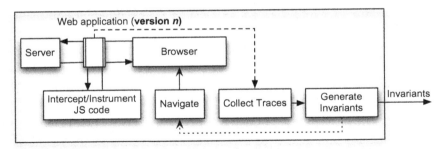

Figure 9 Overview of the JavaScript tracing and invariant generation steps in JSART.

While JSContest requires the developers to manually write the contracts, JSART [36] automatically detects invariants in JavaScript code. The technique is based on dynamic analysis of JavaScript to infer invariant assertions. These obtained assertions are injected back into the JavaScript code to uncover regression faults in subsequent revisions of the web application under test. JSART automatically (1) intercepts and instruments any JavaScript code origination from the server and adds tracing code to the intercepted JavaScript code, (2) navigates the web application to produce execution traces, (3) generates dynamic invariants from the trace data using an extension of the Daikon tool [37], and (4) transforms the invariants into stable assertions and injects them back into the web application for regression testing (Fig. 9).

3.4 Feedback-Directed Testing

Feedback-directed testing is a testing technique in which test cases are randomly generated and executed. The feedback obtained by running the generated test cases is then used to guide the test generation engine to be more effective, for example, in covering the application.

Artemis [18] is a testing technique that uses feedback-directed random testing to generate test inputs for JavaScript applications. Artemis randomly generates test inputs, executes the application with those inputs, and uses the gathered information to generate new test inputs. The execution feedback directs the test generator toward inputs that yield higher coverage.

General web application crawlers that exhaustively explore the dynamic states can become mired in limited specific regions of the web application, yielding poor functionality coverage. Since exploring the whole state space of large web applications can be infeasible (due to state explosion) and undesirable (e.g., time constrains), the challenge to targets is to automatically derive an incomplete test model but with adequate functionality coverage, in a timely manner. FeedEx [38] is a technique that is designed to address this challenge. It has a feedback-directed web application exploration algorithm to derive test models. FeedEx optimizes for four metrics to capture different aspects of a web application test model, namely *code coverage impact*, *navigational diversity*, *page structural diversity*, and *test model size*.

Functionality coverage. A test suite generated from a derived test model can only cover the functionality contained in the test model, and not more. For instance consider Fig. 10. If the inferred test model does not capture events e6 and e7, the generated test suite will not be able to cover the underlying functionality behind those two events. Therefore, it is important to derive a test model that possesses adequate coverage of the web application when the end goal is test suite generation.

Navigational coverage. The navigational structure of a web application allows its users to navigate it in various directions. For instance, s3 and s4 are both on the same navigational path, whereas s3 and s8 are on different branches (Fig. 10). To cover the navigational structure adequately, a test model should cover different navigational branches of the web application.

Page structural coverage. The structure of a webpage in terms of its internal DOM elements, attributes, and values provides the main interaction interface with end users. Each page structure provides a different degree of content and functionality. To capture this structural functionality adequately, a test model should cover heterogeneous DOM structures of the web application.

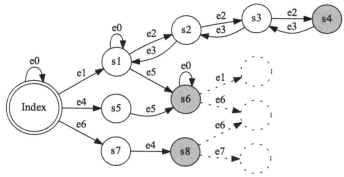

Figure 10 Expanding the state-flow graph.

Size. The size of the derived test model has a direct impact on the number of generated test cases and event executions within each test case. Reducing the size of the test model can decrease both the cost of maintaining the generated test suite and the number of test cases that must be rerun after changes are made to the software. Thus, while deriving test models, the size should be optimized as long as the reduction does not adversely influence the coverage.

Using a combination of these four metrics, FeedEx dynamically monitors the exploration and its history. It uses the feedback obtained to decide *a priori* (1) which states should be expanded, and (2) which events should be exercised next, so that a subset of the total state space is effectively captured for adequate test-case generation.

Leveraging feedback from existing software artifacts to guide the test generation is another technique that has gained more attention recently. Elbaum *et al.* [39] leverage user sessions for web application test generation. Similarly, Sprenkle *et al.* [40] propose a tool to generate additional test cases based on the captured user-session data. McAllister *et al.* [41] leverage user interactions for web testing. Their method relies on prerecorded traces of user interactions and requires instrumenting one specific web application framework.

Milani Fard *et al.* [42] propose Testilizer, a technique that leverages knowledge from existing test cases and uses the feedback to generate targeted test cases. The work behind Testilizer is motivated by the fact that a human-written test suite is a valuable source of domain knowledge, which can be exploited for tackling three main challenges in automated web application test generation.

Input values: Having valid input values is crucial for proper coverage of the state space of a web application. Generating these input values automatically is challenging since many web applications require a specific type, value, and combination of inputs to expose the hidden states behind input fields and forms.

Paths to explore: Industrial web applications have a huge state space. Covering the whole space is infeasible in practice. To avoid unbounded exploration, which could result in state explosion, users define constraints on the depth of the path, exploration time or number of states. Not knowing which paths are important to explore results in obtaining a partial coverage of a specific region of the application.

Assertions: Any generated test case needs to assert the application behavior. However, generating proper assertions automatically without human knowledge is known to be challenging. As a result, many web testing techniques rely on generic invariants or standard HTML validators to avoid this problem.

Testilizer addresses these challenges by taking advantage of existing test cases. It (1) mines the human knowledge existing in manually written test cases, (2) combines that inferred knowledge with the power of automated web crawling, and (3) extends the existing test suite for uncovered/unchecked portions of the web application under test. Testilizer takes as input a set of Selenium test cases TC and the URL of the application, automatically infers a model from TC, feeds that model to a crawler to expand by exploring uncovered paths and states, generates assertions for newly detected states based on the patterns learned from TC, and finally generates new test cases.

3.5 Regression Testing

Regression testing aims to uncover new software bugs, or regressions, in existing areas of an application after changes have been applied to them. As software evolves, one common way to provide assurance about the correctness of the modified system is through regression testing. This involves saving and reusing test suites created for earlier (correct) versions of the software, with the intent of determining whether modifications (e.g., bug fixes) have created any new problems/bugs.

Roest et al. [34] propose a regression testing technique for JavaScript applications that uses a number of ways to control and refine the process of comparing two DOM states occurring in JavaScript applications.

Pythia [20] is an automated regression test-case generation technique for JavaScript applications. It operates through a three step process. First, it dynamically explores and crawls the web application using a JavaScript function coverage maximization greedy algorithm, to infer a test model. Then, it generates test cases at two complementary levels, namely, DOM event sequences and unit tests for JavaScript functions. Finally, it automatically generates test oracles for both levels, through a mutation-based algorithm (see Section 4).

3.6 Cross-Browser Testing

Cross-browser testing seeks to detect inconsistencies in the behavior and layout of a web application across multiple browsers.

Choudhary et al. [43] proposed WebDiff, which analyzes the DOM as well as screenshots of pairs of screens to automatically locate cross-browser issues. The focus is on identifying cross-browser differences in individual screens.

In contrast, CrossT, proposed by Mesbah and Prasad [44], also identifies more systemic cross-browser issues that manifest in the overall trace-level behavior of the web application. CrossT poses the problem of cross-browser compatibility testing of modern web applications as a "functional consistency" check of web application behavior across different web browsers and presents an automated solution for it. CrossT's approach consists of (1) automatically analyzing the given web application under different browser environments and capturing the behavior as a state-flow graph and (2) formally comparing the generated models for equivalence on a pairwise-basis and exposing any observed discrepancies. For example, Fig. 11 depicts the state-flow graphs produced by CrossT for the same web application in Chrome and Firefox. As it can be seen, there are seven state transitions (shown in bold with label 'IMGid:logoff') that lead to state 7 (shown in red; dark gray shade in the print version) that are present in the Chrome version but are missing from the graph in Firefox. All these seven transitions are caused by a click on the logoff tab in the application. The reason for this difference is that the logoff JavaScript function associated with the onclick attribute of the corresponding DOM element is not executed in Firefox. Thus, after clicking on the element, there is no state change and hence no transition detected. This missing state is shown as a red (dark gray shade in the print version) state in Chrome.

CrossCheck [45] is a technique that combines WebDiff and CrossT to leverage from both machine-learning techniques and the power of automated web application exploration and comparison.

3.7 Symbolic Execution and Concolic Testing

Symbolic execution is a static analysis technique that treats input variables as symbolic variables. For every program path detected, constraints are collected (called path constraints) and solved through constraint solvers. Concolic testing combines symbolic execution with dynamic analysis to overcome some of the limitations of symbolic execution and current constraints solvers.

Kudzu [46] is a symbolic execution technique for JavaScript applications. Kudzu is built on top of a constraint solver (called Kaluza) that supports boolean, machine integer (bit-vector), and string constraints, which is used for reasoning about the parsing and validation checks that JavaScript applications perform. Kudzu is particularly focused on string reasoning and finding security vulnerabilities in JavaScript code.

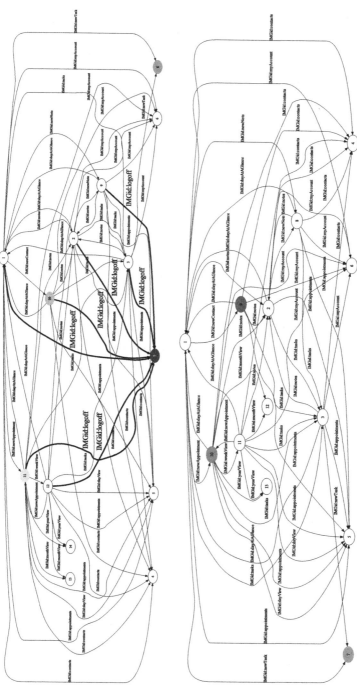

Figure 11 Graphs of the same web application in Chrome (top) and Firefox (bottom) with the detected differences. Colors (different gray shades in the print version) indicate matched states and show differences. Red (dark gray shade in the print version) indicates a state with a missing equivalent state in the other browser.

Jalangi [47] is a framework for light-weight source instrumentation and dynamic analysis of JavaScript code. It also provides a concolic engine for JavaScript. It handles linear integer, and string, and type constraints.

SymJS [48] is a recent framework for automatic testing of JavaScript code. It contains a symbolic execution engine for JavaScript, and an automatic event explorer. It automatically explores events and symbolically executes the related JavaScript code to produce test cases. Its symbolic engine is built on a symbolic virtual machine, a string-numeric solver, and a simple symbolic DOM model.

4. TEST ORACLES

Automating the process of assessing the correctness of the test output is a challenging task, known as the *oracle problem*.

Since in JavaScript-based applications observable state changes are manifested through modifications on the DOM, the DOM as well as the JavaScript code can be asserted for correctness. Ideally, a tester acts as an oracle who knows the expected output, in terms of JavaScript function output or DOM tree elements and their attributes. When the state space is huge, this manual approach becomes practically impossible.

A generic approach used often as a test oracle is checking for thrown exceptions or application crashes. This type of oracle is, however, not very helpful for web applications as they do not crash easily and the browser continues the execution even after exceptions. Many web testing techniques simplify the test oracle problem in the generated test cases by using soft oracles, such as HTML validation [18, 19].

An approach taken in practice to automate the oracle problem is to use the output of a version of the application to obtain a baseline. The shortcoming of this approach is that it presumes that the baseline represents a correct version of the system, from which initial states can be collected and reused as oracles in subsequent test executions. To compare the states between two versions HTML comparators were proposed by Sprenkle *et al.* [49].

For web applications, oracle comparators typically analyze the differences between server response pages. For highly dynamic web applications, this comparison-based approach suffers from a high probability of finding differences between old and new pages that are irrelevant and do not point to an actual (regression) fault. For JavaScript applications, the run-time dynamic manipulation of the DOM tree as well as the asynchronous client/server interactions makes it particularly hard to control the level of dynamism during regression testing. Roest *et al.* [34] propose a solution for this controllability problem. They propose a technique called pipelined oracle comparisons, in which two DOM trees are subsequently stripped of irrelevant information and compared through a series of pipelined comparators, each eliminating one level of irrelevant detail (such as timers, counters, colors, and particular names) or subtrees of the DOM tree.

Mesbah *et al.* [19] propose the use of generic and application-specific invariants as oracles for JavaScript web applications. For instance, Table 1 shows the different generic ways application-specific invariants can be expressed. Invariants can be expressed in XPath, regular, or JavaScript expressions. In addition, there is support for conditions such as the URL or visibility of DOM elements, which can be used to express invariants. The logical operators NOT, OR, AND, and NAND can also be applied, on or between the invariants, for more flexibility. Each invariant type can be constrained to a specific set of states using preconditions. In addition, while crawling through the different states of the web application, with access to the run-time JavaScript, we can also specify invariants on the values of any JavaScript variable.

Figure 12 shows an example of expressing an XPATH invariant with a JavaScript precondition for checking whether the menu item on the home page contains the class attribute "menuNews."

DoDOM [50] detects patterns across different DOM changes and deduces invariants on the DOM tree that should always hold.

JSART [51] automatically infers JavaScript invariants through code instrumentation and dynamic analysis. These invariants are used as test oracles in regression testing. Figure 13 shows examples of in-code assertions generated by JSART. The assertions are at function entry, exit points. The invariants are related to variables as well as DOM elements and their attributes.

Table 1 Expressing State Invariants for JavaScript Applications

	Satisfied If and Only If
XPath expression	The XPath expression returns at least one DOM element
Regular expression	The regular expression is found in the DOM string
JavaScript expression	The JavaScript expression evaluates to true
URL condition	The current browser's URL contains the specified string
Visible condition	The specified DOM element is visible

```
//the news menu item on the home page should always have the class attribute '↵
    menuNews'

Condition newsItem = new XPathCondition("//DIV@id='menu'/UL/LIcontains(@class,
    'menuNews')");
Condition when = new JavaScriptCondition("document.title=='Home'");
crawler.addInvariant("News menu item", newsItem, when);
```

Figure 12 Example of an XPATH invariant with a JavaScript precondition.

```
function setDim(height, width) {
    assert((width < height), 'example.js:setDim:ENTER:POINT1');
    var h = 4*height, w = 2*width;
    ...
    assert((w < h), 'example.js:setDim:EXIT:POINT1');
    return{h:h, w:w};
}

function play(){
    $(#end).css("height", setDim($('body').width(), $('body').height()).h + '↵
        px');
    assert(isIn($('#end').css('height'), {100, 200,
        300}),'example.js:play:POINT3');
    ...
}
```

Figure 13 Generated invariant assertions for JavaScript function parameters, local variables, and DOM modifications.

Pythia [20] uses a mutation-based technique for generating assertions. The technique injects a mutation into the JavaScript code of the application and compares the execution traces obtained from the original and mutated versions. Using this information, it generates test oracles at the JavaScript code level.

Testilizer [42] takes advantage of existing test oracles in manually written test cases of a web application. By analyzing human-written assertions, Testilizer infers information regarding portions of the webpage that are considered important for testing. For instance, an advertisement section might not be as important as a content pane. It uses this information in (1) reusing the *same* assertions from manual-test states for states without such assertions, (2) regenerating assertions with the *exact* assertion pattern structure as the original assertions but adapted for another state, and (3) learning structures from the original assertions to generate *similar* assertions for other states.

5. TEST ADEQUACY ASSESSMENT

There are different ways of assessing the adequacy of a give test suite. Code coverage and mutation testing are two well-known techniques. In this section, we explore tools and techniques for assessing the quality of web application test suites.

5.1 Coverage

Code coverage is the most widely used metric for test-case assessment. The idea is to measure the portion of the program code executed when the test suite is run. Code coverage is particularly useful for detecting under tested portions of the code. Many industrial tools exist today that automate measuring JavaScript code coverage. Examples include Cover,[14] CoverJS,[15] Istanbul,[16] BlanketJS,[17] JSCover,[18] and JSCoverage.[19] All these tools focus on JavaScript code-level coverage (Fig. 14).

Although code coverage has traditionally been a popular test adequacy criterion, it alone is not adequate for assessing the quality of web application test cases. Web application test cases written in frameworks such as Selenium interact with the DOM. Although these actions can trigger the execution of JavaScript code indirectly, the test cases merely check the correctness of the DOM elements and their properties. To address this, Mirzaaghaei and Mesbah [52] propose a set of DOM-based test adequacy criteria for web applications. These criteria aim at measuring coverage at two granularity levels, namely (1) interstate: the percentage of DOM states and transitions covered in the total state space of the web application under test; and (2) intrastate: the percentage of elements covered in each particular DOM state. The goal is not to replace code coverage but to complement it with *DOM coverage*, a metric more tangible for web developers and testers. They propose a tool called DOMCovery, which automatically extracts and measures the DOM adequacy criteria for a given test suite and generates a visual DOM coverage report.

Alshahwan and Harman [53] propose a set of blackbox testing criteria, called test output uniqueness, which include five that are based on the HTML structure and two based on the textual content of webpages. Their key insight behind output uniqueness as a testing criterion is that two test cases that yield different outputs may cover two different paths in the code.

5.2 Fault-Finding Capability

Code coverage alone does not assess the fault-finding capabilities of a test suite. Mutation testing is a fault-based testing technique to assess and improve the fault-finding quality of a test suite. The technique first generates

---

[14] https://github.com/itay/node-cover.
[15] https://github.com/arian/CoverJS.
[16] https://github.com/yahoo/istanbul.
[17] http://blanketjs.org.
[18] http://tntim96.github.io/JSCover/.
[19] http://siliconforks.com/jscoverage/.

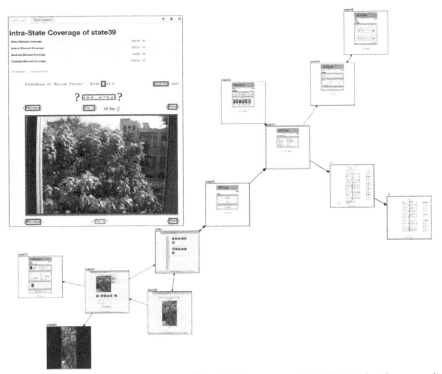

Figure 14 Coverage report generated by DOMCovery: graph highlighted with covered states (green border; light gray shade in the print version) and transitions (green arrow; black shade in the print version). Upper left corner shows one of the DOM states with intrastate coverage details.

a set of mutants—modified versions of the program—by applying a set of well-defined mutation operators on the original version of the system under test. These mutation operators typically represent subtle mistakes, such as typos, commonly made by programmers. A test suite's adequacy is then measured by its ability to detect (or "kill") the mutants, which is known as the mutation score.

Despite being an effective test adequacy assessment method, mutation testing suffers from two main issues. First, there is a high *computational cost* in executing the test suite against a potentially large set of generated mutants. Second, there is a significant amount of effort involved in distinguishing *equivalent mutants*, which are syntactically different but semantically identical to the original program. Equivalent mutants have no observable effect on the application's behavior and, as a result, cannot be killed by test cases.

Mirshokraie *et al.* [54] proposed the first mutation testing technique for JavaScript programs. Their technique and tool, called Mutandis, guides the mutation generation process toward effective mutations that (1) affect error-prone sections of the program and (2) impact the program's behavior and as such are potentially nonequivalent. Mutandis leverages static and dynamic program data to rank, select, and mutate potentially behavior-affecting portions of the program code. It uses the notion of function rank to rank JavaScript functions based on their relative importance based on the application's dynamic behavior. The approach gives a higher probability to functions ranked higher for being selected for mutation. The insight is that if a highly ranked function is mutated, because many other functions depend on its functionality, the result of the mutation will be more likely to be observable and thus nonequivalent. To mutate a selected function, Mutandis selects from a set of JavaScript-specific mutation operators, assembled based on common mistakes made by JavaScript programmers in practice.

Praphamontripong and Offutt [55] proposed a set of mutation operators for HTML and Java Server Pages. Maezawa *et al.* [56] used mutation testing to detect delay-based errors in web applications. Nishiura *et al.* [57] presented a set of genetic mutation operators for JavaScript applications.

5.3 Test-Case Robustness

Another dimension relate to test quality is the notion of test-case robustness. A test case is believed to be fragile when a small change in the application layout causes test cases to fail. In addition, test cases created for one particular browser can easily break when executed on a different web browse. Fragile test cases require extra maintenance effort to remain functional and as such increase the overall cost of a software project. This is especially the case for test cases that check the user interface of the web application. For instance, in Selenium test cases, DOM element locators such as ID or XPath expressions are used to retrieve elements from the webpage. References to elements are needed in order simulate user actions by firing events and to assert properties of the DOM for correctness.

Leotta *et al.* [58, 59] compare web application test cases written in different approaches, such as visual-based using screenshots of the GUI and DOM-based using element locators. They evaluate the robustness of locators among other metrics such as test suite execution time. Their results indicate that DOM-based locators are generally more robust than visual-based identifiers.

Researchers have discussed the fragility of DOM element locators, in particular when XPath expressions are used [32, 60]. Montoto *et al.* [60] propose an algorithm for making XPath locators less fragile by taking into account other properties of DOM elements such as their attributes. Yandrapally *et al.* [61] propose the notion of contextual clues to mitigate the locator fragility problem in DOM-based test cases. Their technique uses a series of contextual clues based on the textual values of elements and their relative positions to locate DOM elements.

6. HANDLING FAILURES

Although testing of modern web applications has received increasing attention in the recent past, there has been limited work on what happens after a test reveals an error. After a test fails, the fault localization process much be undertaken by developers in order to identify the fault responsible for the failure. However, when a web application test assertion fails, determining the faulty program code responsible for the failure can be a challenging endeavor.

AutoFlox [62] is an automated technique for localizing code-terminating DOM-related JavaScript errors—a DOM access function returns a `null`, `undefined`, or incorrect value, which then propagates into several variables and eventually causes an exception in JavaScript code execution. AutoFlox takes a code-terminating line of JavaScript code as input and performs dynamic analysis and backward slicing of the web application to localize the cause of these JavaScript faults.

When a DOM-based test assertion fails, it is particularly challenging to locate the fault in the JavaScript code. Here, the main challenge is related to the implicit link between three different entities, namely, the test assertion, the DOM elements on which the assertion fails (checked elements), and the faulty JavaScript code responsible for modifying those DOM elements. To understand the root cause of the assertion failure, the developer needs to manually infer a mental model of these hidden links, which can be tedious. Further, unlike in traditional (e.g., Java) applications, there is no useful stack trace produced when a web test case fails as the failure is on the DOM, and not on the application's JavaScript code. This further hinders debugging as the fault usually lies within the application's code, and not in its surfacing DOM. Camellia [63] is a tool that helps to uncover these implicit links. First, it automatically links a test assertion failure to the checked DOM elements and subsequently to the related statements in the JavaScript code. Second, it incorporates a dynamic slicing method for JavaScript that reduces the amount of noise encountered by developers when debugging. The slicing method is based on a *selective instrumentation* algorithm to reduce the performance overhead and trace size. Finally, once a test failure is connected to the relevant slice, Camellia visualizes the output to abstract away details and relate the test failure to the corresponding computed JavaScript slice. Figure 15 depicts an example of the visualization output of Camellia for a test assertion.

When a fault is localized, the next natural step would be to repair the fault. Vejovis [64] is a technique that tries to automatically find a fix for a JavaScript fault. First, the authors try to understand common fixes applied by programmers to JavaScript faults. Based on these findings, they propose an automated technique for providing repair suggestions for DOM-related JavaScript faults.

Related to program repair are prevention techniques. For instance, Jensen et al. [65] and Meawad et al. [66] introduce techniques that transform unsafe *eval* calls in JavaScript code to functionally equivalent without the use of *eval*.

7. PROGRAMMER SUPPORT

Current IDEs are known to have serious limitations in supporting developers to understand, write, and maintain JavaScript code. In this section, we overview some of the advancements made to help JavaScript developers to write better code.

Code smells are patterns in the source code that indicate potential comprehension and maintenance issues in the program. Code smells, once detected, can be refactored to improve the design and quality of the code. Current work on web application code smell detection is scarce and industrial tools available to web developers to maintain their code are mainly static analyzers and thus limited in their capabilities to support JavaScript developers. For instance, WARI [67] examines dependencies between JavaScript functions, CSS styles, HTML tags, and images. The goal is to statically find unused images as well as unused and duplicated JavaScript functions and CSS styles. Because of the dynamic nature of JavaScript, WARI cannot guarantee the correctness of the results. JSLint [68] is a static code analysis tool written in JavaScript that validates JavaScript code against a set of good coding practices. The code inspection tends to focus on improving code quality from a

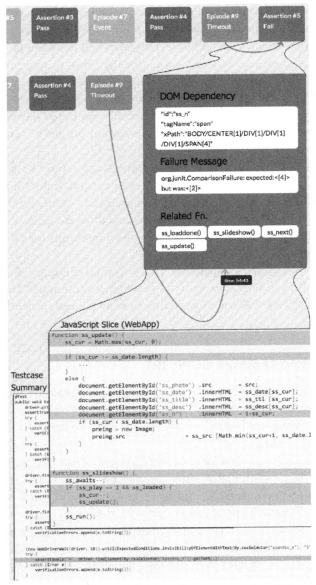

Figure 15 Camellia: connecting DOM-based test assertion failures to related JavaScript code.

technical perspective. The Google Closure Compiler [69] is a JavaScript optimizer that rewrites JavaScript code to make it faster and more compact. It helps to reduce the size of JavaScript code by removing comments and unreachable code.

WebScent [70] detects client-side smells that exist in embedded code within scattered server-side code. Such smells cannot be easily detected until the client-side code is generated. After detecting smells in the generated client-side code, WebScent locates the smells in the corresponding location in the server-side code. WebScent primarily identifies mixing of HTML, CSS, and JavaScript, duplicate code in JavaScript, and HTML syntax errors. JSNose [71] is a recent tool developed that combines static and dynamic analysis to detect a set of 13 smells in JavaScript code: 7 are existing well-known smells, such as lazy object or long function, adapted to JavaScript, and 6 are specific JavaScript code smell types such as Closure Smells, Excessive Global Variables, and Nested Callbacks. Using JSNose, authors conduct an empirical study [71] on 13 online web applications to find out which JavaScript smells are prevalent. Their results indicate that JavaScript code smells are present in online web applications and lazy object, long function, closure smells, coupling between JavaScript, HTML, and CSS, and excessive global variables are among the most prevalent code smells.

Feldthaus et al. [72, 73] provide semiautomatic refactoring support for JavaScript code. To assist IDE services, they propose a static analysis technique [9] that can deduce approximate call graphs from JavaScript code.

Bajaj et al. [74] propose an automated technique, called DOMPletion, which reasons about existing DOM structures, dynamically analyzes the JavaScript code, and provides code completion support for JavaScript code that interacts with the DOM through its APIs.

Alimadadi et al. [6] provide a program comprehension framework, called Clematis, for assisting developers in understanding the complex event-driven interactions in JavaScript applications. Through a combination of automated JavaScript code instrumentation and transformation, Clematis captures a detailed trace of a web application's behavior during a particular user session. The technique transforms the trace into an abstract behavioral model, preserving temporal and causal relations within and between involved components. Finally, the model is presented to the developers as an interactive visualization that depicts the creation and flow of triggered events, the corresponding executed JavaScript functions, and the mutated DOM nodes, within each episode.

8. CONCLUDING REMARKS

JavaScript, the language of the web, has become one of the most popular languages among software developers today. The language is highly flexible and expressive, but at the same time its dynamic, event-driven, weakly typed nature as well as its extensive interactions with the DOM makes it challenging to understand, analyze, and test.

In this chapter, we explored some of the most recent advances made in the literature related to analysis and testing of JavaScript-based web applications. In particular, we covered:

Empirical studies that have tried to shed light on how the JavaScript language is used in today's web applications, how dynamic it is, what consequences its properties have on analysis and testing techniques, and what types of bugs are common in these applications.

Testing techniques that span from industrial tools and practices to more advanced methods targeted toward JavaScript-based web applications such as state-based testing, invariant-based testing, feedback-directed testing, regression testing, and cross-browser compatibility testing.

Test oracles that automate the actual checking of program correctness in test cases, through HTML validation, HTML comparators, pipelined oracle comparators, generic and application-specific invariants on the DOM and JavaScript code, mutation-based oracles, and oracles learned from existing manually written test cases.

Test adequacy assessment which evaluates the quality of a given web application test suite through different methods such as code coverage, DOM coverage, output uniqueness, mutation testing, and test-case robustness.

Handling failures that pertain to different techniques for linking a failure detected by a test case to the actual faulty line of code, localizing a fault, and repairing a detected fault in JavaScript.

Programmer support that presents various approaches that can make it easier for developers to write better JavaScript code such as code smell detection, refactoring, code completion, and program comprehension support.

In this chapter, we have primarily focused on client-side JavaScript. However, JavaScript is also increasingly being used on the server-side through frameworks such as Node.js and for creating mobile apps. In the coming years, JavaScript's usage and popularity are likely to continue to grow and thus we will need more and better analysis and testing techniques to support developers in creating dependable JavaScript-based applications.

REFERENCES

[1] Alexa top sites. http://www.alexa.com/topsites/.
[2] C. Yue, H. Wang, Characterizing insecure JavaScript practices on the web, in: Proceedings of the InternationalWorld WideWeb Conference (WWW), ACM, New York, NY, USA, 2009, pp. 961–970.
[3] Node.js. http://nodejs.org/.
[4] G. Richards, C. Hammer, B. Burg, J. Vitek, The eval that men do, in: Proceedings of the European Conference on Object-Oriented Programming (ECOOP), Springer, Los Alamitos, CA, 2011, pp. 52–78.
[5] S. Hong, Y. Park, M. Kim, Detecting concurrency errors in client-side JavaScript web applications, in: Proceedings of the International Conference on Software Testing, IEEE, Verification and Validation (ICST), Los Alamitos, CA, 2014, pp. 61–70.
[6] S. Alimadadi, S. Sequeira, A. Mesbah, K. Pattabiraman, Understanding JavaScript event-based interactions, in: Proceedings of the ACM/IEEE International Conference on Software Engineering (ICSE), ACM, New York, NY, USA, 2014, pp. 367–377.
[7] S. Porto, A plain English guide to JavaScript prototypes, 2013. http://sporto.github.com/blog/2013/02/22/a-plain-english-guide-to-javascript-prototypes/.
[8] D. Crockford, JavaScript: The Good Arts, O'Reilly Media, Incorporated, 2008.
[9] A. Feldthaus, M. Schäfer, M. Sridharan, J. Dolby, F. Tip, Efficient construction of approximate call graphs for JavaScript IDE services, in: Proceedings of the 2013 International Conference on Software Engineering, ICSE'13, IEEE Press, Los Alamitos, CA, 2013, pp. 752–761.
[10] M. Sridharan, J. Dolby, S. Chandra, M. Schäfer, F. Tip, Correlation tracking for points-to analysis of JavaScript, in: Proceedings of the European Conference on Object-Oriented Programming, ECOOP'12, Springer-Verlag, Los Alamitos, CA, 2012, pp. 435–458.
[11] G. Richards, S. Lebresne, B. Burg, J. Vitek, An analysis of the dynamic behavior of JavaScript programs, in: Proceedings of the ACM SIGPLAN Conference on Programming Language Design and Implementation (PLDI), ACM, New York, NY, 2010, pp. 1–12.
[12] W3C, Document Object Model (DOM). http://www.w3.org/DOM/.
[13] F. Ocariza, K. Bajaj, K. Pattabiraman, A. Mesbah, An empirical study of client-side JavaScript bugs, in: Proceedings of the ACM/IEEE Inter-national Symposium on Empirical Software Engineering and Measurement (ESEM), IEEE Computer Society, Los Alamitos, CA, 2013, pp. 55–64.
[14] W3C, Document Object Model (DOM) level 2 events speci_cation. http://www.w3.org/TR/DOM-Level-2-Events/, 13 November 2000.
[15] F. Ocariza, K. Pattabiraman, B. Zorn, JavaScript errors in the wild: an empirical study, in: Proceedings of the International Symposium on Software Reliability Engineering (ISSRE), IEEE, Los Alamitos, CA, 2011, pp. 100–109.
[16] A. Zaidman, N. Matthijssen, M.-A. Storey, A. van Deursen, Understanding Ajax applications by connecting client and server-side execution traces, Empirical Softw. Eng. 18 (2) (2013) 181–218.
[17] A. Guha, S. Krishnamurthi, T. Jim, Using static analysis for Ajax intrusion detection, in: Proceedings of the 18th International Conference on World Wide Web, WWW '09, ACM, New York, NY, 2009, pp. 561–570.
[18] S. Artzi, J. Dolby, S. Jensen, A. Møller, F. Tip, A framework for automated testing of JavaScript web applications, in: Proceedings of the International Conference on Software Engineering (ICSE), ACM, New York, NY, 2011, pp. 571–580.
[19] A. Mesbah, A. van Deursen, D. Roest, Invariant-based automatic testing of modern web applications, IEEE Trans. Softw. Eng. (TSE) 38 (1) (2012) 35–53.

[20] S. Mirshokraie, A. Mesbah, K. Pattabiraman, Pythia: generating test cases with oracles for JavaScript applications, in: Proceedings of the ACM/IEEE International Conference on Automated Software Engineering (ASE), New Ideas Track, IEEE Computer Society, Los Alamitos, CA, 2013, pp. 610–615.

[21] C. Yue, H. Wang, Characterizing insecure JavaScript practices on the web, in: Proceedings of the 18th International Conference on World Wide Web, ACM, New York, NY, USA, 2009, pp. 961–970.

[22] N. Nikiforakis, L. Invernizzi, A. Kapravelos, S. Van Acker, W. Joosen, C. Kruegel, F. Piessens, G. Vigna, You are what you include: large-scale evaluation of remote JavaScript inclusions, in: Proceedings of the Conference on Computer and Communications Security, ACM, New York, NY, USA, 2012, pp. 736–747.

[23] Z. Behfarshad, A. Mesbah, Hidden-web induced by client-side scripting: an empirical study, in: Proceedings of the International Conference on Web Engineering (ICWE), Volume 7977 of Lecture Notes in Computer Science, Springer, Los Alamitos, CA, 2013, pp. 52–67.

[24] A. Nederlof, A. Mesbah, A. van Deursen, Software engineering for the web: The state of the practice, in: Proceedings of the ACM/IEEE International Conference on Software Engineering, ACM, Software Engineering In Practice (ICSE SEIP), New York, NY, USA, 2014, pp. 4–13.

[25] F. Ocariza, K. Pattabiraman, B. Zorn, JavaScript errors in the wild: an empirical study, in: Proceedings of the International Symposium on Software Reliability Engineering (ISSRE), IEEE Computer Society, Los Alamitos, CA, 2011, pp. 100–109.

[26] A. Marchetto, F. Ricca, P. Tonella, A case study-based comparison of web testing techniques applied to Ajax web applications, Int. J. Softw. Tools Technol. Transfer 10 (6) (2008) 477–492.

[27] A. Andrews, J. Offutt, R. Alexander, Testing web applications by modeling with FSMs, Softw. Syst. Model. 4 (3) (2005) 326–345.

[28] S. Elbaum, S. Karre, G. Rothermel, Improving web application testing with user session data, in: Proceedings of the 25th International Conference on Software Engineering (ICSE), IEEE Computer Society, 2003, pp. 49–59.

[29] F. Ricca, P. Tonella, Analysis and testing of web applications, in: ICSE'01: 23rd International Conference on Software Engineering, IEEE Computer Society, Los Alamitos, CA, 2001, pp. 25–34.

[30] S. Sprenkle, E. Gibson, S. Sampath, L. Pollock, Automated replay and failure detection for web applications, in: Proceedings of the 20th IEEE/ACM International Conference on Automated Software Engineering (ASE), ACM, New York, NY, USA, 2005, pp. 253–262.

[31] A. Marchetto, P. Tonella, F. Ricca, State-based testing of Ajax web applications, in: Proceedings of the 1st International Conference on Software Testing, Veri_cation, and Validation (ICST), IEEE Computer Society, Los Alamitos, CA, 2008, pp. 121–130.

[32] A. Mesbah, A. van Deursen, S. Lenselink, Crawling ajax-based web applications through dynamic analysis of user interface state changes, ACM Trans. Web (TWEB) 6 (1) (2012), 3:1–3:30.

[33] V.L. Levenshtein, Binary codes capable of correcting deletions, insertions, and reversals, Cybernet. Control Theor. 10 (1996) 707–710.

[34] D. Roest, A. Mesbah, A. van Deursen, Regression testing ajax applications: coping with dynamism, in: Proceedings of the International Conference on Software Testing, Veri_cation, and Validation (ICST), IEEE Computer Society, Los Alamitos, CA, 2010, pp. 128–136.

[35] P. Heidegger, P. Thiemann, Contract-driven testing of JavaScript code, in: Proceedings of the 48th International Conference on Objects, Models, Components, Patterns, TOOLS'10, Springer-Verlag, Los Alamitos, CA, 2010, pp. 154–172.

[36] S. Mirshokraie, A. Mesbah, JSART: JavaScript assertion-based regression testing, in: Proceedings of the International Conference on Web Engineering (ICWE), Springer, Los Alamitos, CA, 2012, pp. 238–252.

[37] M. Ernst, J. Perkins, P. Guo, S. McCamant, C. Pacheco, M. Tschantz, C. Xiao, The Daikon system for dynamic detection of likely invariants, Sci. Comput. Prog. 69 (1–3) (2007) 35–45.

[38] A. Milani Fard, A. Mesbah, Feedback-directed exploration of web applications to derive test models, in: Proceedings of the International Symposium on Software Reliability Engineering (ISSRE), IEEE Computer Society, Los Alamitos, CA, 2013, pp. 278–287.

[39] S. Elbaum, G. Rothermel, S. Karre, M. Fisher, Leveraging user-session data to support web application testing, IEEE Trans. Softw. Eng. 31 (3) (2005) 187–202.

[40] S. Sprenkle, E. Gibson, S. Sampath, L. Pollock, Automated replay and failure detection for web applications, in: Proceedings of the ACM/IEEE International Conference on Automated Software Engineering (ASE), ACM, New York, NY, USA, 2005, pp. 253–262.

[41] S. McAllister, E. Kirda, C. Kruegel, Leveraging user interactions for in-depth testing of web applications, in: Recent Advances in Intrusion Detection, Volume 5230 of LNCS, Springer, Los Alamitos, CA, 2008, pp. 191–210.

[42] A. Milani Fard, M. Mirzaaghaei, A. Mesbah, Leveraging existing tests in automated test generation for web applications, in: Proceedings of the IEEE/ACM International Conference on Automated Software Engineering (ASE), ACM, New York, NY, USA, 2014, pp. 67–78.

[43] S.R. Choudhary, H. Versee, A. Orso, Webdiff: automated identication of cross-browser issues in web applications, in: Proceedings of the 26th IEEE International Conference on Software Maintenance (ICSM'10), 2010, pp. 1–10.

[44] A. Mesbah, M.R. Prasad, Automated cross-browser compatibility testing, in: Proceedings of the ACM/IEEE International Conference on Software Engineering (ICSE), ACM, New York, NY, USA, 2011, pp. 561–570.

[45] S.R. Choudhary, M.R. Prasad, A. Orso, Crosscheck: combining crawling and differencing to better detect cross-browser incompatibilities in web applications, in: Proceedings of the International Conference on Software Testing, Verification and Validation, IEEE Computer Society, Los Alamitos, CA, 2012, pp. 171–180.

[46] P. Saxena, D. Akhawe, S. Hanna, F. Mao, S. McCamant, D. Song, A symbolic execution framework for JavaScript, in: Proceedings of the Symposium on Security and Privacy (SP), IEEE Computer Society, Los Alamitos, CA, 2010, pp. 513–528.

[47] K. Sen, S. Kalasapur, T. Brutch, S. Gibbs, Jalangi: a selective record-replay and dynamic analysis framework for JavaScript, in: Proceedings of the European Software Engineering Conference and ACM SIGSOFT International Symposium on Foundations of Software Engineering (ESEC/FSE'013), ACM, New York, NY, USA, 2013.

[48] E.A. Guodong Li, I. Ghosh, SymJS: automatic symbolic testing of JavaScript web applications, in: Proceedings of the Joint Meeting of the European Software Engineering Conference and the ACM SIGSOFT Symposium on the Foundations of Software Engineering (ESEC/FSE), New York, NY, USA, 2014.

[49] S. Sprenkle, L. Pollock, H. Esquivel, B. Hazelwood, S. Ecott, Automated oracle comparators for testing web applications, in: Proceedings of the International Symposium on Software Reliability Engineering (ISSRE), 2007.

[50] K. Pattabiraman, B. Zorn, DoDOM: leveraging DOM invariants for Web 2.0 application robustness testing, in: Proceedings of the International Conference on Software Reliability Engineering (ISSRE), IEEE Computer Society, Los Alamitos, CA, 2010, pp. 191–200.

[51] S. Mirshokraie, A. Mesbah, Jsart: JavaScript assertion-based regression testing, in: Proceedings of the International Conference on Web Engineering (ICWE), Springer, Los Alamitos, CA, 2012, pp. 238–252.

[52] M. Mirzaaghaei, A. Mesbah, DOM-based test adequacy criteria for web applications, in: Proceedings of the International Symposium on Software Testing and Analysis (ISSTA), ACM, New York, NY, USA, 2014, pp. 71–81.

[53] N. Alshahwan, M. Harman, Coverage and fault detection of the output-uniqueness test selection criteria, in: Proceedings of the 2014 International Symposium on Software Testing and Analysis, ISSTA, ACM, New York, NY, 2014, pp. 181–192.

[54] S. Mirshokraie, A. Mesbah, K. Pattabiraman, Efficient JavaScript mutation testing, in: Proceedings of the International Conference on Software Testing, IEEE Computer Society, Verification and Validation (ICST), Los Alamitos, CA, 2013, pp. 74–83.

[55] U. Praphamontripong, J. Offutt, Applying mutation testing to web applications, in: Proceedings of the 2010 Third International Conference on Software Testing, Verification, and Validation Workshops, ICSTW '10, IEEE Computer Society, Washington, DC, 2010, pp. 32–141.

[56] Y. Maezawa, K. Nishiura, H. Washizaki, S. Honiden, Validating ajax applications using a delay-based mutation technique, in: Proceedings of the ACM/IEEE International Conference on Automated Software Engineering, ASE'14, ACM, New York, NY, 2014, pp. 491–502.

[57] K. Nishiura, Y. Maezawa, H. Washizaki, S. Honiden, Mutation analysis for JavaScript web application testing, in: Proceedings of the International Conference on Software Engineering and Knowledge Engineering (SEKE), 2013, pp. 159–165.

[58] M. Leotta, D. Clerissi, F. Ricca, P. Tonella, Capture-replay vs. programmable web testing: an empirical assessment during test case evolution, in: Reverse Engineering (WCRE), 20th Working Conference on 14–17 October 2013, Koblenz, 2013, pp. 272–281.

[59] M. Leotta, D. Clerissi, F. Ricca, P. Tonella, Visual vs. DOM-based web locators: an empirical study, in: Proceedings of the International Conference on Web Engineering (ICWE), Springer, Los Alamitos, CA, 2014, pp. 322–340.

[60] P. Montoto, A. Pan, J. Raposo, F. Bellas, J. Lapez, Automating navigation sequences in Ajax websites, in: Proceedings of the International Conference on Web Engineering (ICWE), vol. 5648, Springer, Los Alamitos, CA, 2009, pp. 166–180.

[61] R. Yandrapally, S. Thummalapenta, S. Sinha, S. Chandra, Robust test automation using contextual clues, in: Proceedings of the International Symposium on Software Testing and Analysis (ISSTA), ACM, New York, NY, USA, 2014, pp. 304–314.

[62] F.J. Ocariza, K. Pattabiraman, A. Mesbah, Autoflox: an automatic fault localizer for client-side JavaScript, in: Proceedings of the International Conference on Software Testing, IEEE Computer Society, Verification and Validation (ICST), Los Alamitos, CA, 2012, pp. 31–40.

[63] S. Sequeira, A. Mesbah, K. Pattabiraman, Linking test failures to faults in web applications, Technical report, University of British Columbia, Software Analysis and Testing Lab, 2014.

[64] F. Ocariza, K. Pattabiraman, A. Mesbah, Vejovis: suggesting fixes for JavaScript faults, in: Proceedings of the ACM/IEEE International Conference on Software Engineering (ICSE), ACM, New York, NY, USA, 2014, pp. 837–847.

[65] S.H. Jensen, P.A. Jonsson, A. Møller, Remedying the eval that men do, in: Proceedings of the International Symposium on Software Testing and Analysis (ISSTA), ACM, New York, NY, USA, 2012, pp. 34–44.

[66] F. Meawad, G. Richards, F. Morandat, J. Vitek, Eval begone!: semi- automated removal of eval from JavaScript programs, in: Proceedings of the International Conference on Object Oriented Programming Systems Languages and Applications (OOPSLA), ACM, New York, NY, USA, 2012, pp. 607–620.

[67] WARI: Web application resource inspector. http://wari.konem.net.

[68] Jslint: the JavaScript code quality tool. http://www.jslint.com/.
[69] Google Closure Compiler. https://developers.google.com/closure/.
[70] H.V. Nguyen, H.A. Nguyen, T.T. Nguyen, A.T. Nguyen, T.N. Nguyen, Detection of embedded code smells in dynamic web applications, in: Proceedings of the International Conference on Automated Software Engineering (ASE), ACM, New York, NY, USA, 2012, pp. 282–285.
[71] A. Milani Fard, A. Mesbah, Jsnose: detecting JavaScript code smells, in: Proceedings of the International Conference on Source Code Analysis and Manipulation (SCAM), IEEE Computer Society, Los Alamitos, CA, 2013, pp. 116–125.
[72] A. Feldthaus, T. Millstein, A. Møller, M. Schäfer, F. Tip, Tool-supported refactoring for JavaScript, in: Proceedings of the 2011 ACM International Conference on Object Oriented Programming Systems Languages and Applications, OOPSLA'11, ACM, New York, NY, 2011, pp. 119–138.
[73] A. Feldthaus, A. Møller, Semi-automatic rename refactoring for JavaScript, in: Proceedings of the 2013 ACM SIGPLAN International Conference on Object Oriented Programming Systems Languages & Applications, OOPSLA'13, ACM, New York, NY, 2013, pp. 323–338.
[74] K. Bajaj, K. Pattabiraman, A. Mesbah, Dompletion: Dom-aware JavaScript code completion, in: Proceedings of the IEEE/ACM International Conference on Automated Software Engineering (ASE), ACM, New York, NY, USA, 2014, pp. 43–54.

ABOUT THE AUTHOR

Ali Mesbah is an assistant professor at the University of British Columbia (UBC) where he leads the software analysis and testing (SALT) research lab. He received his PhD degree in computer science from Delft University of Technology in 2009. His main area of research is in software engineering, and his research interests include software analysis and testing, web-based systems, software maintenance and evolution, fault localization and repair, and empirical software engineering. He is the recipient of two ACM Distinguished Paper Awards at the International Conference on Software Engineering (ICSE 2009 and ICSE 2014) and a Best Paper Award at the International Conference on Web Engineering (ICWE 2013).

AUTHOR INDEX

Note: Page numbers followed by "*f*" indicate figures and "*t*" indicate tables.

SUBJECT INDEX

Note: Page numbers followed by "*f*" indicate figures and "*t*" indicate tables.

CONTENTS OF VOLUMES IN THIS SERIES

Volume 71

Volume 72

Volume 73

Volume 94

Volume 95

Volume 96

Printed in the United States
By Bookmasters